Handbook of
Scenery,
Properties,
and Lighting

Handbook of Scenery, Properties, and Lighting

Volume 2
Lighting
Second Edition

Harvey Sweet

ALLYN AND BACON
Boston London Toronto Sydney Tokyo Singapore

Library of Congress Cataloging-in-Publication Data

(Revised for vol. 2)

Sweet, Harvey.
    Handbook of scenery, properties, and lighting.

    Includes bibliographical references and index.
    Contents: v. 1. Scenery and props -- v. 2. Lighting.
    1. Theater--Stage-setting and scenery.   2. Stage
lighting.   3. Stage props.   4. Amateur theater--Pro-
duction and direction.   I. Title.
PN2091.S8S86   1994 v.2   792'.025   94-10989
ISBN 0-205-14878-6 (v. 1)
ISBN 0-205-14879-4 (v. 2)

Printed in the United States of America
10   9   8   7   6   5   4   3   2   1   98   97   96   95   94

Contents

Preface

A play, opera, ballet, concert, or variety show may be performed anywhere. All that is needed are performers and an audience, but the addition of scenery, properties, and lighting enriches the event for both the actors and the viewers.

This book is directed to the professional as well as the worker in theatre who has a keen interest in noncommercial production but is limited in time, budget, experience, or the physical resources to mount a production. It is a continuation of Volume 1 of *Handbook of Scenery, Properties, and Lighting,* both in content and spirit. Basic information is presented in practical terms for immediate application to any production situation.

The only assumption made in this book is that the reader is interested in practical solutions for lighting staged events. The book begins with a discussion of the purpose, functions, and qualities of stage lighting, which is followed by a discussion about the principles, practices, and strategies of lighting design and then an investigation of color as an element of stage lighting design. Practical concerns and their effect on lighting design are discussed in relation to mounting positions and lighting fixtures. There is a discussion of projection and special effects, which is followed by a simple presentation about the basics of electricity. Finally, lighting control and lighting control equipment are discussed. These chapters will provide the experienced theatre practitioner or the novice with practical solutions to common problems in production.

This book has grown out of numerous questions and experiences of professionals, teachers, and avocational theatre people seeking ways to enjoy the experience of mounting productions within restrictive conditions. Their questions have challenged me to seek practical solutions for traditional problems and find a way to clearly communicate basic working practices. This book is dedicated to all of those devoted, enthusiastic, warm people.

I have been assisted in many ways in the preparation of this book. I am grateful to Marilyn Shaw, who provided critical reading and comment throughout preparation of the first edition. Another who contributed to this book is Jan Robbins, who appears in photographs and whose spirit contributed to the energy in the creation of this work.

I thank Lynda Griffiths for her patient editing and Alice Nichka for her wonderful cover design. I am especially grateful to my former students and my teachers of the past, most notably George Bird and Fred Buerki, who have taught me how to think in a creative way.

Handbook of
Scenery,
Properties,
and Lighting

CHAPTER 1

Lighting Design

INTRODUCTION

Lighting design is one of the most exciting areas of theatrical production. The ephemeral quality of light that is able to contribute and react to a performance can create an effective response in the audience and excitement in the designer. For the designer, it is the sense of being an artist who paints with beams of light rather than with a paintbrush. The artist's product, an illuminated—some might say an elucidated—performance, is almost as essential to a stage production as the performer and the script. The audience will not leave the theatre "whistling the lighting," but effective lighting makes it possible for the audience to see and even easier for them to hear the performance. More than that, the quality of illumination can affect everything that audience members experience. It can intensify the drama, control and direct interest or attention, paint pictures, provide information about the time and place, contribute to the style and mood, and help communicate ideas. When exciting visual effects are created and refined, a sense of artistry and fulfillment is achieved by the designer and a more effective performance is given to those watching and listening. Even when there are severe limits on the availability or use of equipment, time, or staff, lighting can make a significant contribution to a performance.

Light can be constant or it can change throughout the performance, responding to shifts in the dramatic situation, the use of space, or the mood of the production. This essential element can enhance every moment of a performance. When well handled, it makes a production alive and lively.

Lighting a stage production of any type—whether a dramatic play, a musical or opera, a classical or rock concert, or a ballet—may be accomplished with two floodlights on a stand, if necessary, or with several hundred spotlights, floodlights, and moving lights mounted on pipe battens, trusses, and catwalks. Whether a performance is minimally endowed or fully funded, the artistic intent must be carefully determined to fulfill the functions of lighting for stage productions.

There are six **functions of stage lighting:** visibility, mood composition, focus, credibility, and unity. These are the purposes or goals when planning and implementing the lighting design for a production.

Visibility means making it possible to see what is happening on stage. This does not mean that every area of the stage or every performer must be fully illuminated at all times; indeed, it is often desirable to light only a small portion of the stage or a single character. Instead, visibility means that it should be possible to see what is necessary to be seen at any moment of the performance. This may be full illumination or a dramatic light that silhouettes the profile of a dancer.

Mood refers to the emotional effect stimulated by the quality of light. This natural phenomenon is experienced in daily life in the difference in behavior of people on bright sunny days and overcast, cloudy days or dark moonless nights. It is affected by all of the qualities of light.

Composition describes the picture created by the light or the light in combination with the performers, scenery, properties and costumes, and makeup. The stage picture may be painted with a soft flood of illumination, visible shafts of light, cast shadows, or projected images that are consistent throughout the production or that change from moment to moment.

Focus is the ability of light to direct the attention of the audience to a specific location or person on stage by creating emphasis on that person or place. This function is most easily seen when a spotlight brightly illuminates a singer standing in front of an orchestra or chorus; because of the lighting, the audience knows *that* performer is the person to watch.

Credibility is the need for any lighting moment to be plausible within the context of the dramatic situation. This is not to suggest that all stage lighting must be realistic in style—only that the stage picture must be believable. If the script requires absolute darkness yet it is necessary to see the action on stage, as in the last act of *Wait Until Dark*, sufficient light must be present to see the actors without destroying the illusion of absolute darkness.

Unity is the ability of light to tie together the style, colors, and textures of all of the other elements of production—scenery, properties, costumes, and makeup. Since light is usually the last and most easily modified physical production element, it can respond directly to each element of the production as it has evolved.

Each of these functions of light affect every performance, whether they contribute casually or are consciously planned. Fulfilling these functions is achieved by manipulating the **qualities of light:** intensity, direction, movement, color, and texture.

Intensity describes the quantity of light and shadow. The illumination may be bright and evenly distributed with negligible shadows, or it may be at the most minimal level of visibility. Intensity is controlled by the kind and quantity of lighting instruments used, their placement and dimmer setting (if dimmers are available), and any coloring media or accessories used with them. Intensity affects all of the functions of lighting.

Direction refers to the angle at which light strikes the stage. Light may emanate from sources directly in front of the stage to create one effect or may come from instruments to the side or behind the performers, creating other effects; it may be projected at a severe overhead angle or on a very flat plane. The direction of light affects illumination and the way shadows are cast on and by the performers and the setting. This modifies the three-dimensional appearance of the stage and everything on it. Light projected from acute angles tends to make things look more three-dimensional; light projected from flat angles tends to make the stage appear very two-dimensional. Direction affects the functions of visibility and credibility and has an especially strong effect on mood.

Movement is any change in light that suggests motion. This could be as subtle as the sun slowly passing from dawn to dusk, the arbitrary fading or switching or pools of light located around the stage, the motion of a moving shaft of light, the gyrations of a strip of light bulbs turning on and off like a movie marquee, or changes of color or intensity that imply motion. As the light is modified, the attention of the audience is directed to the movement that enhances the interest of the audience by keeping the stage picture vital, exciting, and changing throughout the performance. When carefully planned, the movement can control focus, directing the attention of the audience to people and places on stage and subtly altering the stage picture.

Color, whether used in a realistic or highly artificial way, affects moods and attitudes and even perceptions of temperature. It affects all of the functions of lighting but makes its greatest contribution to mood. Color can be consistent throughout a production or can be in flux, responding to changes in the dramatic action and shifts in the mood of the performance.

Texture is a sense of planned variation in the pattern of lighting. Illumination may be very smooth and consistent all over the stage, or the lighting may be arranged to create bright pools of light or color in an otherwise dim space, causing the performers to move through a texture of light and shadow. Patterns of shadows may be intentionally projected on the stage to create variegated shapes resulting in textures of light and shadow, or the beams of light in the air may be arranged to appear woven or as a grain in coarse fabric. These effects are created by controlling intensity, directly modifying a beam of light with filters, patterns, or diffusers or by placement of the lighting instruments. Each of these effects will provoke a different response in the audience. Texture affects visibility, mood, and credibility.

Lighting design is a creative process in which the artist develops a design idea: pictures in his or her mind's eye that can be achieved by controlling the qualities of light. The designer's choices are made in harmony with the directorial concept, the script, and the nature of the physical space and equipment available to the production.

PLANNING

Planning the lighting for a production is a process of determining what effects are needed and desirable based on the nature of the production. It is also necessary to identify the capabilities of the facility, equipment, time, and talent to implement the lighting. Limitations, such as the absence of equipment or rules forbidding the relocation or refocusing of lighting instruments, should be considered challenges (not barriers) that demand greater creativity to implement an effective design. Whether free to make maximum use of facilities, equipment, and talent, or somehow restrained, the basic approach to lighting design is similar.

The process of lighting design can be arranged in three categories: planning, installation, and cueing. **Planning** is the process that requires the greatest amount of time. It constitutes analysis of the script, any music, and the performance (as seen in rehearsal), and a careful determination of all the physical limitations placed on the production. **Installation** requires the greatest amount of labor. It includes putting the appropriate equipment attached to the correct controls in the proper locations, and focusing and coloring the lights as necessary. **Cueing** is the portion of the work that is done under the greatest pressure. This is the period when the planning is tested and the design is perfected.

Analysis

Analysis is the first step in developing a lighting design. Even before a production goes into rehearsal, the person responsible for the lighting should have a clear understanding of what the performance is about and what ideas the production is attempting to express. Often a performance will simply be entertaining without any deep thematic expressions. Variety shows are typical events of this kind. On the other hand, some dramatic performances—including plays, operas, and ballets—are composed of complex stories expressing universal themes that the director and the rest of the production company wish to communicate to the audience. Events of those types require that the person planning and designing the lighting attain a clear understanding of what the production intends to achieve.

Script

Script analysis begins, of course, with a reading of the text. An initial reading should lead to an understanding of the theme and help establish a sense of mood—a feeling about the content. Some plays or libretti are so powerful that the person feels delighted or depressed, warm and loving, or perhaps suicidal after reading the text. It is important to be aware of how the text makes the reader feel. The mood that the piece stimulates in the reader will probably be similar to the mood of the audience on seeing the performance. A sense of mood about the play, opera, or ballet is essential to planning the lights because mood is such a strong effect of lighting.

A second reading of the text should allow determination of the practical needs of the script. The reader should perform a technical analysis that identifies the time of day and any changes in the location of the action, changes in mood, passage of time or season, and any other mechanical concerns that would establish lighting demands. This analysis should also include a discovery of the need for table lamps, chandeliers, and other lighting fixtures that appear as practical props on the set in more realistic productions; the required presence or absence of sunlight, moonlight, or lights through windows; a fireplace that might project light on a scene; or any other **motivational lighting** that would dictate the apparent source of light for a scene.

These two analyses, determination of theme and mood and identification of the practical needs of the performance, determine the expectations established by the script. When the director or choreographer is also serving in the roles of scenic designer, costume designer, and lighting designer, as often occurs in school and community theatre, most of this information will already be gathered and analyzed. When the director is not fulfilling all of these responsibilities, the person serving as lighting designer must complete these analyses and also come to an agreement with the director and other designers about the ideas, moods, and feelings expressed in the show. These are concepts that should guide all artistic decisions for the production.

Performance

Analysis of the script is only a starting point for planning the design. It is necessary to experience the production when it is well along in rehearsal (even in its rough rehearsal condition) to get a sense of how the performance feels. In addition, it is important to see how the stage is used to determine any special lighting requirements. Some parts of the stage may need exceptionally bright illumination, or deep shadows may be appropriate; climactic scenes or important speeches or actions may require special lighting to give them focus at a moment in the show. It is also important to know if characters stand on tables or lie on the floor or find themselves in other unusual positions that may require special treatment of the lights.

After the script has been analyzed and the production has been reviewed in rehearsal, it is necessary to gather additional information in preparation for planning the lighting.

Production Situation

The layout of the setting must be carefully analyzed to determine where lighting instruments may be placed and to identify any obstructions or hazards created by the design of the building or the location or movement of scenery or drapes. If drawings are available, the setting should be studied in both a plan and sectional view. If not available, the setting should be surveyed in place to make these determinations.

An inventory of available equipment is needed. This should be a simple list that identifies the kind and size of the spotlights and floodlights that are available and a notation about the wattage of lamps in each fixture. If equipment is to be borrowed or rented, it is very important to check the kind of plugs in the facility and the kind of plugs on the equipment that is to be obtained. If the plugs do not match, it may be necessary to acquire or make adapters that will allow the borrowed or rented equipment to be connected to power. Replacing plugs on the borrowed equipment is another option. Changing plugs on equipment belonging to someone else should be done only with permission. If plugs are changed, it is equally important to replace the connectors that were removed and to be sure that they are properly wired before returning the equipment.

In some facilities, lighting equipment is permanently installed and sometimes permanently focused. This may be a result of administrative policies or due to limited access to the equipment. In those situations, it is imperative to discover the rigidity of the restrictions. It is sometimes possible to persuade administrators to modify policies if they can be convinced that (1) it is appropriate and necessary to refocus the lights, (2) the person making the request understands what he or she is doing and is capable of doing it, and (3) the equipment will be returned to its original location and focus after the event. If this persuasion fails, it is necessary to take maximum advantage of the equipment in its restricted use, keeping the goals of the production in mind.

When productions are staged in facilities with built-in mounting positions and wiring, a diagram of these locations and circuits facilitates planning. When a production is mounted in a space where built-in equipment is not installed, it is necessary to know what portable mounting equipment is available and what restrictions may be imposed on its installation. It is important to determine whether pipes may be temporarily suspended overhead or if booms may be placed in aisles. It is also necessary to discover the availability of sufficient cable and connectors to hook up the lighting equipment.

The location, capacity, and type of the control board that is to be used must be identified. This information is essential to the planning, for it determines the size and quantity of lights that can be used and the degree of complexity of light cues. This information is equally important when planning lights to be controlled by a permanently installed system or a portable control system.

There are also several other things that need to be known when planning to use a portable control system.

1. *The type, size, and location of electrical service available to power the dimmers.* Some small portable systems can plug into several separate 120 volt 20 amp circuits by means of standard extension cords, while other systems require 220 volt single- or three-phase service that requires special cables wired directly to the main electrical panel of a building. The availability of the proper kind and size of electrical service is imperative for any lighting control system. It must be carefully checked and determined in advance before making arrangements to borrow or rent any equipment.

2. *Whether the dimmers and control console are a single integrated unit or are individual components that can be placed at separate locations.* An integrated system usually must be placed backstage to hook up to power and to distribute electrical service to the lights in a practical way. If an integrated system is placed in the audience, usually an exceptional amount of cable is needed to hook up the lights to the system. In addition, noise from dimmers and fans may distract the audience. On the other a hand, remote-control systems with a separate control console and dimmer bank permit both the dimmers and the control board to be placed at the most convenient locations. Often, the dimmers are placed backstage and the controller is placed at the rear of the audience. No matter which system is used, this information is imperative to determine the size and amount of cable needed to bring power to the dimmers and the quantity and length of extension cords to distribute power to the lights.

3. *The kind of connectors used and the number of outlets for each dimmer.* As with the instruments, it is important to know the kind of connectors the dimming equipment requires to plan the use of cables and adapters or whether to change connectors on equipment. The number of outlets a dimmer has will also determine the need for multiple connectors such as two-fers (as in two-for-one, explained in Chapter 6).

Whether using portable or permanently installed equipment, it is necessary to know the capacity of each dimmer. The quantity and size of dimmers will restrict the number of lights that may be turned on at one time. Working with a system that has a limited number of dimmers does not prohibit the possibility of repatching lights during the show if the system has a patch panel or if the dimmers of a portable system are accessible.

The final group of planning requirements is sometimes the most frustrating. To plan the lighting for a production reasonably, it is necessary to know the amount of time that will be available to install the equipment, focus the lights, and develop the cues for the show. In addition, it is helpful to know the availability and degree of knowledge of the staff that will assist with the installation, focus, and operation of the lights. When staff is limited in either knowledge or experience, or when time is highly restricted, or when both staff and time are limited, the complexity of a lighting design may have to be modified.

Achievement of an effective design depends on a knowledge of what is possible and how to adapt to limitations. It often is a matter of combining technical knowledge about electricity, light, and lighting equipment with artistic judgments about the production.

Developing the Design Idea

Once analysis has been completed, it is possible to begin to develop the actual lighting design. This stage of the process may start by planning specific images to be produced by light or it may begin with the placement of equipment. Whether the placement of equipment is planned for the production or imposed on the production by restrictions on the use of equipment in the facility, lighting design images may develop from the potential created by the equipment as it is placed. Whether images determine placement of the lights or the lights determine the images possible—and often both approaches become mixed in the development of a design—the lighting design should ultimately fulfill the six functions of stage lighting discussed earlier in this chapter: visibility, mood, composition, focus, credibility, and unity.

The first and most important task of a lighting design is to make the performance visible to the audience. Sometimes this may be the only function the lights for a production are able to fulfill because of the restrictions on equipment, staff, or time.

Visibility is a relative value. It does not mean flooding the stage with light but rather creating lighting conditions that reveal form, features, texture, and color appropriate to each moment of the show. This may be a very bright illumination that exposes every detail on stage, or it may be very dim light that softly models the performers with deep shadows. There are three concepts that must be considered when dealing with the function of visibility: plasticity, threshold of visibility, and figure-ground relationships.

Plasticity is the ability to distinguish visually three-dimensional form. A lighting design must make it possible to see the shape and texture of people and things on stage. A plastic or three-dimensional view is achieved by ensuring the presence of shadows as well as light, for it is the *combination* of highlight and shadows that reveals form. A lighting design must provide this contrast. This necessitates control of the quantity, color, and direction of light.

When there is too little illumination, it is impossible to see at all. As more light is added, it becomes easier and easier to distinguish the shape and texture of objects. At a certain point, the amount of light present will become so great that shadows will begin to disappear and then, due to an *excess* of light, it is impossible to distinguish the shape or texture of objects. To achieve plasticity, the lighting design must permit sufficient illumination to reveal form but also enough shadow to make the forms distinguishable.

Adjusting the quantity of illumination is only one way to control plasticity. The direction and angle at which light strikes a figure or object also affect the three-dimensional appearance of the object. Light coming from only one side of a form will place half of it in highlight and the opposite half in deep shadow. If light is aimed straight at a person or object from the front, shadows will be washed out and it will be difficult to distinguish form. If light is placed overhead or below a figure, deep shadows will be cast by the nose, lips, and eye sockets. By placing lights at angles that will help reveal form, a great sense of plasticity is achieved. Figure 1–1 shows the effect or lights at various positions around a form and the degree of plasticity they achieve.

Visibility sometimes means providing enough light to see, but this is a relative value, for human eyes are sensitive mechanisms that are able to adjust to extreme conditions. This is experienced in daily life. Perhaps the most dramatic example occurs when going into a darkened movie theatre on a sunny afternoon. When first entering the theatre, it is nearly impossible to see the aisle and even more difficult to distinguish empty seats. In a few moments, the eyes begin to adjust and it becomes easier to see in this darkened atmosphere. By the time the movie is over, the eyes have thoroughly adjusted to the dark and it is very easy to see in the diminished light of the theatre. The level of illumination has not changed, but the response of the eye has changed. The ability to see at any level of illumination is called the **threshold of visibility**, which identifies the point at which sufficient light is present ot make it possible to see. The threshold changes as the iris of the eye opens and closes to adjust to present conditions. An audience will be temporarily unable to see the stage when illumination is minimal if the preceding moment was very brightly lit; on the other hand, a quick change in illumination from a very dark stage to a very bright stage will be painful and it will be difficult for the audience to see until their eyes adjust. In other words, the ability to see in any quantity of light is related to the amount of light that was present immediately before. This is a relative factor that must be considered whenever planning the lighting.

The relative amount of light on a figure and the background before which it is seen is called the **figure-ground relationship**, and this also affects visibility. When the background has a lot of light falling on it, objects in the foreground may appear to be in shadow or silhouette even though they are well illuminated. The proportion of light falling on the figure and the background is out of balance. The problem may be solved by *reducing* only the amount of light on the *background* to improve the figure-ground relationship.

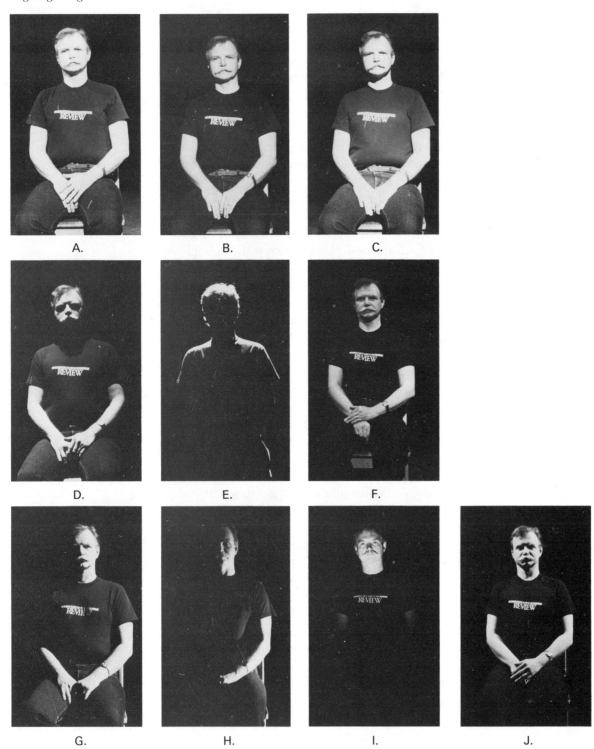

A. B. C.

D. E. F.

G. H. I. J.

FIGURE 1–1   **145**

Each photograph shows the model illuminated by a single source of light from a specific location. (A) Front 30° vertical angle; (B) front 45° vertical angle; (C) front 60° vertical angle; (D) directly overhead—a downlight; (E) back 60° vertical angle; (F) side 45° angle; (G) side even with the shoulder; (H) side about shin high; (I) front at floor; (J) both sides 60 vertical angle.

Once the function of visibility has been fulfilled, it is possible to plan effects that will achieve the other functions of lighting design. Creating and altering **mood** are some of the most important of these. It is the creation of an atmosphere that evokes a psychological effect in the audience. Mood is created and manipulated through lighting by controlling the quantity, direction, and color of the illumination. Although each of these qualities of light may be discussed individually, it is the combination of intensity, direction, and color that contributes to the sense of mood as well as to composition, focus, credibility, and unity.

Direction refers to the angle at which light strikes the stage. Light may come from sources directly in front of the stage to create one effect or from instruments to the side or behind the performers, creating other effects. It may be projected at severe overhead angles or on a very flat plane parallel to the stage floor. The direction of light affects plasticity but also contributes to mood, focus, and credibility. Like all other qualities of light, the direction of light also contributes to a sense of composition, or the creation of a picture.

Whether used in a realistic or highly artificial way, **color** makes a dramatic contribution to a lighting design. When color is used subtly, it can create a realistic atmosphere that reinforces the sense of credibility and also contributes to the mood of the production as well as influencing focus and composition. Used in an artificial way, color in light can contribute to striking dramatic effects that enhance a dramatic moment or become independent compositions of light.

Control and manipulation of each of the qualities of light—in conjunction with each other—should create stage pictures that enhance the dramatic effect of any production. The results may reinforce a sense of reality about a drama or add visual excitement to a concert. Limits on equipment, staff, or time may mean that the use of light simply allows the audience to see. However, even in these restricted situations the effect of lighting can be maximized with careful planning and an understanding of ways to utilize the equipment to the greatest advantage.

LIGHTING DESIGN

Each of the functions of lighting design—visibility, mood, composition, focus, credibility, and unity—can be achieved in a variety of ways. A number of systems of design have developed based on the way they fulfill one or more of the functions of light or as a result of limits on equipment, mounting positions, or the way a performance space is used. Obviously, a production in a proscenium theatre that positions the audience only on one side would place different kinds of demands on the lighting than a performance mounted on an arena stage with the audience surrounding the performance.

The real issues in each of the lighting design systems are where the equipment is placed, how it is colored, and the effect of those choices on visibility, mood, composition, focus, and credibility.

In discussing each of the lighting design systems, a number of terms will be used that require specific understanding.

Key light is a term that the theatre industry has borrowed from television. It refers to the most intense directional illumination high lighting a figure. The alternative to key light is **fill light**. This is the softer, less intense illumination that is used as soft general illumination to fill in shadows.

High-angle illumination refers to sources of light placed at a vertical angle of 60° or more (Figure 1–2), while **low-angle** illumination refers to lighting instruments located in the 15 to 30° range.

FIGURE 1–2
Low-angle illumination is at a vertical angle of 15 to 30°, and high-angle illumination is at a vertical angle of 60 to 75°.

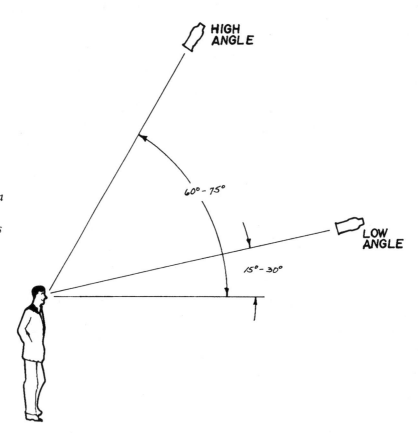

Backlight (Figure 1–3) is placed behind a performer at a high-angle overhead. It is often positioned to project at a vertical angle between 60 and 75° so that it brightly illuminates the rear of the figure but casts a short shadow in front of the figure. Backlight separates a figure from the background by placing highlight on the shoulders, head, and back of the torso. It contributes significantly to a sense of plasticity.

Downlight (Figure 1–3) is usually placed directly above a figure and focused straight down on the stage. Downlight makes the top of the head and shoulders glow with illumination but causes deep shadows to be cast in the eye sockets and under the nose, chin, and any other protrusions. Although it creates a sense of plasticity, downlight often causes a sense of distortion due to the deep shadows. Used at low intensity and mixed with light from other positions, downlight can wash the stage with color without creating too severe distortion.

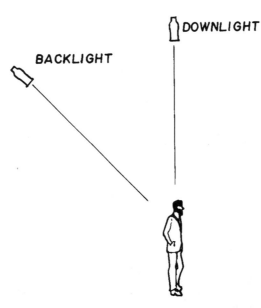

FIGURE 1–3
Downlight and backlight.

Sidelight (Figure 1–4) is placed directly to the left and/or right of a performer. It may be located above the performer at a high angle, at a 45° angle, level with the performer, or near the floor.

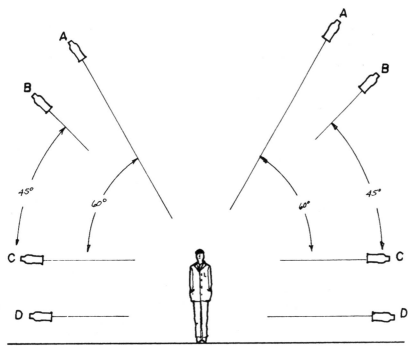

FIGURE 1–4
Positions for sidelight. (A) High-angle sidelight at an approximate vertical angle of 60°; (B) sidelight at an approximate vertical angle of 45°; (C) shoulder-high sidelight; (D) shin-high sidelight, known as "shin kickers."

13

Hard and **soft** refer to the quality of beams projected by a light (Figure 1–5) and the shadows they create as a result of the quality of light projected. A hard beam of light can be projected from ellipsoidal reflector spotlights and follow spots. Soft beams of light are cast by fresnels, strip lights, and scoops. The judgment about whether a beam is hard or soft can be made by looking at either the edge of the beam or the shadow cast by a figure in the beam of light. If the edge of the beam or the edge of the shadow of a figure in the beam is sharp and crisp, it is a hard beam of light. If the edge of a beam of light fades off rather than sharply cutting off or the shadow is fuzzy, it is a soft beam of light. It is easy to blend together soft beams of light; it is very difficult to achieve blending with hard beams of light.

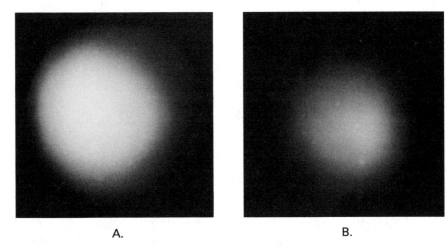

FIGURE 1–5
(A) A hard-edged beam of light; (B) a soft-edged beam of light.

A.   B.

As part of the process of developing the lighting design, the acting area for the performance is divided into a number of focus areas. A **focus area** is a location on stage where a single light or a group of lights is aimed. Each focus area may be distinct and isolated. However, it is usually most effective when each area overlaps and blends into adjacent focus areas. Although a focus area approximately 8'–0" in diameter provides the most practical degree of control, the actual size of the area is determined by the kind of lighting instruments that will be used and the throw. If scoops are the only lighting instruments available, the focus area may be 15'–0" to 25'–0" in diameter; a 6" fresnel will project an effective beam of light that is 8'–0" in diameter at a throw of about 15'–0", and a 6 × 9 ellipsoidal will project an approximate 8'–0" circle of light at about a 25'–0" throw. See Table 4–1 in Chapter 4 for more detailed information about the effective pool of light projected by various instruments. Each focus area may be illuminated with only one or with several lighting instruments from various positions.

Warm and **cool** describe the sense of temperature that certain colors of light or pigment convey. In general, colors that have a red or yellow quality communicate a sense of warmth, and colors that have a blue or green characteristic communicate a sense of coolness.

Dilute and **saturated** describe the strength of a gel color. A very deep color would be considered saturated, whereas one that is very pale would be considered dilute.

Systems of instrument placement and the use of color have developed to fulfill the functions of lighting design. They are guides from which to develop a lighting design. The systems vary the quantity, placement, direction, and color of light.

No matter which system is used, *the function of visibility can only be achieved satisfactorily by placing some lighting instruments in front of the stage*—that is, in locations above the audience on each side of the stage on which audience members are seated. This may only be one side of the stage for a proscenium production or it might be on four sides of the stage for an arena production.

In any of the lighting systems described here, usually it is preferable to use ellipsoidal spotlights or PAR can fixtures (see page 103) of the appropriate size from mounting positions in the auditorium. Fresnels are preferred for front and downlight on stage, but ellipsoidals and PARs work equally well. Either ellipsoidals, fresnels, PARs, or beam projectors are effective as backlight, and ellipsoidals and PARs are the most satisfactory sidelights. These uses of equipment are preferred because of (1) the ability of ellipsoidals and PARs to project a concentrated beam of light that can be controlled with shutters in the ellipsoidal and barn doors on the PARs to eliminate any stray illumination and (2) the ability of fresnels and beam projectors to project strong but easily blended beams of light.

Should the preferred or traditional equipment not be available, many of the functions assigned to ellipsoidals or fresnels can be fulfilled with other equipment—if there is some acceptance of uncontrolled illumination or a lack of concentration of the beam. If necessary, scoops or strip lights can replace any of the downlight or sidelight. The pattern of the light will be uncontrollable. However, two or three scoops may be able to create an effective wash of colored illumination that has a distinct directional quality, which may help create the sense of dawn or dusk or contribute to plasticity. The depth and sharpness of shadows will be diminished with the use of floodlights, but the general effect of the angle of projection can be achieved to make a more interesting lighting design. If absolutely necessary, fresnels or even scoops may be used in auditorium positions for front light to at least ensure adequate visibility. In other words, even when one of the approaches described here calls for an ellipsoidal or a fresnel in a specific location, the instrument may be replaced with a scoop or some other instrument if the preferred equipment is not available and spill is acceptable. One nonstandard use of equipment should be avoided: it is difficult to use scoops in backlight positions because the broad beam tends to flood uncontrolled into the audience. If an instrument that projects a more concentrated beam is not available for this application, backlight should be eliminated from the design.

SYSTEMS OF LIGHTING DESIGN FOR THE PROSCENIUM THEATRE

Individual creativity is one of the hallmarks of an artist. Knowledge of standard or typical means of expression provides any artist with a place to begin thinking and from which to expand. In some cases, traditional techniques or approaches provide a strong foundation upon which to build a design idea. This section presents an array of approaches to lighting design based on the position of fixtures and potential selections of color for illumination. The quality of light produced by any of these approaches may be altered significantly simply by changing the type of fixture used or employing colors in unique combinations. Several ways are presented because no one way is correct for any situation. Any choice is valid so long as it enhances the performance. The following "systems" are offered as points of departure for further exploration by the artist-lighting designer. In these descriptions, the word *point* describes the number of directions from which sources of light will be projected.

Single-Point Lighting

Some facilities and production companies are extremely limited in the amount and type of lighting equipment available. It is not unusual to discover that a small school, or a church has only one or two scoops or a borrowed follow spot to illuminate the stage. Lighting in these situations must simply provide sufficient illumination for visibility. Selection of the location for this equipment is critical since the one light must do a great deal of work. This is single-point lighting in the most extreme sense: a single fixture to illuminate the entire acting area.

Single-point lighting generally means using only one lighting instrument to illuminate each focus area of the stage. Usually a design restricted in this way can provide visibility and, by carefully controlling intensities, fulfill some of the other functions of lighting design as well.

When a single lighting instrument is used to illuminate each focus area, it should be placed directly in front of the area at a vertical angle of approximately 45° to create the "most natural" visibility lighting (Figure 1–6). Each instrument should project a beam of light that blends into all adjacent focus areas. Color may or may not be used in this system depending on the intensity of the light. If there is insufficient illumination when the lights are colored, gel should not be used. However, if the lights are bright enough, a dilute gel such as No-Color Pink or a somewhat stronger color such as Flesh Pink might be selected to help create a sense of warmth or coldness. If the beams of light do

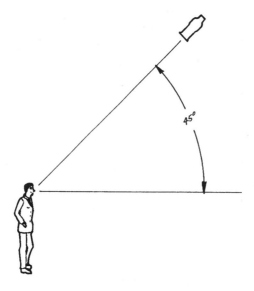

FIGURE 1–6
A 45° angle is the optimal vertical angle for front light.

not blend effectively with each other, a diffusion gel such as Tough Silk, Frost, or Hamburg Frost may be used to soften edges of the light.

Lights projected directly from the front at a vertical angle of 45° provide satisfactory illumination that casts seemingly natural shadows. This results in a moderate sense of plasticity and little distortion. This vertical angle is usually steep enough to prevent the shadows cast by actors from falling on each other or on the scenery. Mounting positions, however, may necessitate moving lighting instruments to higher or lower vertical angles. As the angle of projection becomes lower, larger and darker shadows will be projected upstage. At a vertical angle of approximately 30°, the audience will begin to see two shows: the actors performing one show, and their shadows performing another show on the background. In contrast, however, as the angle of projection rises above 45°, there is an increase in the depth of shadows on faces and figures. A vertical angle of 60° is still practical; however, any angle greater than that will result in reduced visibility and unnatural appearances to the performers. These extreme angles of illumination can create lighting that is very distracting to an audience. They should be used only when a special effect is desired.

Two-Point Lighting

Although it is possible to illuminate the stage with a single lighting instrument focused on each area, this system is extremely limiting. Much more effective and flexible lighting designs can be created using two-point lighting. Obviously, this requires additional lighting instruments, circuits, and control equipment.

The simplest extension from one-point to two-point lighting maintains a light directly in front of each focus area at a vertical angle of approximately 45° and places a second instrument directly behind each focus area at a vertical angle of 60° to 70° (Figure 1–7). The front light

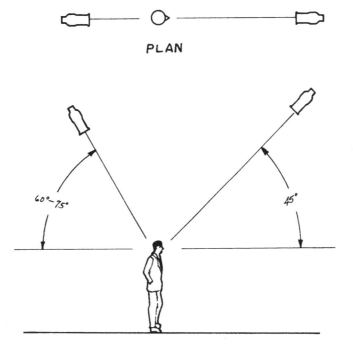

PLAN

FIGURE 1–7
Preferred angles for front and backlight.

60°–75°   45°

provides visibility and some sense of plasticity; it is usually colored with a dilute gel that gently warms or cools the beams without distorting the colors of costumes or scenery. The backlight creates a glow at the back of the head, the shoulders, and around the torso of the performers. This visually separates them from the background and strengthens the sense of plasticity. The backlight may be colored with any gel. Dilute colors, similar to those used for the front light, will add a kind of sparkle or glow to the stage; saturated colors, such as Sky Blue or Medium Red, can be used to paint the stage with strong colors of light. Since these strong colors are projected from behind, the appearance of the performers, illuminated with dilute colors from the front, will not be distorted. This is an effective way to put deeply colored illumination on the stage without making the costumes or the actors look ugly or unnatural. By balancing the relative intensity of the front light and the backlight, the stage may appear to shift in color while always maintaining a natural appearance to the performers.

This system can be enriched by having more than one backlight on each focus area (Figure 1–8). If a production makes radical shifts from one mood to another or from one time of day to another, it may be desirable to color the stage both deep blue and deep red at different times while maintaining a natural appearance to the performers. This can be accomplished by **double-hanging** the backlight—that is, placing two lighting instruments under separate control behind each focus area and coloring each instrument with a different-colored gel. Although this extension of the system adds a third instrument to each focus area, the light still only comes from two points, in front and behind each focus area.

FIGURE 1–8
Double backlight combined with a single front light for each focus area.

This two-point lighting system can be modified in a number of ways.

1. (Figure 1–9) Rather than placing the front light directly in front of the focus area, it could be moved toward a side. The backlight could be kept in place directly behind the lighting area or it could be moved on the same axis to remain directly in line with the front light. This variation will result in stronger shadows on the faces of the performers, and as the backlight moves toward the front, increasing color distortion will be visible.

FIGURE 1–9
Front light rotated off-axis.

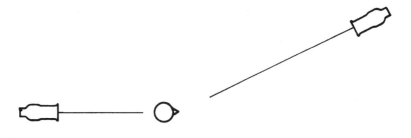

2. (Figure 1–10) Rather than placing the lighting instruments directly opposite each other, the backlight could be relocated to a side position. In this way, the front light continues to provide undistorted, moderately three-dimensional illumination, but the high-angle sidelight paints dramatic shadows and colored beams on the performers and scenery.

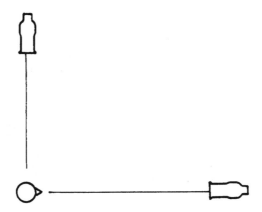

FIGURE 1–10
The backlight revolved 90° to become sidelight.

3. (Figure 1–11) The sidelight can be moved to a low angle that washes the torso with color and casts long shadows on the scenery or into the opposite wing. Once again, the front light provides illumination and the sidelight performs a three-dimensional modeling and coloring function.

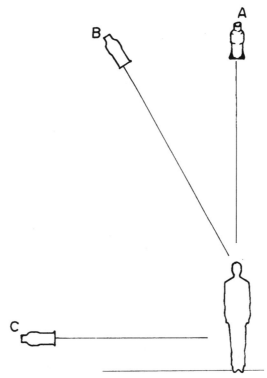

FIGURE 1–11
Front view. (A) Front light; (B) high-angle sidelight; (C) low-angle sidelight.

19

4. (Figure 1–12) The front light is maintained directly in front of each focus area and provided with a dilute color gel. Any lighting instrument, but preferably an ellipsoidal or a fresnel, is mounted directly above each focus area and equipped with a dilute or very intense color that washes down on the figures in each area. When ellipsoidals are used for downlight they cast deep, harsh shadows that tend to suggest scary monster lighting. If the ellipsoidals are replaced with fresnels, the lighting becomes much softer, casting fuzzy shadows that are neither as deep nor as harsh as those created by the ellipsoidals. In a pinch, scoops or strip lights can be used in the downlight position. The shadows they cast are much softer; they tend to just flood the stage with colors of light, rather intensely illuminating a performer.

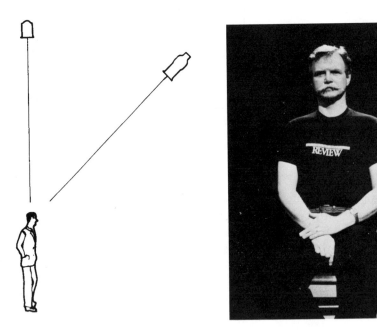

FIGURE 1–12
Front and downlight.

Certainly other variations of two-point lighting can be devised, working with subtle and broad differences in color and direction.

A completely different two-point system is the result of research by Professor Stanley McCandless. He explored the effect of various lighting positions and colors to determine ways to achieve the most realistic appearance for stage lighting. This resulted in the development of the **McCandless System.**

The theory behind the McCandless System is that light is directional, based on the location of the source of light. During daylight outdoors, the light that is on the sunny side of a person is bright and warm in color while the opposite side is in shadow. Shadow is the absence of light. On stage, this would place one side of a performer in bright light and the opposite side in darkness. Rather than placing half of the performer in darkness, the McCandless System projects light to the side opposite the source of light in a shadow-like color. In this way, a performer is illuminated on both sides: one side with highlight representing the source of light and the other side with light representing the coolness of shadow. If the scene occurs indoors, the same rules apply, but the source of light may be a lamp, chandelier, fireplace, or light through a window. The side of the stage that faces the source of light will be illuminated with a warm color and the side facing away from the source of light will be illuminated with a cool color.

Each focus area in this system will be illuminated with one warm light from the side of the stage from which the source of light seems to be projected and one cool light on the opposite side. The most effective angles at which to project this light are 45° to the right and 45° to the left of each focus area at a vertical angle of 45° (Figure 1–13). Ellipsoidal spotlights should be placed in front of the stage and adjusted to a soft focus that allows the beams of light to blend into each other but still permits shutters to cut off light at the wings and the edges of the stage. Fresnels should be used onstage since they are shorter-throw instruments that blend together extremely well.

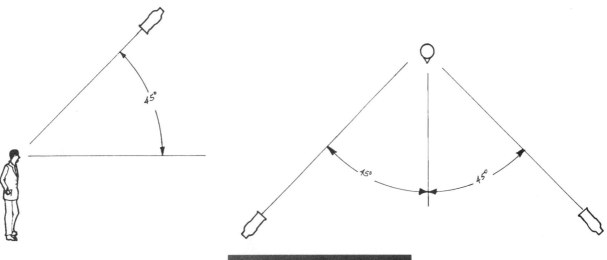

FIGURE 1–13
The "McCandless Lighting System." The vertical angle for all fixtures is 45° and an instrument is placed 45° to both the right and left of the center of each focus area. No color is used in the photograph, so it shows the 45° angles with white light only. Normally, a warm color is used on one side and a cool color is used on the opposite side.

21

The system works fairly well when sufficiently dilute colors are used in the lights from each side. However, if the colors are too saturated, they may cause a performer facing stage right to appear pink while the person facing stage left appears blue. In a sense, the actors may change colors or appear to walk through stripes of colored light if the gel is too saturated or the beams do not blend together smoothly. This is especially important and often difficult to accomplish with the ellipsoidals used to illuminate downstage areas from auditorium mounting positions.

A few additional things are needed to complete the McCandless System: motivational light, specials, door specials, and backing lights. These also may be incorporated in other lighting systems.

Motivational light is the apparent source of illumination in a scene. In realistic lighting it should be apparent whether it is a floor lamp or sunlight streaming through a window. A floor or table lamp should be controlled by a dimmer so the glare from the light bulb is not too intense and distracting for an audience. If it is not possible to put the lamp on a separate dimmer, then a low-wattage light bulb should be used in the fixture. The result gives the appearance that the lamp is on and producing the light for the scene; however, the actual illumination from the lamp will not be sufficiently strong even to create a realistic pool of more intense light in the vicinity of the fixture.

A **special**—that is, a light that is not used for area lighting but serves a special purpose—should be added to the design to project the realistic pool of light around the lamp. When the source of light is a chandelier, some additional considerations must be given to projecting the pool of more intense realistic looking light in the vicinity of the fixture. Since a fresnel mounted directly above a chandelier as a down-light will cast a shadow of the fixture on the performers and floor beneath it in an unrealistic way, another means must be established to project the pool of light seemingly cast by the chandelier. The most effective technique is to place four fresnels above the chandelier and aim them just beneath the fixture to the opposite side of the light, so the beams of light cross just beneath the fixture (Figure 1–14).

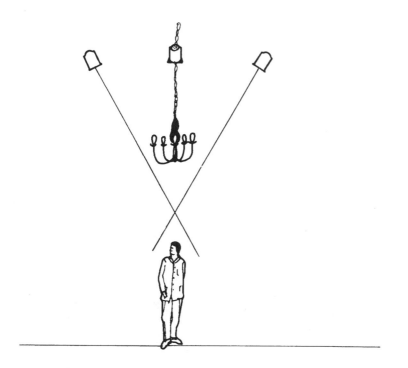

FIGURE 1–14
To project the sense of realistic illumination from a chandelier, at least four fresnels are positioned so their beams cross beneath the practical fixture.

Sunlight is easily projected through a window by aiming any light from offstage through the opening on the setting. Ellipsoidals, fresnels, and beam projectors are especially effective for this purpose. However, if only scoops are available, they will be satisfactory but may spill badly on the back and around the edges of the setting. The effect of sunlight through a window can be enhanced by placing a gobo in an ellipsoidal to project the pattern of the bars in a window on the floor or walls of the setting (Figure 1–15). Selection of the appropriate color gel is very important to give credibility to this effect.

If a scene occurs in the woods or some other outdoor setting, motivational light is still necessary. This may be strong rays of sunlight brightly coloring the stage from a specific direction or filtered sun or moonlight streaming through the leaves of a forest and casting mottled

FIGURE 1–15
*Sunlight can be implied by projecting a window pattern with light on the floor or wall of a setting. (*The Dining Room, *Theatre UNI, University of Northern Iowa.)*

speckles of brightly colored light in an atmosphere that is otherwise misty green or shadowy blue.

Door-backing lights are usually needed with McCandless lighting designs. These are lighting instruments located behind door openings to illuminate the area just offstage of the door so that a performer does not appear to be walking into a black void when exiting from the acting area (Figure 1–16). Small fresnels, R40 lamps mounted in swivel bases, or any other small fixture might be used for this purpose. The light fixtures can be hooked or screwed to the back of flats on the latch (opposite the hinge) side of the door. The light should be focused at the performers as they walk through the door opening. The instrument should be colored with the same gel as the acting area lighting, or if a distinctive environment is to be implied, a different color gel may be used.

Once performers are in the door opening, they are in a lighting area that is between the door-backing light and the acting-area light. There often is no illumination in that area. This problem is solved by adding a **door special** to the design. The door special is usually an ellipsoidal spotlight placed at a high angle directly in line with the door.

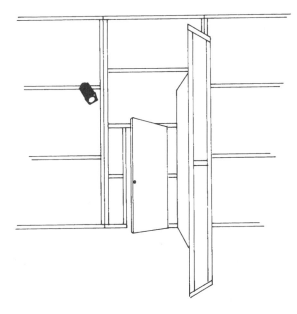

FIGURE 1–16
A door-backing light should be mounted above the door on the side opposite the hinge.

The shutters on the instrument should be adjusted to limit the beam of light to the inside of the door opening. This will illuminate the performer in the space between the door-backing light and the acting-area light. The instrument should be equipped with the same color gel as the acting area lighting. It should be set at a level bright enough to light a performer in the door opening without turning into a bright, independent rectangle of light.

The McCandless System limits highlight to only one side of the stage. Often this is an appropriate arrangement, but when passage of time is important to the action or the scene moves to a locale with distinctly different illumination, the apparent source of light might move—even to the opposite side of the stage. This may occur when the play spans the period from dawn to dusk or when sunlight comes through a window on stage right during daytime scenes but a lamp on stage left is the motivational light during evening scenes. These kinds of changes in illumination can be accommodated by hanging a **Double McCandless** design, which places two lights on each side of the stage for each focus area (Figure 1–17). This results in a warm and a cool light focused on each area from each side of the stage. Obviously, the system requires almost twice as much lighting equipment as a regular McCandless plot.

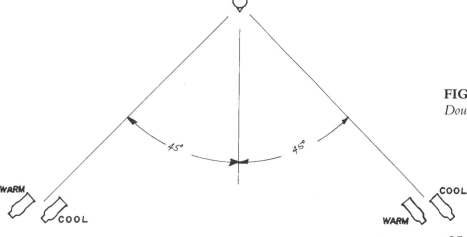

FIGURE 1–17
Double McCandless light plot.

25

This system of design can lead to some dramatic and exciting lighting cues. If a play takes place from dawn to dusk, the opening moments can use the cool lights from both sides of the stage, with the sunrise side at a higher level of intensity. As the sun rises, the cool light on one side is replaced with warm light from that side, for instance, stage right. As the sun continues to rise to the warm, bright light of early afternoon, the entire acting area could be illuminated by changing intensities of warm light from both sides of the stage until late afternoon lighting takes over. This would consist of cool light from stage right in this case, and warm light from stage left where the sun is beginning to set. Early evening could be illuminated with a combination of cool light from both sides of the stage plus some warm light from stage left emulating the lingering glow of the setting sun. Finally, the lighting returns to the original condition of the cool light of night from both sides of the stage. Achieving this series of cues requires enough lighting instruments to hang a Double McCandless design, a sufficient number of dimmers to control all of the lights at one time, and preferably a memory control board or excellent control board operators who can execute slow, smooth changes in the lights.

A version of the Double McCandless concept can be achieved if the shift in the action of a play from day to night occurs during an intermission and the lighting instruments are easily accessible. Simply, the color media in the lighting instruments can be reversed so that the lights on stage right change from the warm to the cool color, and those on stage left become the warm lights for the second act. Although this approach does not permit the range of subtlety that a true Double McCandless System offers, it does provide the possibility of making an obvious shift in the lighting from one time of day to another.

Three-Point Lighting

Both the McCandless System and the Double McCandless System are effective when the beams of light are arranged to blend together in smooth even patterns and the warm and cool gel colors support each other. Although saturated washes of colored light are sometimes desired, the McCandless System does not allow the use of strong colors in the lights from either side of the stage since they will distort the realistic sense that the system is attempting to create. Projection of strongly colored illumination can be accomplished in another way. The lighting can be enriched by adding a backlight to each focus area (Figure 1–18). The backlight serves two purposes: (1) it visually separates the performers from the background, adding to the sense of three-dimensionality; and (2) it permits a highly saturated color of light to be used without distorting the realistic effect created by the McCandless System. The combination, then, of a warm light 45° to the right front and a cool light 45° to the left front of each focus area at an elevation of 45° above the performer, plus a backlight directly behind each focus area at a vertical position between 60° and 75°, can greatly enhance the effectiveness of the McCandless System. If a play takes place in the evening, the backlight can bathe the stage in deeply colored blue light, yet the performers can remain illuminated "realistically" from the front without any color distortion.

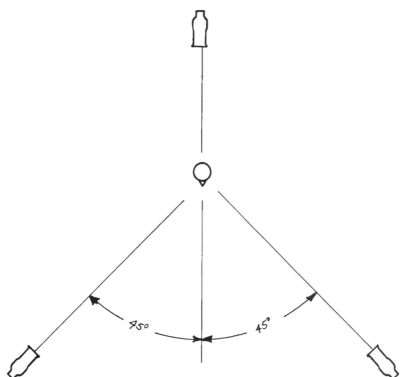

FIGURE 1–18
A McCandless light plot
with backlight added.

Other ways of utilizing three-point lighting for the proscenium stage are less systematized, with seemingly unlimited possibilities. As with most two-point systems, three-point lighting usually uses a dilute color for front light to provide illumination in each focus area, and the remaining lights fill or cast shadows, project strong colors, and create intense highlights. Since there is one additional lighting instrument needed for each area, the equipment requirements are increased by approximately one third and additional dimmer space is needed. Each approach described below is, in a sense, a combination of some of the two-point systems described above.

1. (Figure 1–19) Three fixtures are evenly distributed on three separate axes located 120° apart, with one light located directly in front of each focus area at a vertical angle of 45°. A low saturation color is used in the front light to achieve undistorted illumination. The other two lights are located to the rear-side of each focus area at a vertical angle of 60° to 75°; these lights may use highly saturated colors that complement or contrast each other. The backlights may be used independently of each other while in combination with the light from the front, or they may be used concurrently to illuminate from both side-rear positions, mixing with the front light.

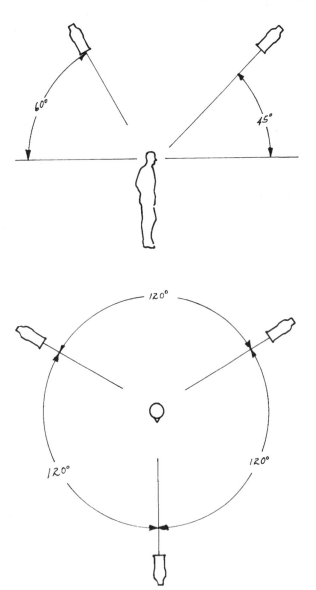

FIGURE 1–19

Area lighting from three sources on equally spaced axes. The front light should be at a vertical angle of 45° and the backlights at a steeper vertical angle.

This approach provides excellent illumination with almost no distortion of color or unnatural shadows. The backlight allows the stage to be washed in two different colors at varying degrees of intensity, and when the colors mix together they may create a third color. As the intensity of the front light and each of the backlights is modified, an immense number of new combinations of highlight, shadow, and color can be created. At times, front light might dominate; at other times, the backlight in combination might be dominant or one or the other backlight might be made most intense. This is a way to control color, plasticity, and movement of the light.

2. (Figure 1–20) Similar to the three-point system above, a front light is located directly in front of each focus area and the backlights are placed at the rear but only 15° to 30° to either side of the centerline of each focus area; the high vertical angle is maintained for the backlights to minimize casting long shadows downstage. This increases the angle between the front light and the backlights and locates the backlight more directly behind each focus area, which results in the backlight serving as a strong and colorful highlight on the head, shoulders, and torso of a figure rather than projecting color down each side of the figure.

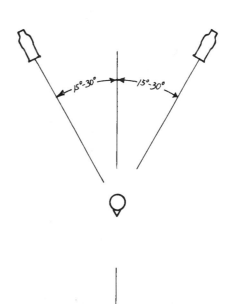

FIGURE 1–20
A lighting design using three fixtures per area. The backlights are placed off the centerline to the rear of each focus area.

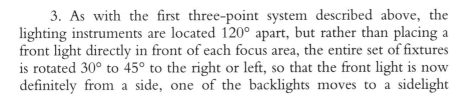

3. As with the first three-point system described above, the lighting instruments are located 120° apart, but rather than placing a front light directly in front of each focus area, the entire set of fixtures is rotated 30° to 45° to the right or left, so that the front light is now definitely from a side, one of the backlights moves to a sidelight

position, and the other backlight moves to an off-centered backlight position. The vertical angle of the sidelight could be maintained or adjusted to a very high or low angle.

This approach will result in a strong sense of three-dimensionality, especially if a highly saturated color is used for the instruments that become sidelight. The artificiality and depth of shadows created by this system can be minimized by reducing the saturation of the gel in the side position. A workable combination of colors might use a deep blue in the backlight, a lighter blue in the sidelight, and no gel at all in the off-axis front light for a more natural illumination with a high level of plasticity and visual interest.

4. (Figure 1–21). A somewhat different approach to three-point lighting returns to the basic two-point system with one fixture directly in front of each focus area, another directly behind each focus area, and then adding a third fixture, preferably a fresnel, directly above each focus area as a downlight.

The front light provides illumination for visibility, and the backlight helps to establish a sense of plasticity and separation from the background, as well as projecting a strong color. The downlight can be used to project a soft wash of intense or dilute color, casting interesting shadows that may be partially filled in with the front light. The effect of this lighting changes dramatically as the fixtures used for the downlight are replaced. Ellipsoidals will cast stronger, deeper, crisper shadows, while scoops or strip lights will project very soft, almost shadowless light.

FIGURE 1–21
A figure illuminated with three evenly spaced lights (120° apart) plus a downlight.

5. (Figure 1–22) This approach to three-point light also locates an instrument directly in front of and behind each focus area, but rather than mounting the third instrument directly overhead, a fixture may be placed directly to one side of each focus area at a vertical angle between 30° and 75°.

Once again, the front light provides undistorted illumination for visibility; the backlight contributes to plasticity and separation from the background and permits the use of saturated color. The sidelight should be used with a dilute or moderately saturated color, stronger than the front light but not as saturated as the backlight. These instruments will highlight one side of the torso and face to create an extremely strong sense of three-dimensionality; however, the color from the side may cause some distortion of flesh tones and costume colors. This design may be used with any setting when the vertical angle of the sidelight is 60° or above; at lower angles it is difficult to use this sidelight with realistic interior settings because strong, unnatural shadows are cast across the stage on other performers and on the walls.

FIGURE 1–22
A figure illuminated with a front light, backlight, and one sidelight.

6. (Figure 1–23). Another practical three-point lighting design locates one instrument directly in front of each focus area at a vertical angle of 45° and an additional instrument directly to each side of each focus area at a vertical angle of 60°. The front light should use a very dilute color, while moderate to strongly saturated colors may be placed in the sidelights.

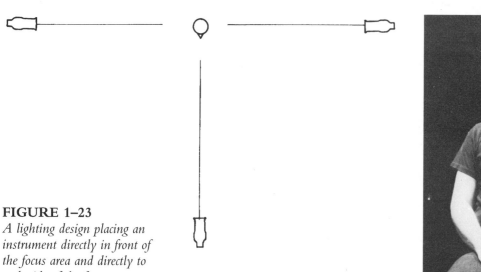

FIGURE 1–23
A lighting design placing an instrument directly in front of the focus area and directly to each side of the focus area.

The front light provides undistorted illumination, while the sidelights can be used to cast strongly colored light on the stage. The sidelights can be used to create mood or as three-dimensional modeling light. While the beams of the sidelight wrap around to the front of a performer, the front light will minimize any color distortion. When the intensity of the front light is reduced, the sidelights will be more apparent and will strongly color the stage and performers. This lighting creates deep shadows that contribute to the three-dimensional effect of the lighting. With the absence of backlight, the performers will not be quite as effectively separated from the background.

7. Low-angle sidelight is combined with front light and backlight. Front light and backlight are located in the usual positions and the sidelight is mounted at shoulder or shin height on booms or trees in the wings. The use of color can be highly varied in the sidelight; it is often in sharp contrast to both the front and backlight.

This very low-angle sidelight removes the lighting from any usual sense of realism. Because the light is especially effective for revealing the torso in a very plastic way, it is usually reserved for special effects or for lighting mime or dance performances.

8. (Figure 1–24) An interesting, although somewhat shadowy effect can be created by locating an ellipsoidal at 60° to 75° to the right and left of each focus area mounted at a vertical angle of 75°. A downlight must be placed directly above each focus area to fill shadows. Since this lighting tends to be very shadowy and unrealistic, use of color may be equally unrealistic. Usually, however, this lighting is most

FIGURE 1–24
A figure illuminated with high-angle sidelight and downlight.

effective if dilute colors are used in the sidelight and the strong colors are reserved for the downlight.

This approach to lighting tends to provide strong figure-modeling light that emphasizes plasticity. It can be effective for nonrealistic productions, dance, or mime.

9. (Figure 1–25) Front light at a vertical angle of 60° may be combined with another front light on the floor and a third instrument positioned as a backlight. The floor light and front light should use dilute colors, while the backlight may be a dilute or highly saturated color. The floor light must be used at a low level of intensity to avoid creating unnatural shadows for a somewhat realistic effect, or strong colors can be used for nonrealistic effects.

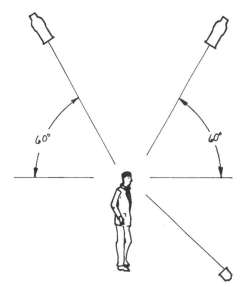

FIGURE 1–25
A lighting design using high-angle front light, floor front light, and backlight.

Four-Point Lighting

In four-point lighting, any three-point lighting system is simply extended by adding an additional position to enhance the effectiveness of the lighting and increase the possibilities for variety in lighting moments. A greater number of lighting angles are available and more colors can be used as the number of sources of light increases. Also, there is a greater possibility of effectively using shadow and reduced illumination by emphasizing backlight or sidelight while maintaining a glow of illumination from the front for the purposes of visibility. A great deal of variety is possible. Once again, the selection of appropriate colors is a serious concern in the development of the design. In general, front light should be dilute to minimize distortion of flesh tones, while backlight and side light may be as dilute or as saturated in color as desired. The following brief summary of some approaches to fourpoint lighting should exemplify ways to apply this expanded use of equipment.

FIGURE 1–26

A lighting design using four evenly spaced instruments located 90° apart. (A) Each instrument located on an axis parallel with and perpendicular to the audience; (B) each instrument located on an axis diagonal to the audience; (C) a figure illuminated with four-point lighting on parallel and perpendicular axes.

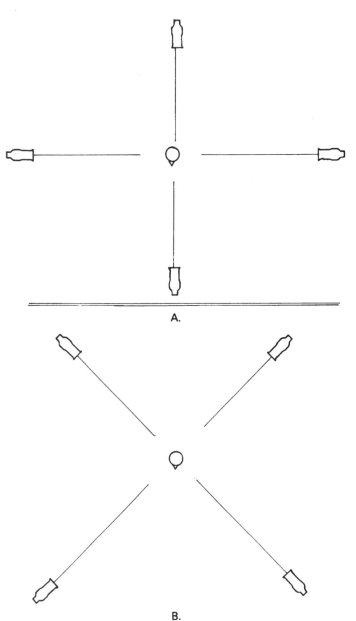

A.

B.

C.

1. (Figure 1–26) Place four instruments 90° apart to establish front, back-, and sidelight. The instruments may be located on axes parallel with the proscenium arch and perpendicular to it or may be revolved to different orientations, but maintaining the 90° spacing between instruments.

2. (Figure 1–27) Three lighting instruments can be located 120° apart on any convenient orientation, with a fourth instrument used as a downlight, a low-angle sidelight (shin kicker), or as a footlight from the front.

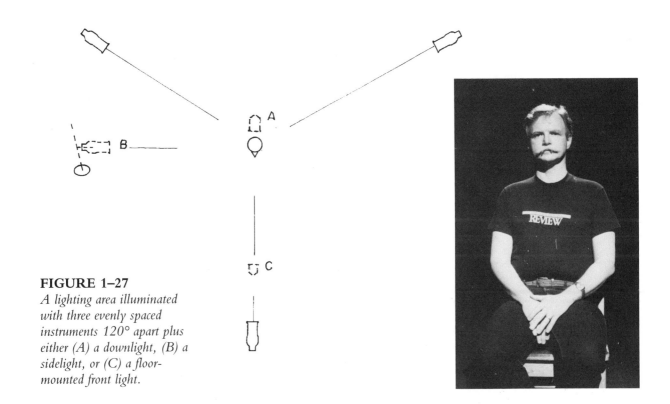

FIGURE 1–27
*A lighting area illuminated
with three evenly spaced
instruments 120° apart plus
either (A) a downlight, (B) a
sidelight, or (C) a floor-
mounted front light.*

Multipoint Lighting

Four-point lighting simply combines any variety of lighting positions to extend the plot for greater diversity, subtlety, and control. **Multi-point** lighting (Figure 1–28) extends the plot even further by combining any five or more lighting positions in the same design. Multipoint lighting may be used for any kind of production but is especially effective for performances that emphasize movement, such as dance and mime.

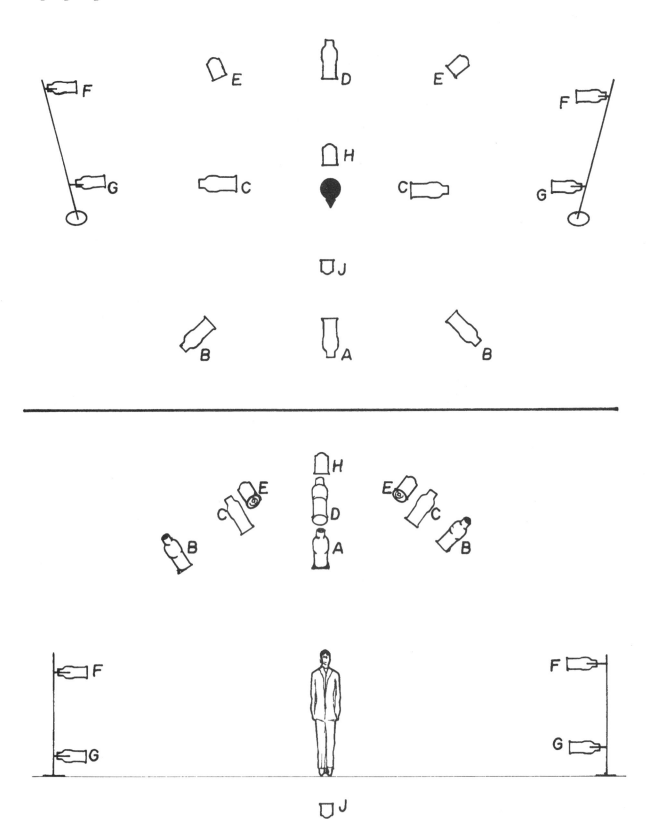

FIGURE 1–28
Multipoint lighting. (A) Front—directly in front of each focus area; (B) 45° to the side of each focus area; (C) high-angle sidelight; (D) backlight; (E) side backlight located 45° to the side rear of the focus area; (F) shoulder or low angle sidelight; (G) shin kickers located at the side near the floor; (H) downlight; (J) front floor light.

SYSTEMS OF LIGHTING DESIGN FOR THE NON-PROSCENIUM THEATRE

The lighting systems thus far described have all been for the proscenium theatre. When planning lighting for the nonproscenium theatre, such as an arena or thrust stage, many of the same design approaches can be used, but there are additional concerns. Because the arena theatre, with the audience completely surrounding the stage, is the most extreme example of a non-proscenium theatre, it shall be used to exemplify the needs and systems involved in non-proscenium lighting. The location of the audience on all sides of the stage makes lighting for visibility necessary on all sides of the performance area. There can be no dark side of the stage or a side that is deeply colored throughout the performance.

The absolute minimum lighting for an arena theatre uses three-point lighting to provide visibility to all members of the audience. There are two systems that will accomplish this:

1. (Figure 1–29) Place three instruments 120° apart at a vertical angle of 60° to focus on each lighting area. The higher vertical angle of 60° is used in the non-proscenium theatre to reduce the likelihood of lights shining into the eyes of the audience. Each instrument should be provided with a dilute color. All instruments might use the same gel, or, preferably, the lights from each position will be equipped with a different but still dilute color. A combination of No-Color or Flesh Pink, Surprise Pink, and Pale Blue will not only provide plasticity but will also permit two of the colors to be set at a lower intensity so the stage can be predominantly pink or blue at some time to suggest day or night. As the performance progresses, the emphasized lighting can shift from one color to another. In this way, the area light provides both

FIGURE 1–29

Minimum non-proscenium lighting usually requires three evenly spaced fixtures located 120° apart at a vertical angle of 60° to avoid glaring into the eyes of the audience.

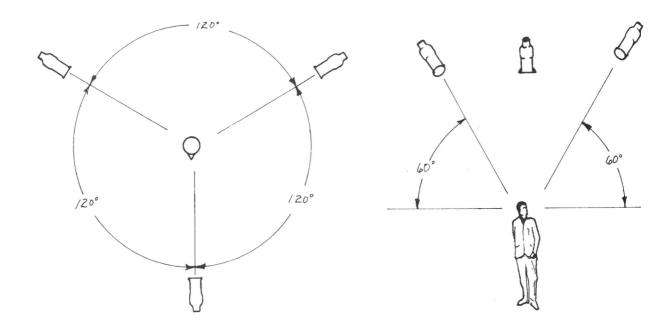

illumination and color. Ellipsoidals or fresnels equipped with barn doors are preferred for this lighting because they permit cutting off the beam of light from the eyes of the audience.

2. (Figure 1–30) Another approach to three-point lighting for the arena stage locates two instruments opposite each other on an axis at a vertical angle of 60° and adds a downlight for each focus area to fill in the shadows. Dilute colors must be used for the instruments opposite each other. The downlight may be strongly colored. If equipment is available, two or more sets of downlights can be used, one with a saturated color, the other with a dilute color. This system creates fairly strong shadows and may make it difficult for people sitting on one or

FIGURE 1–30
Another non-proscenium lighting design uses a front and backlight plus a downlight for each focus area.

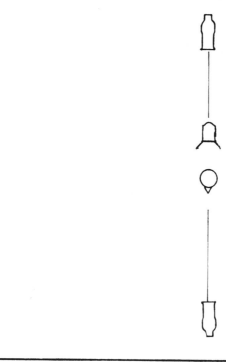

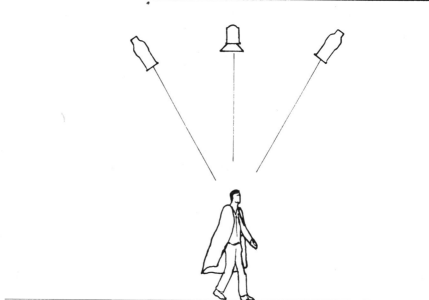

two sides of the theatre to see, but if the downlight is sufficiently soft it will fill the shadows and blend the other light. Ellipsoidals or fresnels with barn doors can be used for the lights on the axis and fresnels can be used for the downlights. Strip lights and scoops can also be used for the downlight but they will project a lot of spill on the audience.

Each three- or four-point lighting system described can be modified for use on the arena stage, so long as illumination is provided for each side of the audience and the vertical angles of lights are adjusted to keep glare out of the eyes of the audience. Each of the lighting systems applicable to lighting an arena production is equally appropriate for lighting almost any other non-proscenium form that locates the audience on more than one side of the stage.

Any of these approaches to lighting non-proscenium spaces can be elaborated by (1) adding instruments to create special focus areas, (2) combining standard positions from one system with standard positions from another system, or (3) multiplying the system so that, for instance, two 120° systems are illuminating the stage, with one set of lights in dilute colors and another set in saturated colors.

These systems are guides from which to begin developing a lighting design for a show. Selection and modification of the appropriate system for a particular facility, production situation, and show depend on the analyses performed as the initial tasks in planning the lighting.

THE DESIGN PROCESS

Whether a facility or program possesses a great deal of equipment or just a few lighting instruments, the process of lighting design can be a simple or complex task. It may be accomplished by simply turning on previously mounted, focused, and colored lights; by standing on stage and pointing at locations to hang the lights; by concurrently selecting circuits and colors as each instrument is placed; or by means of careful advance planning during which all details are worked out on paper. The approach taken is a personal choice related to the working situation. However, ultimately the same set of decisions have to be made—whether they are made on paper in advance of the work or under the pressure of getting the show up. The design process described here utilizes advance planning—each designer must select from this process those things most appropriate to his or her own working methods.

Beginning the Design Process

There are a number of ways to begin the design process. It can start (1) by determining the overall dramatic effect to be achieved; (2) with an idea of specific cues to be performed; (3) with a list of the lighting fixtures, control equipment, and other hardware available; or (4) with a commitment to the "design system" to be utilized. The analyses of the script and the production situation should help determine which of the approaches is most appropriate.

Starting to design by having an idea of the dramatic effect desired helps determine which of the design systems will become the foundation for the lighting. If, for instance, a production is to be mounted on a proscenium stage and it is most desirable to create a sense of reality throughout the performance, utilization of the McCandless System might be the most desirable approach. This system, after all, has been developed to create the greatest sense of realism and will achieve that goal if angles and color choices are carefully controlled. On the other hand, if it is most important to create very dramatic shadows during significant moments in the production, a two-point or three-point lighting system that incorporates downlight might be a better choice. If a dance or mime show is being staged, lighting that heavily emphasizes plasticity, perhaps a three-point system utilizing high- or low-angle sidelight, might be best. Once the overall effect has been determined and a lighting system has been selected (keeping in mind the hardware available), it is simply a matter of developing the design on paper.

As an alternative, starting to design by having specific cues or lighting moments in mind can lead to the selection of a lighting system as well. For instance, if it is important to create a sense of night but still clearly see the faces of the performers with a minimum amount of distortion, a two-point lighting system using a light pink or other dilutely colored front light and a medium or dark blue backlight would be sensible. It might be important during a production to place characters in clearly defined pools of downlight. Once again, a two- or three-point lighting system that incorporates downlight could make the best use of the equipment to provide visibility and to create the desired effect. In other words, the desire for specific lighting moments can dictate the choice of the design approach.

The factor most often determining the possible approaches to lighting design is the limit on available instruments, control equipment, and mounting positions. When only two scoops are available to light a production, there is little choice but to place the instruments in front of the stage to make it possible to see the show. If there is equipment available to provide at least basic illumination for visibility, it is possible to design the lighting to enhance the effect of the performance.

Paper Work

Planning the lighting design on paper begins with drawing a light plot. A **light plot** is a map of where lighting instruments are to be placed. The plot usually incorporates a plan of the setting with the "focus areas" identified and the lighting instruments shown in scale in their actual locations. Normally, each mounting position is given a name, such as "1st Electric," or "House Right Box Boom," and each fixture is numbered in that location, counting from number 1 for each mounting position. The numbering may be from either stage right or house right toward the opposite end of the pipe and is normally from the top to the bottom of vertically arranged fixtures on trees or booms. The fixture number is normally placed within the outline of the instrument. Professional lighting designers apply specific standards to draw light plots. These standards are summarized in Appendix B.

Light plots may be drawn by hand or generated by computer-aided drafting and design (abbreviated CAD or CADD). Specific CAD programs may be purchased for this purpose or traditional CAD programs may be customized for lighting design. Hand-drawn plots are normally developed using lighting templates (Figure 1–31) containing a scaled outline of theatrical lighting fixtures. Additional marks and notations enlarge the vocabulary of symbols on most templates so that the same outline with various patterns of slashes or bars may represent various fixtures on the light plot.

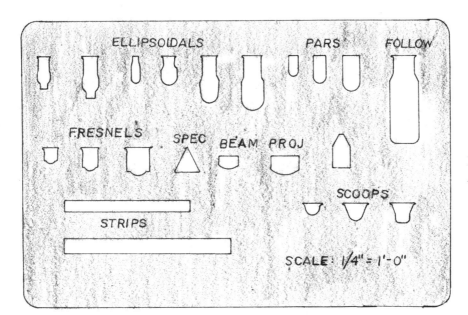

FIGURE 1–31
A typical lighting template.

As a minimum, a light plot will show the location and type of fixtures used and the fixture number. The plot must also include an indication of drawing scale and a legend by which to interpret the drawing symbols. It is preferable to develop these drawings in accordance with traditional theatre drawing standards.

In both professional and nonprofessional theatre, a light plot can be developed with different amounts of information. The style of plot is related to the working style of the designer, the availability of computer support, and the capabilities of the staff installing the lighting design. There are two extremes of light plot style: (1) (Figure 1–32A–C) a drawing showing the location of each fixture and the fixture type, which also includes all detailed information about the fixture, including lamp, color selection, accessories (barn door, patterns, color scroller, etc.), circuit number, dimmer number, and the function of the fixture in the lighting design; or (2) (Figure 1–32D) a drawing that simply shows the location of the fixture, which also identifies the fixture type and provides an instrument number by which to reference the instrument to a detailed but separate fixture schedule. Designers with access to computers and lighting design software most often use the latter approach since it makes the light plot easier to read. Using the computer also makes modification of the details about a lighting instrument or group of instruments in the design an efficient task easily handled in the computer.

An advantage of the "complete" light plot (Figure 1–32A) is that only one piece of paper is necessary to have all of the information about the design. That single sheet (or in the case of large installations, two or three sheets) can be reproduced as a blueprint. Although this is efficient in some ways, the drawing has to be done very clearly for the light plot to be legible (CAD-generated light plots are easiest to read). Also, as the lighting design evolves, the drawing should be updated with the new information. This can damage the original drawing if a lot of changes are made in one area and can be quite time consuming. In contrast, the simpler light plot can be produced in a smaller scale, if desired, since less information is included on the drawing (once again, CAD-generated light plots are the easiest to read). Both the lighting designer and the electricians, however, have to handle multiple sheets of paper to track information about each lighting instrument as the design is installed and modified.

There are various points of view about some issues related to drawing the light plot. Some designers prefer to draw fixtures evenly spaced and parallel with each other (a quick and efficient method when generating a light plot in CAD), whereas other lighting designers prefer to place the fixtures on the plot at the approximate angle they will be focused and either evenly spaced (such as 18" on-center) or more randomly spaced as seems appropriate to the specific application. The designer can assist the installing electricians by providing dimensioning information about the location of fixtures. This may be done by (1) evenly spacing the instruments and calling out a specific on-center dimension, (2) drawing a bar graph scale adjacent the light pipes on the plot,or (3) using traditional extension and dimension lines, showing actual measurements between the center of each lighting fixture on the pipe. Since it is a matter of personal choice, a designer may present the light plot in any manner that is clear, efficient, and communicative.

Some electricians, while preparing for installation, will take a copy of the light plot and cut it into sections showing each lighting pipe. The electrician or the lighting design assistant may add information to a simpler plot, such as lamp, accessory, or color needs of each fixture. The installing electricians then have complete information on a single drawing to locate the appropriate fixture complete with its accessories and to plug it into the appropriate circuit.

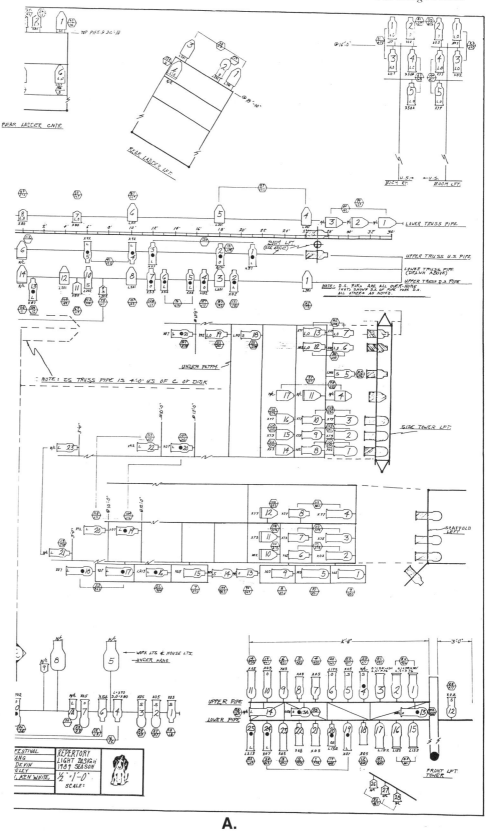

A.

FIGURE 1–32
Light plots. (A) Half of a hand-drawn light plot for the Colorado Shakespeare Festival; (B) a portion of a CAD-generated light plot for the Colorado Shakespeare Festival (C) a hand-drawn light plot for a proscenium production at the Cleveland Playhouse; (all courtesy of Richard Devin); (D) a hand-drawn light plot showing only fixture type (identified by the symbol), fixture location, and fixture number.

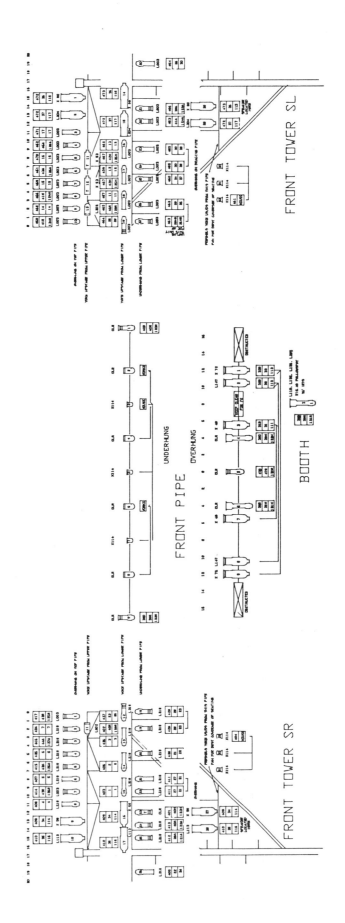

B.

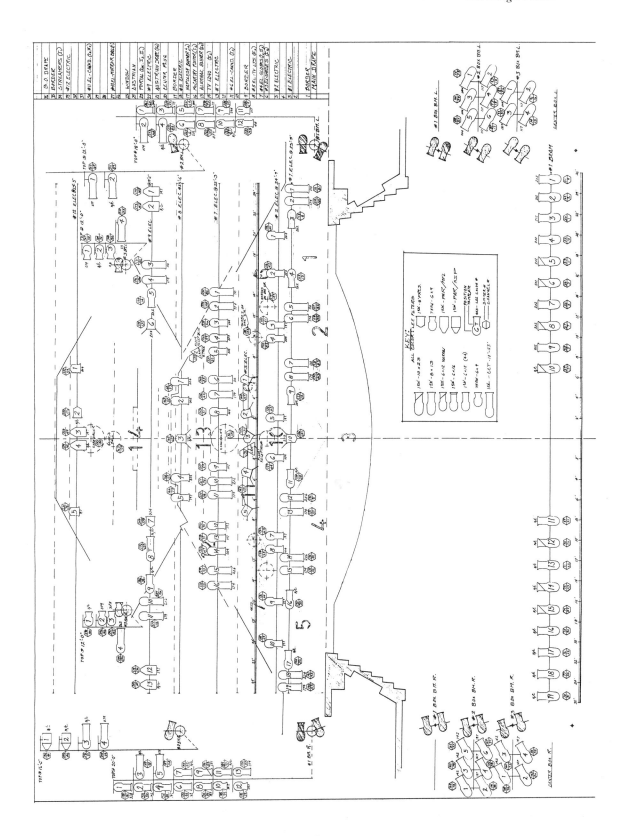

C.

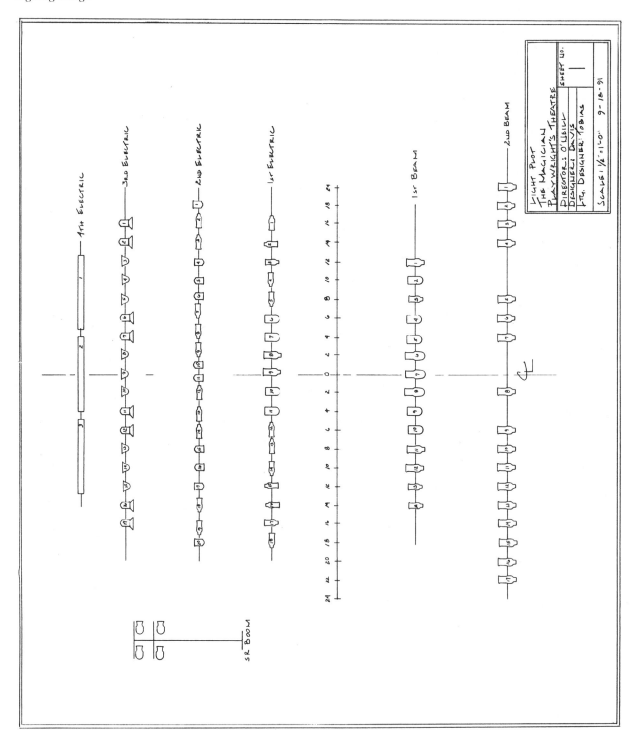

D.

The fixture schedule is an essential document that accompanies the light plot. The **fixture schedule** is a chart of detailed information about each fixture on the light plot (Figure 1–33). The schedule references the lighting instruments by the fixture number that is inserted in the outline of each fixture drawn on the plot. Although many versions of a fixture schedule may be created (with computer-generated fixture schedules), normally, the primary version is arranged by fixture number. Alternate versions of computer-generated fixture schedules may order the information by fixture type, color, accessories,

FIXTURE SCHEDULE
UNKNOWN SYMPHONY

NUMB	FUNCTION	FIXTURE	LAMP	WATTS	ACCESSORIES	CIRC	DIM	COLOR	NOTES
FIRST BEAM									
1	1 front	20 ellipse	fel	1000		9	51	L202	as far stg lft as poss.
2	2 front	20 ellipse	fel	1000		2	49	L202	
3	6 front	20 ellipse	fel	1000		1	52	L202	lowest yoke holes
4	7 front	20 ellipse	fel	1000		1	52	L202	lowest yoke holes
5	12 front	15 ellipse	fel	1000	patternR7805	10	59	L202	under focus
6	11 front	15 ellipse	fel	1000	pattern R7805	10	59	L202	under focus
7	front wash	8" fresnel	bvv	1000	barn door	4	55	G150	
8	front wash	8" fresnel	bvv	1000	barn door	5	54	G150	
9	front wash	8" fresnel	bvv	1000	barn door	5	54	G150	
10	front wash	8" fresnel	bvv	1000	barn door	4	55	G150	
11	front wash	8" fresnel	bvv	1000	barn door	6	56	G150	
12	front wash	8" fresnel	bvv	1000	barn door	6	56	G150	
13	14 front	15 ellipse	fel	1000		2	53	L202	lowest yoke holes
14	13 front	15 ellipse	fel	1000		2	53	L202	lowest yoke holes
15	9 front	20 ellipse	fel	1000		3	56	L202	lowest yoke holes
16	8 front	20 ellipse	fel	1000		3	56	L202	lowest yoke holes
17	3 front	20 ellipse	fel	1000		8	51	L202	as far stg rt as poss.
2	4 front	20 ellipse	fel	1000		7	49	L202	
HOUSE LEFT BOOM									
1	left wash	6 x 9		750	pattern R7882	75	98	G690	overfocus
2	left wash	6 x 9		750	pattern R7882	75	98	G690	overfocus
3	left wash	6 x 9		750	pattern R7882	75	98	G690	overfocus
4	left wash	6 x 9		750	pattern R7882	76	99	G690	overfocus
5	left wash	6 x 9		750	pattern R7882	76	99	G690	overfocus
6	left wash	6 x 9		750	pattern R7882	76	99	G690	overfocus
HOUSE RIGHT BOOM									
1	left wash	6 x 9		750	pattern R7882	75	98	G1570	overfocus
2	left wash	6 x 9		750	pattern R7882	75	98	G1570	overfocus
3	left wash	6 x 9		750	pattern R7882	75	98	G1570	overfocus
4	left wash	6 x 9		750	pattern R7882	76	99	G1570	overfocus
5	left wash	6 x 9		750	pattern R7882	76	99	G1570	overfocus
6	left wash	6 x 9		750	pattern R7882	76	99	G1570	overfocus
FIRST ELECTRIC									
1	15 down	6" fresnel		500	top hat	102	15	G960	
2	16 down	6" fresnel		500	top hat	102	15	G960	
3	17 down	6" fresnel		500	top hat	103	15	G960	
4	18 down	6" fresnel		500	top hat	103	15	G960	

FIGURE 1–33
Fixture schedule.

47

circuits, dimmers, or any other data range. Whether handwritten or computer generated, the following categories of information are normally included on a fixture schedule:

> MOUNTING POSITION or LOCATION
>> Typical locations would be 1st Catwalk, Balcony Rail, or 3rd Electric
>
> FIXTURE NUMBER
>
> FIXTURE
>> Type of fixture and when appropriate, lens configuration
>
> LAMP
>> Type of lamp and might also include color temperature or other special characteristics
>
> WATTAGE
>> Lamp wattage
>
> VOLTAGE
>> If low-voltage or high-voltage lamps are used, they may require a transformer or may affect the dimmer selection
>
> ACCESSORIES
>> Barn doors, patterns and patterns holders, gobo rotators, color scrollers, or other effects, devices, top hats, diffusers, or any other fixture accessories
>
> FUNCTION or FOCUS
>> Purpose of the light, such as "Area 7 front" or "door special"
>
> COLOR
>> Color media color selection normally by brand and number
>
> CIRCUIT
>
> DIMMER
>
> WORKS WITH
>> A fixture may be planned to always operate concurrent with other fixtures and use the same circuit for power
>
> NOTES

Not all of these categories are necessary for every fixture schedule and other categories may be needed for some schedules. The schedules need to be customized for the application, the needs of the designer and the production staff.

Other paperwork that contributes to the lighting design process is a **hook-up** (Figure 1–34). This is a chart used to indicate which fixtures or circuits are connected to what dimmers. The hook-up shows the crew which circuits or lighting instruments to connect to each dimmer at the patch panel or the dimmer pack. The hook-up will also show what patches to change during a show.

THE MANDRAKE

HOOK UP

DIMMER	CIRCUIT	FIXT NOS	FUNCTION	WATTS	NOTES	TOTAL LOAD
1	14	BEAM 1, 6	FRONT 6,7	1000		2000
2	15	BEAM 9	FRONT 2	1000		2000
	16	BEAM 14	FRONT 1	1000		
3	22	BEAM 4	FRONT 5	1000		1000
4	108	Ist E 1, 19	FRONT 22	750		1500
5	109	1ST E 2, 18	FRONT 21	750		1500
6	212	FLR RT 1	SIDE 21	500		500
7	213	PRACTICAL	SET LIGHT	75		75
8	2	BEAM 3	FRONT 5	1000		1000
9	3	BEAM 4	FRONT 4	1000		1000
10	146	4th E 12,13	BACK 4	500		2000
	147	4th E 10, 9	BACK 3	500		
11	1	BEAM 10	FOLLOW	5000	6K DIMMER	5000
12	2	BEAM 11	FOLLOW	5000	6K DIMMER	5000
13	99	1st E 12,13	DOWN BLU	500		2000
	100	1st E 14, 15	DOWN BLU	500		

FIGURE 1–34
A hook-up sheet.

To keep track of which dimmers control what lights while developing the lighting cues for the show, it is handy to have some kind of summary of the information on the light plot, and fixture schedule; this may be a cheat sheet or a magic sheet. A **cheat sheet** is a chart listing each focus area and the lights that illuminate them for various functions, such as front lights, backlight, and downlight (Figure 1–35A). A **magic sheet** (Figure 1–35B) is a map of essentially the same information. Each of these charts summarizes the information on the light plot and the hook-up from the point of view of the designer rather than a crew member. Both the cheat sheet and the magic sheet are used by the designer to select circuits for fading up or down during a cue. They are simple means of shorthand to keep track of information.

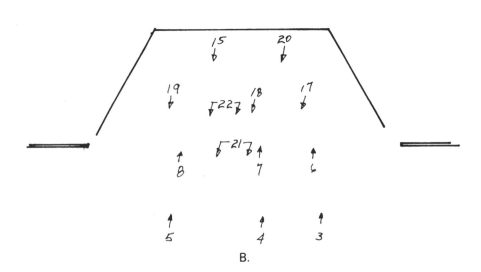

CHEAT SHEET			
AREA	FRONT	BACK	DOWN
1	3	17	21
2	3	17	21
3	4	18	21
4	5	19	21
5	5	19	21
6	6	20	22
7	6	20	22
8	7	20	
9		15	
10			

A.

B.

FIGURE 1–35
(A) Cheat sheet; (B) magic sheet.

In complex production situations, additional paperwork includes a **gel-cutting list**, which summarizes the size and quantity of each gel color to be cut, and a **shop order**, which is a complete inventory of the equipment needed for a show arranged in order of equipment, accessories, cable, lamps, mounting equipment, lighting control, and so forth.

After the show has been planned on paper, it is time to implement the design. When qualified staff is available, the advanced planning that has been done on paper can simply be handed to crew members who will mount and hook up the lights and prepare the gel.

Light Cues and Lighting Moments

Once the lights have been hung, cabled, and focused, the only tasks remaining are developing the lighting moments and integrating them into the performance. A **lighting moment** is the arrangement of lights composing a stage picture; it relates directly to the activity and mood of the performance at that time. A lighting moment may be the product of a single cue or several cues piled together. A **cue** is a change in the intensity of one or more lights.

If the person designing the lights for a production is not also the director and scenic designer, it is important that each of these people meet well in advance of developing the specific light cues for the show. Their purpose is to identify the quality and timing of specific lighting moments. In preparation for that communication, the lighting designer should see the show in rehearsal to understand how the stage is used and to get a sense of the performance as a whole as well as individual moments of the performance. The lighting designer, then, brings an understanding of the script, the planned performance, and the production limitations to the development and implementation of the design.

The easiest and most practical process for developing light cues, if time allows, is to schedule a **dry tech** rehearsal without actors where each lighting moment is built and modified until the light appears correct. This is often a session with only the lighting designer, director, stage manager, and the crew participating so there is only minimal pressure. The director and stage manager may stay away from the first dry tech rehearsal and attend a second rehearsal where they are shown the lighting moments, which are then further modified to fit the vision of the director. Finally, the cues are tried out during the technical and dress rehearsals with the actors, when additional adjustments are made and timing between lighting moments is perfected. A **technical rehearsal** is the first rehearsal or two during which lights, sound, and scene shifts are integrated in the production. The technical rehearsal usually occurs just before costumes and makeup are added to a show for the **dress rehearsals.**

Other approaches can be taken to the process of cue development. Lighting moments can be developed by writing down predicted **levels**—that is, the intensity settings—for each dimmer, and then these are tried out and modified at rehearsals. Or lighting moments can be built and adjusted during technical rehearsals with all of the cast and crew present rather than at separate rehearsals. However, this is tedious for the actors and crew members and puts a great deal of pressure on the lighting designer and light board operators. It is almost always best to develop lighting cues independently of the cast and then to integrate them at a later rehearsal. After the cues for a production have been developed, they must be perfected, making minor adjustments in lighting levels to balance the stage, adjust focus, modify color or mood, and correct the timing between cues. This polishing process often continues through the final dress rehearsal for the production.

No matter what kind of lighting control equipment is used or how reliable the light crew is, it is a good idea to track the lighting cues. **Tracking** is a process of writing down the level of each dimmer for each cue independent of the board operator. In this way, a reliable record of the show is maintained in case the board operators did not record information accurately. This also guarantees a back-up copy of the lighting cues in case something happens to the cue book or there is an equipment failure on a memory system.

The light board operator(s) must keep a careful record of what they are to do for each cue, whether they are working on a single-scene manual board, a two-scene preset console, or a sophisticated memory system. The board operators need to know (1) what they must do, (2) when they must do it, and (3) at what rate they must do it. The simplest cue sheet is written with bold markings that are easy to read, such as the one shown in Figure 1–36. The number at the top right corner of the page is the cue number. If a production uses a stage manager who calls the light cues, additional information about when a cue is to occur is only needed when several cues occur in quick succession. In that case, a notation such as "Q11 follows immediately" or "Go w/ Q12" should occur some place on the page. Should the light board operator have to take cues on his or her own, then the cue line from the script and page number in the script should also be noted near the top of the page. On the remainder of the page, the left-hand column contains the dimmer numbers, the center column indicates the action, and the right-hand column lists the levels to which the dimmers are to come. The number at the bottom of the page, "4 count," is the rate of fade. (A "count" is approximately one second.)

This cue would be read:

Cue Number 10
    Dimmers 4, 5, 9, and 11 go up to a level of 8
    Dimmers 1 through 3 and 14 through 16 go up to a level of 5
    Dimmer 10 goes down to a level of 4½
    on a 5 count

Although a board operator will adapt this system of cue recording to his or her own style, a few shorthand symbols are commonly used:

    Q = the word *cue*
    FOA = fade out all lights currently on
    Bump = instantly bring up or down (count of 0)
    BO = black out
    Restore = bring the previous lighting moment back

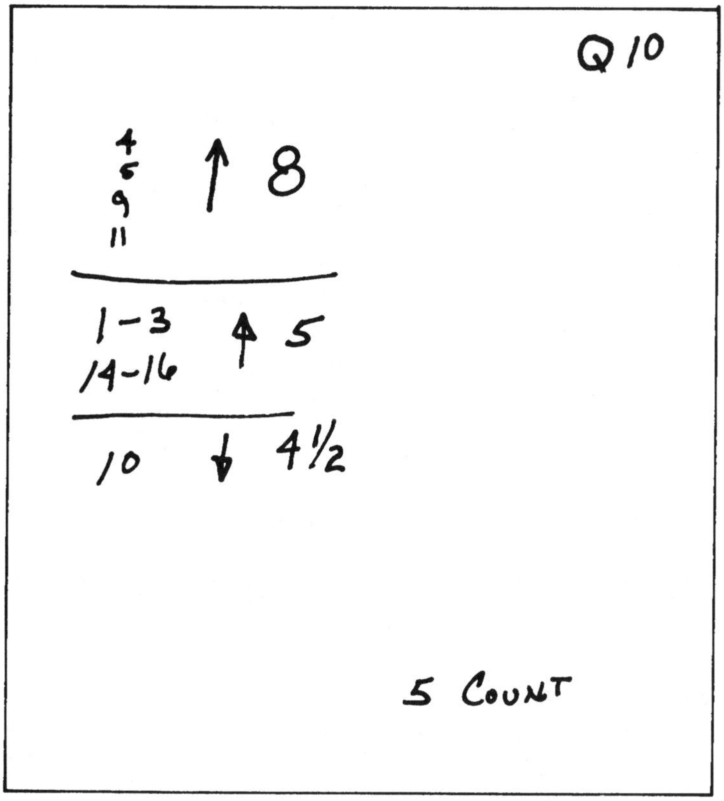

FIGURE 1–36
Board operator's cue sheet.

Writing cues for a two-scene preset board requires two sets of information: (1) the cues that instruct the board operator to move individual pots, submasters, and masters to new settings, similar to the cues above; and (2) the set-ups for each of the presets. Recording preset levels and assigning submastering may be done in a manner similar to writing cues, as in Figure 1–36 or a form might be developed that is boldly marked with settings for the individual pots, as in Figure 1–37. Cues for a memory board can be recorded in a manner similar to that used for the manual board with a simple indication of the kind of action and timing. Most board operators prefer to have as little information on a cue sheet as possible so they will not be distracted by unnecessary data.

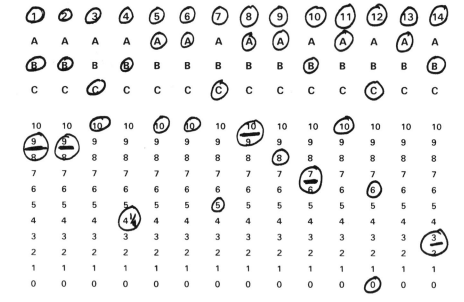

FIGURE 1–37
Presetter's cue sheet.

It is handiest to write each cue on a separate sheet of paper placed in a looseleaf binder. As cues are modified during the rehearsal process, it is easy to replace pages as necessary. The final book of cues should be clear, accurate, and easily understood.

Cueing

Often, the stage manager for a production will call the light cues, in other words, instruct the board operator (and all other backstage personnel) when to perform an action. This is preferred for most productions. It permits the tightest coordination among lights, sound, scenery, special effects, and the performers because they are all directed by a single person who should be especially familiar with the production. Cue calling is a demanding task that requires precise timing and language to achieve the most effective results. There are two levels to the cue calling process: warnings and cues. A **warning** usually is given by the stage manager between 15 seconds and 1 minute before a cue is to occur. The warning alerts the crews as to an action to be performed and allows them to prepare themselves for the activity, whether it is the light board operator checking cue sheets or a stagehand untying a rope. The second step is to give the cue. There must be a clear distinction in the language identifying warnings and cues and distinguishing among cues for sound, lights, scenery, and performers.

The following guidelines have been developed in professional work to help keep information as clear as possible. These guidelines are equally viable for nonprofessional productions.

1. All board operated cues are identified by number, so that light cues would be called *lights 1* and sound cues would be called *sound 1*. Scene shifts or drape opening and closing are usually simply identified by the activity, such as *curtain* or *shift*.

2. When new cues are added between existing cues, rather than renumbering all of the cues for a show, the new number is given an alphabetic notation, such as *lights 1-A*.

3. When giving a warning, the stage manager must always begin the phrase with "warning cue…." Since the word *warning* is given first, it alerts all who are listening to pay attention, but does not panic them into improperly running a cue at that moment.

4. When initiating a cue, the stage manager must always phrase the information so that the sentence ends with the word *go!* The cue will happen when the word *go!* is said. A simple warning/cue sequence is "Warning lights 14." "Lights 14, go!"

5. The stage manager should anticipate initiating a cue so that it is possible to take a very brief pause between naming the cue (*lights* 14) and initiating the cue (*go*).

6. When light and sound cues are to occur on a single "go," the stage manager can set up the cue in this manner:
"Warning lights 14 and sound 7"
"Lights 14 and sound 7, go!"

7. If several things occur on a single "Go," such as a light cue, sound cue, curtain closing, and telephone ring, the stage manager must carefully set up the cue during the warning and give a very clear "go." The following arrangement works well:
"Warning lights 14, sound 7, curtain closed
and telephone all on my next go."
"Lights 14, sound 7, curtain and phone, go!"

8. If this complex cue were followed almost instantly by another complex cue, the stage manager could carefully set up the cue in this manner:
"Warning lights 14, sound 7, curtain closed
and telephone all on my first go.
Lights 15, sound 8, snow, and drop out on my second go."
"Lights 14, sound 7, curtain, phone, go!"…."Go!"

The clarity, precision, and consistency of this style of communication will ensure the greatest coordination between each of the elements of production.

CONCLUSION

An extensive array of equipment may be used to light a play, opera, ballet, musical, or variety show, or a production may be illuminated with one or two floodlights controlled at a wall outlet. The quantity and type of equipment available may make the task of planning the lighting for a production easier and the potential for subtlety greater, but whether a great deal of equipment is available or only a limited inventory, at some point someone must decide where to place and aim the lights, when to turn them on, and when to turn them off. If dimming is available, the intensity of each light and the rate of change must be decided as well as choices about color and beam quality.

The art of lighting design, without regard to the quantity or type of equipment available, is an important task that may contribute to the overall effectiveness of any production. Light should not only make the performance visible, it should enhance the dramatic or comedic effect of every moment of the production. This is accomplished best with a practical understanding of lighting equipment and how to utilize that equipment in artful ways. Lighting design, then, is the art of making a performance visible, theatrical, and dramatic as a result of judicious planning, a clear understanding of the script and the performance, and the artistic application of technology.

CHAPTER 2

Color

INTRODUCTION

One of the most exciting and challenging elements of design is the use of color. Color in lighting has an extremely powerful effect. Although we may not be conscious of it, the color of light contributes to our moods and attitudes. We sense this daily as we respond to the radiance of sunshine, the green glow of filtered light in a forest or a glen, the soft blue haze of light on a shimmering lake, the dreary greyness of cloudy days, the startling flash of police lights, or the unnerving glare of a blinking neon sign. The intensity, the movement, and, most of all, the color of all of these different kinds of light have a psychological effect on us. They may cause a sense of warmth or cold, vitality, happiness, depression, melancholy, joy, anger, or tension. In performance, the choice of colors for lights similarly affects the mood of the audience. The color of lights for a show must be selected so that the lighting enhances the dramatic effect of the performance and complements the colors of the settings and costumes.

Color is one of the most challenging elements of design. The colors selected for scenery and costumes should be pleasing to the eye and appropriate for the mood of the show. However, it is of no consequence what colors are chosen for the scenery or costumes for a production if the lighting does not complement those colors. Selection of appropriate lighting colors can harmonize all of the visual elements of a show, or poorly chosen colors can turn the colors of the setting or the costumes into bright, glowing blobs, or a murky muddy mess. Obviously, with this ability to aid or damage the effectiveness of the sets, costumes, and production as a whole, the selection of color for lights must be done with great care.

An understanding of the theory of color in pigments, which is explained in Volume I, and the theory of color in light, which is discussed below, can aid this selection process.

COLOR THEORY

The color of a surface is the result of a combination of the pigments mixed to create the color of the surface, the color of the light that strikes the surface, and the way the human eye sees the lighted surface. To begin to understand how color works in light and how light interrelates with the color of objects and surfaces necessitates some understanding of the composition of light.

Additive Color Mixing

White light is a combination of all the colors of light that may be distinguished by the human eye. Those colors can be identified by passing a beam of white light through a prism (Figure 2–1). This results in stripes of colored light similar to a rainbow and constitutes the **visible spectrum of light** arranged in **wavelengths**, a measurement of light energy (Figure 2–2). When all of the visible colors of light are present and merged, the beam of light is white; when only a portion of the colors are present, the beam acquires a color. When starting with no light and adding wavelengths, new colors of light are formed until all of the wavelengths are present, resulting in white light. The adding together of wavelengths of light or colored beams of light is called **additive color mixing**. The stage can be illuminated with a single color light, such as blue borderlights, or beams of several colors can be mixed with each other to create a new hue or even the effect of white light.

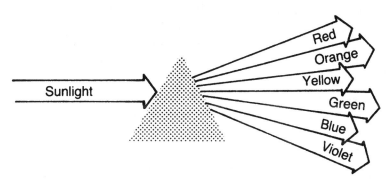

FIGURE 2–1
Sunlight passing through a prism.

FIGURE 2–2
The visible spectrum of light arranged by wavelengths.

White light can be created by mixing together individual beams of red, blue, and green, which are the **primaries of light**. In theory, the primaries of light can be mixed in various proportions to create all other colors of light. It is for this reason that many stages are equipped with red, blue, and green borderlights, cyc lights, and footlights. While the theory is operable in the laboratory, on stage it is difficult to control the proportions of these colors to attain specific colors of illumination. It is also difficult to obtain sufficient intensity from these primary-colored lights to illuminate an acting area adequately in many colors. Stage lighting is almost always more efficient when fixtures are equipped with the exact colors desired rather than trying to mix beams of the primaries to create specific colors of light.

No matter what colors are used for lighting, the effect of mixing colored beams of light must be taken into consideration when planning a show. Consideration must be given not only to the way the colored beams of light mix with each other but also to their effect on scenery, costumes, and makeup.

The Interaction of Additive and Subtractive Color Mixing

When white light falls on a surface, the surface may absorb or reflect any portion of the visible spectrum of light. The *color of the surface* determines which wavelengths of light are absorbed and which wavelengths are reflected. Beginning with a surface that is white and therefore contains no hues and no color absorbers, the more hues that are mixed together to make the color of a surface, the more wavelengths of light will be *absorbed*. Mixing *pigments* to create a color is called **subtractive color mixing** because pigment absorbs—or subtracts—wavelengths of light from the reflection pattern. Those wavelengths of light that are not absorbed by the pigment are reflected by it.

Under white light, the entire visible spectrum of light is present to be reflected or absorbed, so what is seen as the color of a material is the actual mixture of the pigments. If, however, only a portion of the visible spectrum of light is present, the *combination* of the color of the object and the color of the light produces the apparent color of the object. This happens because not all colors of illumination are available to be absorbed or reflected, and the apparent color of the surface onto which the light falls is altered.

Here are several examples of this theory in operation (see Figures C–1 through C–11):

1. If a white object is seen under white light, it will appear white. There are no color absorbers in the object since white pigment contains no hues, and all of the visible spectrum of light is present to be reflected.

2. If a blue ball is seen under white light, all of the visible spectrum of light is present. The ball absorbs all colors of light *except blue*, which is reflected, and the ball is seen as a blue object.

3. If a white cup is seen *under only red light*, it will appear red. While the white cup contains no color absorbers, the full spectrum of visible light is not present and the surface can only reflect the color of light projected on it. Since only red light is present, only red light can be reflected and the cup will appear red. This would be equally true if only violet, orange, blue, or any other single color of light were projected on a white surface.

4. If a blue ball is seen *under blue light*, it will appear intense blue. Since only blue light is projected on the ball and the surface of the ball is blue, all of the light striking the ball will be reflected and none of it will be absorbed. The ball will appear blue. The eye may be tricked: the intensity of the reflection may cause the ball to appear white if no white objects are near the ball.

5. If a blue ball is seen *under only red light*, it will appear black. Since there is no red pigment in the blue ball and no blue wavelengths in the red light, the ball will absorb all of the light projected and no light will be reflected. The ball also would appear to be black if it were seen under a pure green light.

6. If a yellow vase is seen *under only red light*, it will appear red because there is no green light present to complete the mixture of light.

7. If a yellow vase is seen *under green light*, it will appear green since there is no red light present to be reflected.

8. If a yellow vase is seen *under only blue light*, it will appear brown or black since there is no blue in the yellow pigment.

When two or more variously colored sources of light are projected, the beams will mix to create a new color of light. Anything illuminated by the mixed beams will react to all of the wavelengths of light that are present as if projected from a single source.

9. When a white cup is seen *under equal proportions of red, blue, and green light*, the cup will appear white. Since these are the primaries of light, the entire visible spectrum is present to be absorbed or reflected. The cup reflects all of the light since white pigment contains no color absorbers.

10. If a blue ball is seen *under equal proportions of red, blue, and green light*, the ball will appear blue. Since these are the primaries of light, the entire visible spectrum is present to be absorbed or reflected. The ball absorbs all but the blue light, which is reflected as if it were illuminated by a single source of white light.

11. If a blue ball is seen under *both red and blue light*, it should appear blue because there is no red pigment in the ball to reflect the red wavelengths. The ball may appear to be more violet because the red and blue beams of light mix with each other to create a new color. A portion of the red wavelengths will not be absorbed in this new mixture.

12. If a blue ball is seen under *both red and green light*, it will appear black because there are no reflectors of either color present in the ball.

13. If a yellow vase is seen under *both red and green light*, it will appear to be a slightly greyed yellow color as the beams mix with the pigment.

It is difficult to predict the exact response of any combination of pigment and lighting color due to the impurity of colors in both media. For instance, many blue pigments contain touches of red and many pink lighting colors contain mixtures of green. All combinations of colors must be carefully tested to determine the results of the color mixes. Since the colors of the beams of light and the colors of surfaces intermix in human vision, the selection of colors used must be done very carefully.

Selecting Lighting Colors

It is tempting to avoid the problem of mixing colored light with scenery and costumes by using only white light. However, unfiltered white light is often too harsh to create an appropriate atmosphere, establish an appropriate sense of time, or evoke the appropriate mood. For these reasons, colored light should not be avoided, but colors should be carefully chosen with sufficient testing and experimentation to determine which tints and shades are most effective.

Manufacturers of color media provide swatch books that are usually available free. They may be used to help select and test lighting colors. There are three ways to test a color or combination of colors to determine their appropriateness when projected on skin, costumes, or scenery.

1. When two colors are to be used in combination, hold a swatch of each in front of each eye. Look first through one eye at one color, then through the other eye at the second color. Try to hold one color over each eye and look equally through them both at the same time. Look at your own hand, and at the actual scenery, costumes, and makeup for the show. Determine if:

   a. The right sense of warmth or coolness and the proper mood seem to be created.
   b. The colors of pigments become distorted. Do colors turn muddy? Do they glow? Are patterns lost or do they jump out?

There should be a minimum of distortion to colors or patterns. Skin should seem to look normal with neither a pallor nor exceptional ruddiness.

2. A better way to test the color media is to hold it about one foot away from the surface to be illuminated and shine a flashlight through it. If more than one color is to be used at a time, both colors should be projected concurrently on skin, makeup, costumes, and scenery for evaluation. Each color should be viewed separately and when they overlap. The same judgments regarding appropriateness and color distortion should be made with this approach as above.

3. An even more effective way to test the appropriateness of lighting colors is to put the color media in a spotlight and project the light on an actor, the costumes, and the scenery. This will give the truest sense of the effect of the color. Keep in mind that the quantity, type, and location of instruments will modify the effect of the color media:

   a. More fixtures with the same color will project the color more intensely.
   b. Lights closer to the stage will project a stronger color than lights at a greater distance from the stage.
   c. Spotlights will project a more concentrated beam of color than floodlights.

To aid in the selection of the appropriate color for various effects, one manufacturer, Rosco Labs, has published a *Color Media Guide*, which is reprinted in Appendix A. This guide provides suggestions of ways to use colors on stage.

COLOR MEDIA

Lighting instruments are given color by placing a filter over the light. The filters remove some colors from the white light projected by the fixture and allow the apparent color of the filter to be projected through it. There are three categories of light-coloring media: liquid, glass, and disposable sheets.

Liquid

Lamp dip is a liquid color medium that adheres to glass. It can be used to paint glass slides for projections or to color light bulbs rated at less than 100 watts. Dip is available in eight colors.

Glass

Glass color media are widely used on strip lights. **Rondels** or **roundels** are round glass lenses that look like the red, yellow, and green filters on traffic lights. They are mounted in a metal frame or held in place with a spring ring over individual lights. They are available in several different colors. Rondels are preferred for strip lights because they project permanent, nonfading, deep colors that are frequently used in borderlights, cyc lights, and footlights. Rondels or similar glass media are also manufactured for use with some PAR lamps and other specialized fixtures. Heat-resistant Pyrex rondels are convex lenses textured on the inside to diffuse the beam in either a medium or wide pattern. Another style of rondel is a flat lens constructed from narrow strips of glass mounted in a metal frame. Spaces between the strips of glass are designed to permit expansion as the glass heats.

Another form of glass color media is **dichroic colors**. These are color filters made from heat-resistant glass coated with a very thin film of highly selective crystals that either transmit or project very specific wavelengths of light. Dichroic filters commonly are used on architectural and theatrical lighting fixtures with very high temperature light sources. These are the most permanent light color medium available, resisting fading in almost all conditions. The greatest hazard to using dichroic colors is that the glass may break from mishandling. Dichroic color media tends to be quite expensive and is viable mostly for permanent installations or extremely long-run productions. The palette of dichroic filters remained quite limited after the medium was first introduced, but it is now possible to obtain "standard" dichroic colors in a moderately broad range. In addition, custom colors can be made to order. A notable characteristic of dichroic filters is that the filter often appears to be a far different color from the light projected through it. Thus, the only way to know what color a dichroic filter produces is to project light through it.

Disposable Sheets—Gel

The final category of color media is disposable sheets known as **gel**. This is a relatively inexpensive consumable material that is available in a broad range of colors. This category got its name from the original product that was used to color lights: gelatine. There are now two different kinds of plastic materials used in place of gelatine.

An older and mostly ignored coloring media is made from acetate, which is sold under several brand names, such as Roscolene and Dura 60. This is a fairly thick plastic sheet that is quite durable and is water resistant. Acetate coloring media are available in over 60 colors. This medium will withstand the heat generated by most old-generation lighting instruments, although deep colors tend to fade quickly. It is not a practical medium for use with lighting instruments equipped with quartz lamps. Heat will cause colors to fade and warp. Once any color filter has faded or warped, it should be discarded.

The most durable color media available are made from polyester and polycarbonate plastics. They are sold under brand names such as Roscolux, Gamcolor, and Lee Filters in over 100 colors. This material is thin, flexible, and very durable. It will not be damaged by water nor will it deteriorate with age. Since it is quite thin, it will not absorb as much heat as the thicker acetate medium, which makes the polyester/polycarbonate plastics practical for use with fixtures equipped with quartz lamps. These filters have become the standard of the industry.

DEALING WITH GEL

Each kind of gel is available in several colors that are identified by a color name and a two- or three-digit number. The numbers are distinct to each brand, so that colors numbered with two digits, such as 09 or 43, are from one manufacturer and 200-series colors, such as 211 or 258, are manufactured by another company. There is no standardization of colors, color names, or color numbering between manufacturers.

No matter which type of gel is used, the procedures for working with the materials are consistent. Gel is supplied in sheets measuring 20" × 24" or in rolls 24" wide. It is cut to size and inserted in a metal frame that slides into the color holder slots on the front of the lighting instrument. Most instruments are designed to allow two color holders or a color holder and an accessory such as a barn door to be inserted in the slot at the same time. Gel should be cut about ¼" smaller than the outside dimensions of the color holder. This is easily done by placing the gel on a firm surface that can serve as a cutting board. A thick sheet of illustration board is a perfect base for cutting gel. The color holder is placed on top of the gel so that two sides are just ¼" off the edge of the color media. A matte knife is drawn around the other two sides of the frame, resulting in a piece of gel that will fit neatly inside the color holder with nothing hanging over the edges. It is convenient to identify each cut piece of gel with its color number (Figure 2–3). Use a grease pencil to write the number in one of the corners of the sheet. If deeply colored gels are marked in areas through which light projects, the numbers will actually melt through the gel.

Most color holders consist of a piece of folded metal with a large hole in the center to allow the light through. To insert the gel, the two sides of the color holder are spread apart and the gel is slipped between them. Sometimes it is preferred to fasten the top edge of the color

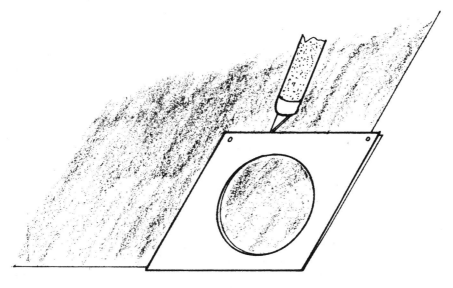

FIGURE 2–3
Cutting gel to fit a color holder.

holder to prevent the thin media from warping. The top edge of the frame can be fastened using brass paper brads that are inserted in each of the small holes at the top of the frame. Tape of any kind should *not* be used to keep the gel in place or the sides of the color holder together. The tape may burn and the glue will deposit an extremely gummy residue on the metal frame. Some frames used on scoops, beam projectors, follow spots, and rainlights are two-part circles that must be connected with brass brads to hold the pieces together. Metal color holders are used with almost all theatre lighting instruments. A color holder made from a heat-resistant fiber material may be used in place of the metal frame. Since it is made of a material that feels like cardboard, should it fall down the fiber color holder will not cause injury, which is possible should a metal color holder fall out of an instrument.

The lighting instrument, color holder, and gel are designed to allow air circulation to cool the color media. Only one sheet of gel should be put into each color holder. When two sheets of gel are placed in the same holder, they will not cool sufficiently and may fade or melt quickly.

Gel should be replaced once it begins to fade seriously. This may occur rapidly with some deep colors. Since the purpose of gel is to create color on stage, it is useless if the color has faded out of the material. Warped, cut, or damaged gel should be disposed of, for it will distort the light rather than effectively color it.

Whole sheets of gel should be stored flat on a shelf or in an enclosed container. The tissue that is usually shipped with the media should separate each layer of gel. It is a good idea to keep the colors in order by numerical designation and to mark the color number on a corner of each sheet with a grease pencil if not already labeled. Since acetate and polyester/polycarbonate are reusable media, pieces cut to fit color holders can be saved for later productions. The gel can be left in the color holders and saved that way, but this requires an exceptional number of color holders. It is usually more convenient to remove the gel from the frames and to store the undamaged pieces flat on shelves in file folders or in large mailing envelopes. The folders or envelopes can also be placed in a file cabinet or some other storage rack. For future convenience, each sheet should be labeled with its color number and each color stored in its own folder. Be sure that the cut sheets are placed in storage so they are flat, smooth, and wrinkle-free.

DIFFUSION MEDIA AND COLOR CORRECTION

Diffusion is a category of gel that modifies the beam of light but does not color it. It is used to make a concentrated or hard-edged beam into dispersed and softened light.

Frost (Figure 2–4B) is used to disperse a concentrated beam of light in all directions. Placed in front of a fresnel or an ellipsoidal spotlight, the edges of the beam will spread out almost like a floodlight but with a strongly concentrated center area of illumination. When used with floodlights such as scoops, the beam spreads out in all directions and easily blends with all other stage light. There are several densities of frost gel available to achieve increasingly greater diffusion of the beam of light. Frosts are also available in a variety of colors, including lighting primaries and several colors often used for cyc lighting.

Silk (Figure 2–4C) is characterized by striations or a grain that causes it to look as if strands of fiber run through it. When placed in front of a beam of light, it will disperse the beam only in one direction, perpendicular to the direction of the striations; the beam will remain virtually unchanged in the opposite direction. If the grain is placed in a vertical direction, the beam of light will spread horizontally; if the gain is placed in a horizontal direction, the beam will spread vertically. Silks are very handy to soften the patterns of scoops on a cyc or to blend the edges of beams from ellipsoidals. Silks are also available in lighting primaries, cyc colors, and some other lighting colors.

Diffusion media may be used as a full color frame to modify an entire beam of light or as a half or quarter frame to affect only one edge of the beam. For instance, if an ellipsoidal must project a hard line on one side of the beam to cut off at the proscenium but the other edge should blend into the rest of the stage light, a half-frame of silk with the grain running vertically may be used to soften the onstage edge of the beam of light while the offstage edge remains sharply focused. Another use might be to soften only the top edge of a beam projected from a scoop to remove the scallop pattern that often occurs on cycs. In this case, silk or frost could be placed in the top third of the color holder to diffuse only that portion of the beam without affecting the remainder of the beam of light.

Both silk and frost may be combined with colored gels in front of an instrument but must be placed in separate color holders. They are also available in traditional border and cyc lighting colors so that only one sheet needs to be placed in the light to achieve both color and diffusion.

A small group of products available to the theatre and an extensive array of gels made for television and cinema are called **neutral density**. These are gels that are designed to reduce the quantity of

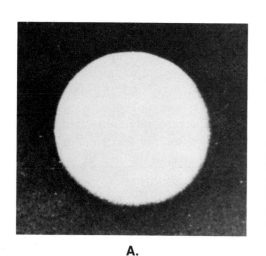

A.

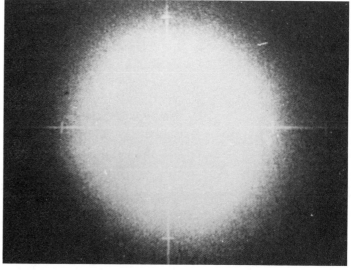

B.

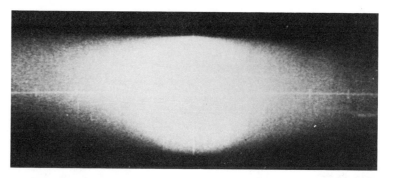

C.

light projected by an instrument without significantly affecting the color of the light. The traditional names for the colors most often used in the theatre are *grey*, which is used to reduce intensity in the cool ranges, and **chocolate** or **special chocolate**, which is used to reduce intensity in the warm color ranges. These gels may be used with other colors or by themselves.

In addition, a number of other neutral-density and color correction gels are made for television and film. These filters are identified by their traditional function such as "minus green" or "plus orange," which are used to balance the color fluorescent lights and other fixtures. These filters do not introduce a great deal of color, but they definitely tint the light in small amounts. There are times when these color correction filters can produce the most appropriate color for a theatre performance.

A typical application for neutral-density gel is when two lights controlled by the same dimmer are illuminating adjacent areas of the stage but one is brighter than the other. Since the brighter light cannot be faded down separately from the less intense one, balancing the intensity of the two lights is impossible using the dimmers. The problem may be solved by adding a piece of neutral density, either grey or chocolate, to the brighter light. The neutral-density gel will reduce the output from that lighting instrument without changing the color of the light.

FIGURE 2–4

The effect of diffusion filters. (A) Unfiltered ellipsoidal spotlight beam; (B) ellipsoidal spotlight beam with frost filter; (C) ellipsoidal spotlight beam with silk filter. (Courtesy Rosco Laboratories, Inc.)

COLOR SCROLLERS

Many touring companies and an increasing number of resident theatres are using color scrollers as a lighting fixture accessory. A color scroller (Figure 2–5) is an automatic color changer that mounts in the color holder of a lighting fixture. Upon receiving a remote signal, the scroller will draw colors in front of the lens until the appropriate color has been reached. Scrollers are designed for various sized lighting fixtures and can be equipped with eight to sixteen different colors on the scroll. The rate of change from color to color can be remotely controlled so that very fast changes can occur during a momentary blackout or slower changes can be incorporated into lighting cues to shift the light on stage from one color to another. The scrollers tend to be very quiet and reliable, but like most machines they are not perfect. Use of scrollers can reduce the number of lighting fixtures required on a production, since now any single fixture equipped with a scroller can project at least eight different colors of light.

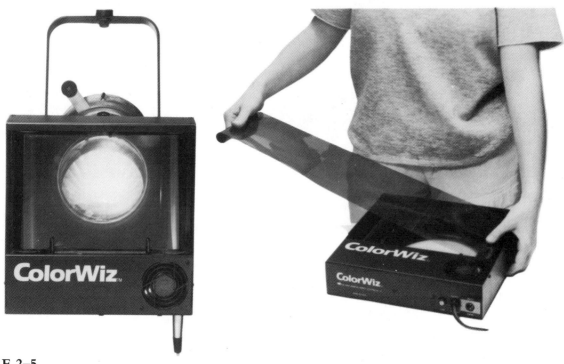

FIGURE 2–5
Color scroller for a 6"
spotlight. (Courtesy The
Great American Market)

FIGURES C–1 through C–11

Each of these photos shows the same set of paper color swatches under different lighting colors to represent the interrelationship of colored light and colored pigment. The color swatches are shown under white light in Figure C–1. The gel color (or colors) is identified with each photo. Roscolux was used with a tungsten-halogen source. The order of the color swatches is: red, violet, blue, green, yellow, orange, and medium grey.

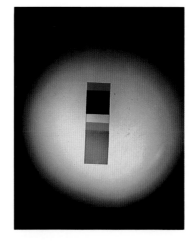

FIGURE C–1
No gel. White light.

FIGURE C–2
Red gel. Roscolux #27.

FIGURE C–3
Green gel. Roscolux #91.

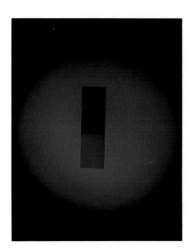

FIGURE C–4
Blue gel. Roscolux #80.

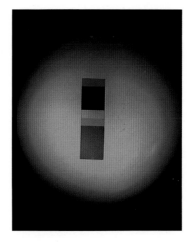

FIGURE C–5
Orange gel. Roscolux #23.

FIGURE C–6
Lavender gel. Roscolux #58.

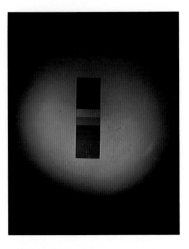

FIGURE C–7
Yellow gel. Roscolux #10.

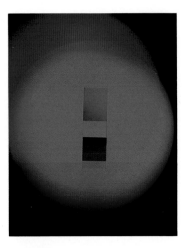

FIGURE C–8
*Red plus blue gel. Roscolux
#27 and #80.*

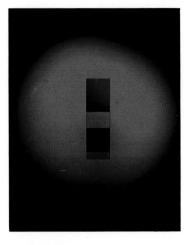

FIGURE C–9
*Red plus green gel. Roscolux
#27 and #91.*

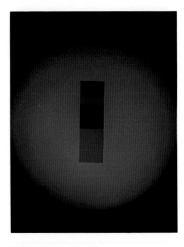

FIGURE C–10
*Blue plus green gel. Rosco-
lux #80 and #91.*

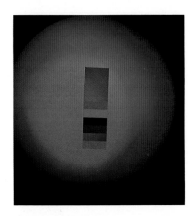

FIGURE C–11
*Red plus blue plus green gel.
Roscolux #27 and #80 and
#91.*

Each of the following photos are of the same setting for a production of Hang Onto Your Head. *Figure C–12 shows the set under nearly white lighting. The set was painted dark blue and spattered with red, yellow, and green paints to reflect and change with the lighting colors as shown in Figures C–13, C–14, and C–15.*

FIGURE C–12
The set under nearly white light.

FIGURE C–13
The set under magenta lighting.

FIGURE C–14
The set under amber lighting.

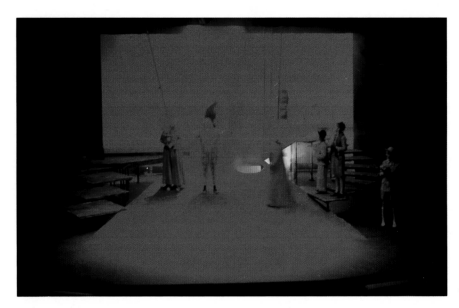

FIGURE C–15
The set under red lighting.

CONCLUSION

Color has one of the greatest psychological impacts of all the visual elements of a production. The color of light can enhance or detract from a performance. It can change the color of the setting or costumes, influence the mood of the audience, or be used to paint the stage with atmospheric lighting that helps to create a sense of time or place. The importance of color in light cannot be neglected and must always be given consideration when planning a show. The selection of color must be made with care so that the performance is enhanced rather than damaged. The process of selecting the colors must be done carefully with a full understanding of the effect of the color on the scenery, costumes, and makeup, as well as the psychological effect of the lighting on an audience.

CHAPTER 3

Mounting Positions and Equipment

INTRODUCTION

An effective lighting design is dependent on many elements. Where the lights are installed significantly affects the success of a lighting design since it controls the angle of the beams of light and the distance the light must travel to the stage. Theatrical lighting fixtures are portable equipment that may be moved and focused to meet the needs of the current production or, in some situations, they may be permanently installed. The ideal situation permits lighting instruments to be placed anywhere in a performance space. To accommodate this flexibility, a well-equipped facility allows easy access to built-in locations to hang lights and also provides for portable mounting positions. This degree of flexibility is usually reserved for sophisticated facilities. Although many theatres are equipped with at least limited lighting positions, many other facilities and most nontraditional performance spaces, such as a gymnasium or cafeteria, do not have permanent mounting positions for theatrical lighting instruments. In those situations, temporary mounting and electrical distribution equipment must be used.

REQUIREMENTS FOR LIGHTING POSITIONS

The locations for mounting lights, whether permanent or temporary, should fulfill certain requirements:

1. Mounting positions should allow lights to be focused onto the stage from the front, back, and both sides of the performance space. As an absolute minimum, it should be possible to hang lights overhead-in-front of the stage to provide illumination for visibility.

2. It should be possible to mount lighting instruments to project light from the front of every area of the stage at a vertical angle of approximately 45° to 60° (Figure 3–1). This angle produces the most effective illumination for visibility, casts a minimum of distracting shadows on the performers and scenery, and projects light that establishes a sense of three-dimensionality to the actors, scenery, and stage space.

3. Mounting equipment, usually 1½" (inside diameter) schedule 40 or 80 (strength) pipe, must be sufficiently strong so it will not bend or fracture. The pipe must be securely installed so that it will not fall when heavily loaded with lights and cable. Normally, pipes used for lighting are supported at least every 10'-0" of their length.

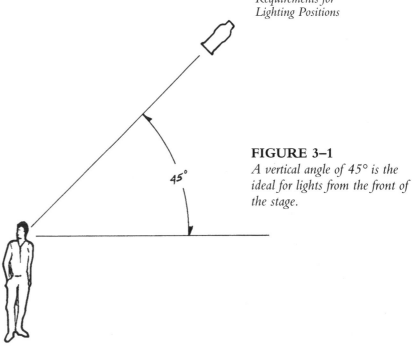

FIGURE 3–1
A vertical angle of 45° is the ideal for lights from the front of the stage.

4. Mounting pipes must be installed in a manner that prevents them from rotating.

5. Mounting positions must be accessible to workers so that lights can be hung, focused, and maintained. Preferred access is by means of catwalks, which place stagehands on a secure floor that allows them to hang and focus the lights easily. In lieu of catwalks, there must be a way to place a scaffold or ladder on a stable base within safe access of each lighting instrument.

6. Mounting pipes must be installed with sufficient clearance above to permit pipe clamps to slide over them and enough clear space below to allow fixtures to tip all the way down for focusing.

7. It is normally preferable (when possible) to have lighting positions masked or hidden from the view of the audience. It is too easy for audience members at dramatic productions to be distracted by the glare of the lights. There are productions where it is desirable to have the lights in view of the audience. This is especially true for rock concerts where the light fixtures are treated as scenery or special effects.

8. Electrical power must be available at each mounting position. This may be permanent equipment to distribute power or a temporary installation of extension cables.

Mounting Equipment

Theatrical lighting instruments are designed to be hung with clamps or with bolts on pipes, track, or flat surfaces. The usual means to mount lights is to fasten a pipe clamp over a 1½" pipe that is hanging horizontally. This may be a permanently installed lighting pipe in the ceiling of the auditorium, a batten that is part of the counterweight

FIGURE 3–2

*Standard pipe clamp attached
to a pipe.*

system over the stage, or a pipe temporarily hung anywhere for this purpose. The pipe may be welded in position, suspended from chain or rope, or rigged with aircraft cable. Lighting instruments hook to the pipe with a special clamp designed to fasten securely to pipe 1" to 2" in diameter (Figure 3–2).

The second means of mounting replaces the pipe clamp with a bolt or lag screw and washer. The bolt may fasten to a steel clip that slides in a **Unistrut track** (Figure 3–3A) which is permanently installed on the surface of a wall or ceiling, or the track may be part of a portable structure. The bolt might also fasten to a sliding-tee hanger rigged off the side of a vertical pipe (Figure 3–3B), or a bolt can be fastened through a wooden or steel base that is placed on the floor (Figure 3–3C). Finally, a bolt or a lag screw can be used to attach the lighting instruments to the side of a wooden beam in the ceiling or to bolt a light to the wall or floor.

FIGURE 3–3

*Other means of hanging
lighting instruments include:
(A) attaching the yoke to a
Unistrut track with a bolt and
special Unistrut nut; (B)
using a side arm mounted on
a vertical pipe and a sliding
tee to which the yoke is
fastened with a bolt; or (C)
bolting the yoke to a piece of
plywood which may be
screwed or nailed to the floor
or weighted to hold the light
in place.*

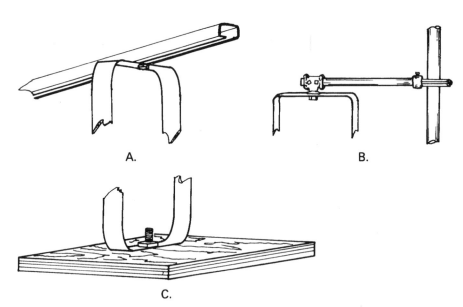

A.

B.

C.

Mounting with either a pipe clamp or a bolt must be sufficiently secure to carry the weight of the lighting instruments. The mounting must also allow the lights to be aimed and focused and then firmly fastened in place.

Any lighting fixture should be additionally secured with a safety cable or safety chain when it is installed in an overhead location where it might fall on someone, whether audience, cast, or crew member. Suppliers of theatrical fixtures provide safety cables or chains with almost all new lighting fixtures. The safety cable is a thin wire rope that can be easily threaded through the yoke of the lighting fixture and wrapped around or hooked to the pipe upon which the fixture is hung. (Some stage electricians prefer to attach the safety cable directly to the body of the lighting fixture rather than simply passing it through the yoke.) It is strongly recommended that all accessories such as color holders, color scrollers, barn doors, and top hats are secured with a safety cable or chain also. Safety chains serve the same function as the wire rope safety cable; however, they tend to be heavier and bulkier.

TRADITIONAL PROSCENIUM THEATRE MOUNTING POSITIONS

A number of traditional lighting positions have evolved in the proscenium theatre. Instruments placed in these locations provide the best illumination for visibility and dramatic effects. The four traditional lighting positions in the auditorium are the balcony rail, ceiling beams, box booms, and rear-of-house/control booth.

Front-of-House Mounting Positions

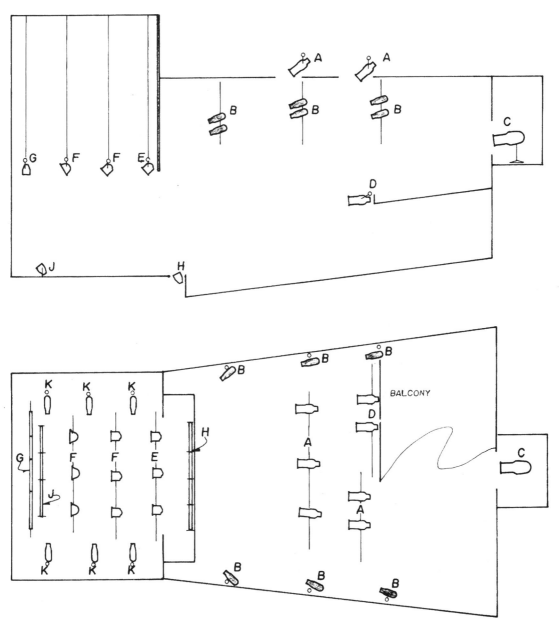

FIGURE 3–4

Traditional mounting positions of lights in the proscenium theatre. Top is a centerline section and bottom is a plan view. (A) Beams; (B) side wall slots or vertical mounting pipes sometimes called "box booms"; (C) control booth; (D) balcony rail; (E) first electric pipe; (F) succeeding electric pipes approximately 8'-0" on center (dimensions vary greatly on different stages); (G) cyc electric pipe; (H) footlights; (J) electric ground row; (K) booms, trees, or light ladders mounted in the wings.

Balcony Rail

The **balcony** rail is a lighting position that developed in the commercial (especially Broadway) theatre to meet the needs of touring productions. In this location, a mounting pipe is temporarily or permanently attached to the front edge of the balcony. This position gets the instruments out of the sightlines of the audience and provides relatively easy access to the fixtures once they are hung in place. Light coming from this location usually reaches the stage at a very flat angle that causes actors to cast long, dark shadows on each other and on the scenery. For this reason, the balcony rail is less than an ideal lighting position but in many theatres it is the only front-of-house location for lights and must be used to provide visibility.

Beams

The best front-of-house lighting positions are the **beams** located in the ceiling of the auditorium. These may be enclosed false beams that mask the lights from the audience, hidden or exposed catwalks spanning the ceiling, or simply pipes suspended overhead. Most theatres with permanent lighting positions have at least one beam position at which to mount lights to illuminate the front third of the stage. Of course, on deeper stages lights in the beams might only illuminate the downstage fourth or fifth of the acting area, and multiple beam positions might be provided. Stages with deep aprons usually need a minimum of two beam positions, one to mount lights that illuminate the apron and the other to mount lights that illuminate the area immediately upstage of the proscenium arch.

A well-designed beam position not only provides a pipe on which to mount the lighting instruments but also a means to get to the lights. The ideal solution is catwalks accessible by stairways or ladders.

When catwalks are not part of a facility, it is necessary to hang and focus lights above the auditorium from a scaffold or ladder. Scaffolding can sometimes be set up to clear the seats and provide a solid platform on which to work. Most often this is not possible and lights over seats can only be reached by a ladder. If a four-legged ladder on wheels can be maneuvered around the seats and the floor is not too severely sloped, the working situation is not too difficult. With a stagehand positioned at each corner of the ladder to keep it solidly in place, the ladder with the person at the top can be rolled from light to light and equipment passed up the ladder in a basket on a rope. If a ladder on casters will not fit between the seats, it may be necessary to use an extension ladder to get to the lights. In this situation, at least two people must brace the base of the ladder while the technician works overhead. In many places, state or local safety rules may prohibit the use of extension ladders as a means of access to light fixtures. Once again, equipment can be passed up the ladder in a basket on a rope. The stagehand must come down the ladder and the ladder relocated between work on each pair of lights. The ladder must be maneuvered around and must straddle the seats each time it is moved, but now it must also be kept balanced so it does not fall over while moving. Since the floor of an auditorium is usually sloped or stepped, the ladder may have to be blocked up under one leg to make it level. Finally, lighting pipes over the audience are usually very high, so ladders must be extended a long way, adding to the danger of the situation. Preparing the lighting for a production becomes very tedious when it is possible to hang or focus only one or two lighting instruments at a time, then climb down the ladder, move it, and climb back up the ladder to work on the next lights.

Box Boom

Audience seating boxes are often located along the side walls of older theatres. Although these are hardly ideal positions from which to watch a production, they provide good locations for some front-of-house lighting. A **box boom** is a vertical lighting pipe placed in the audience seating boxes near the sides of the proscenium arch. Originally, these positions were used to supplement balcony rail lighting. Although they may still do that, presently they are also used to provide mounting positions for front-of-house side light. These lighting positions may be temporary vertical pipes in stands, **booms**, placed in the seating boxes, bare pipes attached to the side walls of the auditorium, or one, two, or three **side wall slots** with vertical pipes built into the auditorium walls and hidden in some architectural manner. Since the pipes located in these positions are vertical, lighting instruments mounted on them will extend straight out from the pipe at 90°, making it very difficult to focus the light. A method has been devised to minimize this difficulty. A side arm is installed at each position a lighting instrument is to be mounted. A **side arm** is a pipe attached perpendicularly to a boom. It may be a piece of pipe screwed into a threaded coupling on the boom or it might be a piece of pipe attached to a lighting pipe clamp (Figure 3–3B) that fastens to the side of the boom. Either method works to provide a horizontal pipe from which to mount the lighting instruments on the boom. A boom with side arms is often called a **tree** (Figure 3–5B).

Rear-of-House/Control Booth

A final auditorium lighting position is at the rear of the seating area or in a booth at the back of the house. In addition to placing spotlights here, these positions are usually used for follow spots. A platform or scaffold may be constructed to raise the lights high above the audience and improve the angle of the beam to the stage. The disadvantage of placing follow spots in the audience is the noise generated by the fan of most of these instruments as well as the noise and activity of the follow spot operator, which may distract the audience from the performance.

On-Stage Mounting Positions

There are at least six traditional on-stage lighting positions in the proscenium theatre: the first electric pipe, succeeding electric pipes, the cyc electric pipe, electric ground row, on-stage side-lighting positions including booms and ladders, and, occasionally, footlights.

The **first electric pipe** is the furthest downstage location at which to hang lights on stage. It usually is located directly upstage of the act curtain. Lighting instruments placed on this pipe provide front light to the middle third of the stage and back light to the downstage third of the acting area. The first electric pipe often carries the greatest quantity of lighting instruments of all pipes on stage.

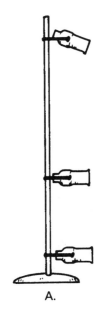

A.

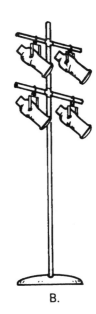

B.

FIGURE 3–5
(A) Boom; (B) tree.

77

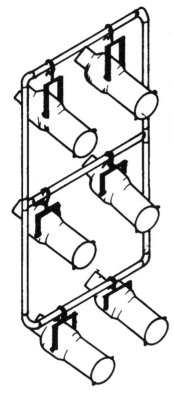

FIGURE 3–6
Light ladder.

Succeeding electric pipes, the second, third, and fourth electrics, are placed 6'-0" to 10'-0" apart counting upstage from the first electric pipe. A moderately equipped stage 30'-0" deep has at least three electric pipes. Generally, instruments on the second electric pipe are used to provide front light for the upstage areas and back light for the middle one-third of the stage. The third electric pipe is often used to mount back light for the back one-third of the acting area and, perhaps, to provide front light for a drop at the back of the stage. Side light, down light, and special effects might be mounted on any of the electric pipes.

The **cyc electric pipe** is usually located just a few feet ahead of the back wall of the stage. It is usually equipped with scoops or strip lights to provide a wash of illumination and color on the upper portion of a cyclorama or painted drop. An **electric ground row**, usually assembled from strip lights, is mounted on the floor directly under the cyc electric to illuminate the bottom portion of a cyclorama or drop.

Booms, trees, and light ladders (Figure 3–5) are used in the wings to mount high and low-angle side light. The booms are assembled from vertical pipes up to 20'-0" tall screwed into very heavy steel bases. It is almost always necessary to load extra weight onto the boom bases to counterbalance the weight of the lighting instruments. Side arms may be added to the vertical pipe to make a tree. A rope should be tied to the top of a boom or tree over 10'-0" tall and fastened overhead or to the wall to keep the vertical pipe from tipping. To clear floor space for scenery or to place side lighting at a steeper angle, a boom may be replaced with a light ladder. A **light ladder** (Figure 3–6) is a pipe frame forming two or more rectangles on which lights are mounted. It is suspended from the gridiron or ceiling with ropes or hung at the end of electric battens to provide high angle side-lighting positions.

Footlights, when used, are located on the floor along the front edge of the stage. Some stages have built-in footlight troughs and others have disappearing footlights that may be turned upside down to extend the stage floor all the way, to the edge. Stages without built-in footlights may use strip lights in this location when needed. Although footlights continue to be used on some stages, they generally have been eliminated except to create special effects or to fill in heavy shadows on the faces of performers. When used, they must be kept at low levels of intensity so they do not distort the appearance of a performer by reversing the normal pattern of highlights and shadows on the face. Footlights are still used in some auditoriums as the sole source of front light because of a lack of appropriate front lighting positions or a sufficient quantity of lighting instruments.

NON-PROSCENIUM THEATRE MOUNTING POSITIONS

Permanent mounting positions in non-proscenium theatres, such as arena or thrust stages, are usually of two types. They may be lighting pipes laced in patterns that conform to the shape of the outer edge of the stage (Figure 3–7A) or they may be a gridiron of pipes over stage and over either a portion or all of the audience (Figure 3–7B). The grid

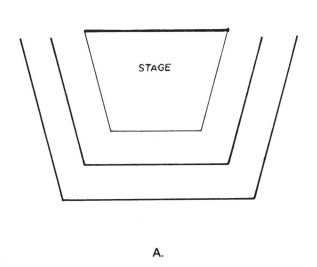

A.

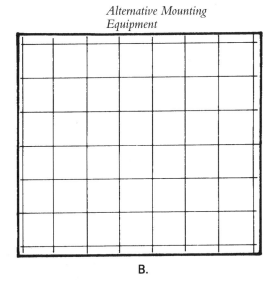

Alternative Mounting
Equipment

B.

FIGURE 3–7
*Traditional mounting positions
for nonproscenium theatres:
(A) Positions may conform to
the shape of the stage or (B)
may be laid out in a grid of
pipes located four to eight feet
on-center in each direction.
Combinations of these patterns
are often found in many
theatres.*

is usually laid out with pipes placed no less than 4'-0" apart in each direction and up to no more than 8'-0" apart in each direction. The gridiron system is used in flexible theatres, television studios, and on stages where very little scenery will be flown overhead. Either of these systems may be used alone or combined and either design may be accompanied with catwalks or only allow ladder access from the floor. Overhead mounting positions may be supplemented with booms and trees positioned near audience aisles or behind audience seating sections. If no other means of installing lighting fixtures is possible and sufficient height is available, an arena stage could be illuminated using no more than four trees evenly spaced around the perimeter of the stage.

ALTERNATIVE MOUNTING EQUIPMENT

When a performance space is not equipped with lighting positions, it may be adapted by temporarily adding pipes. The easiest way to do this is to suspend a 1½" pipe with properly installed aircraft cable from a solid overhead structure that a structural engineer has confirmed is able to carry the weight.

The pipe should be supported at 8'-0" to 10'-0" intervals. In some buildings, the overhead structure is a solid beam rather than an open web through which chain can be passed. In these situations, the chain can be attached to a **beam hanger** (Figure 3–8). This is a small clamp available from theatrical suppliers that fits around the bottom plate of I-beams and provides a hanger from which chain or cable can be suspended to carry the lighting pipe.

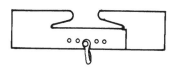

FIGURE 3–8
*A beam clamp from which a
pipe may be suspended by wire
rope or chain.*

79

If it is not possible to install a support cable or chain at least every 10'-0", or if the pipe that is being installed is to carry an extremely heavy load, the pipe can be replaced with a truss (Figure 3–9). This is a welded triangular arrangement of pipes and rods that provides a sturdy mounting over a long span with a minimum of support.

FIGURE 3–9

A square truss which is often used for tour rigging of stage lighting fixtures. Square and triangular trusses are available in a variety of sizes. (Courtesy James Thomas Engineering Ltd.)

Trees, ladders, and booms are handy portable mounting equipment. Other portable devices that may be used to mount lights are manual and power-operated towers. A **tower** (Figure 3–10) serves in place of a boom or ladder. It has a large base that may or may not be mounted on casters. A tower has a sturdy cross-member from which a number of lighting instruments can be suspended. The cross-member may be Unistrut track or simply a piece of pipe. The center column of the tower telescopes and allows the top to be raised as much as 20'-0" above the floor. Manual systems are constructed with pipes that slide inside of each other, with a locking collar to hold them in place. There are some towers that utilize a manual or electric winch system and others that can be raised with air pressure or carbon dioxide.

A few manufacturers of stage equipment have developed tower-and-truss systems that permit assembling a portable frame on which to hang lighting and drapes. The systems use at least four towers and six trusses to enclose the stage (Figure 3–11).

Although well-designed and well-equipped theatres may have some or all of the traditional mounting positions and equipment, many organizations work in minimal facilities or must adapt gyms, churches, cafeterias, or classrooms to perform. Those kinds of spaces seldom have

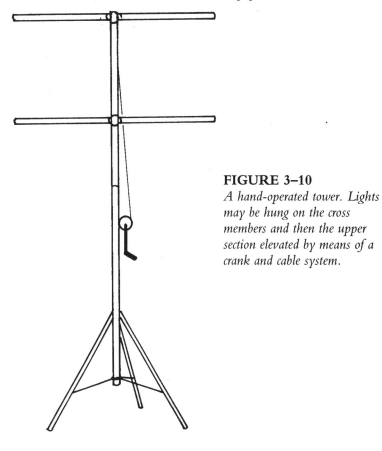

FIGURE 3–10
*A hand-operated tower. Lights
may be hung on the cross
members and then the upper
section elevated by means of a
crank and cable system.*

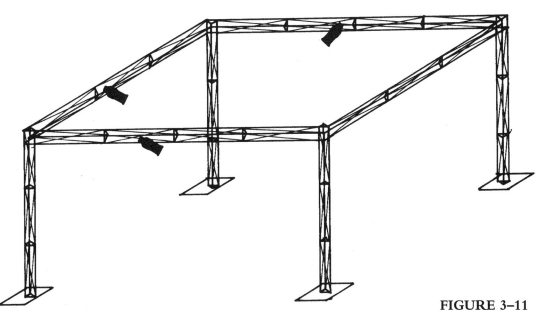

FIGURE 3–11
*Typical ground support tower
and truss rigging for temporary
mounting positions of lighting.*

81

established positions for mounting lights or means to distribute electrical power, and the organizations also lack the budget to purchase standard equipment to use for rigging. A few inexpensive solutions are possible to solve the problems of finding locations for lights in these situations.

When working in a gym, the stage is often located behind a basketball backboard that is suspended from overhead on pipes and raised out of the way on cable. *With permission*, several of the pipes that frame the backboard can be used to mount spotlights. It may be necessary to add a supporting rope between the backboard and the ceiling to compensate for the added weight. Sometimes it may be tricky to get a ladder to a location on the frame where the lights can be attached.

Many gym programs use pipes mounted in tires or wheels filled with cement to support volleyball nets. These same net standards can be used as lighting booms. If they are not available from the athletic program, similar standards can be constructed. Concrete is poured into a tire that has a piece of 1½" pipe positioned in the center of it. The pipe must be perfectly vertical. The object is to create a flat, solid base that weighs between 50 and 100 pounds. The pipe should be as tall as the performance space allows, up to 20'-0" if a rope can be fastened to the top of the boom and tied to a structural member overhead, or up to only 12'-0" if there is no way to tie off the top of the boom.

When working in a gymnasium, cafeteria, or other larger space that does not have permanent mounting positions for lights, lighting towers can be constructed by assembling construction scaffold. These sturdy steel frames can be built into tall towers from which follow spots can be operated or on which other instruments can be mounted. Scaffolds should always be used with their outriggers. This can be especially handy when a multipurpose room is being used for production and an alternate use of the space requires an unobstructed floor for other activities. The scaffold can be assembled on wheels and simply rolled into the corner when the room is used for other purposes. Two or more scaffold towers can be used with a truss or pipe securely fastened in the gap between them. Many school systems and government agencies own their own scaffold that might be available for production. If it is not possible to borrow this equipment, scaffold can be rented. It comes complete with floor plates or casters, frames, braces, and floor boards. Whenever scaffold is used to mount lights, a grounding wire should be connected to the steel frame.

GETTING TO MOUNTING POSITIONS

Some facilities used for production have complete catwalk systems and easy means of access to all of the lights over the audience. However, many facilities, whether temporary or permanent, require climbing a ladder or some other temporary structure to get to the fixtures above the auditorium and over the stage to hang, cable, and focus them. There are a number of different ways to get to lighting positions; some are safer than others, some are more convenient, and some are more efficient.

Ladders are the most obvious way to get to high places. They are generally available even in the most primitive working situations. *When working on lights—or anything electrical—aluminum ladders should* **not** *be used.* In the event of an electrical short, an aluminum ladder may carry electrical power and endanger the lives of anyone in contact with it. A wood or fiberglass ladder of the appropriate height should be used.

There are a number of ladder-safety rules that should be strictly observed.

1. A sufficiently tall ladder should be used. It must allow someone to stand *no higher* than the second step from the top to reach the lights comfortably without overreaching a safe point of balance.

2. Do not use the top of any ladder as a step.

3. A ladder no taller than necessary should be used. Excessively tall ladders are difficult to handle and very likely will run into and damage scenery and drapes or bump the lights.

4. Do not move a ladder with a person on it unless the ladder is securely fastened to a stable rolling platform or frame.

5. When someone is working on a ladder, a person should be stationed at each leg of the ladder to brace it and prevent it from moving or tipping.

6. Do not stack tables or chairs up to support the legs of a ladder to make it taller.

7. Only use a ladder when it is level and square and the legs are securely resting on the floor.

8. Do not overreach the balance point when working on a ladder.

9. Climb only on the side of the ladder with steps.

10. No more than one person at a time should be on a ladder.

11. Never leave tools unattended on any shelf or step on the ladder.

12. Observe the safety and caution statements printed on the top and sides of the ladder.

There are four different kinds of ladders that are convenient for focusing stage lights: extension ladders, A-ladders, A-frame extension ladders, and stair-climbing ladders. Good ladders are expensive; only the finest-quality ones should be used.

An **extension ladder** (Figure 3–12) is the simplest and the most dangerous type of ladder to use. A simple frame with rungs slides in the carriage of a wider frame with rungs. A pair of spring-loaded brackets designed to slide past each rung or to hook in place as needed allows the ladder to be extended to and fixed at a working height. These ladders are available in heights from 8'-0" when closed and extending to about 14'-0" when opened, to as great as 24'-0" when closed, opening to approximately 40'-0" when fully extended. Extension ladders are very heavy.

FIGURE 3–12

An extension ladder should be kept at a fairly steep angle and placed against a firm support. A worker should always be at the base of the ladder when it is in use to ensure that the bottom does not slip.

83

To Set Up an Extension Ladder

1. Usually, three or four people are needed to set up a tall extension ladder. Place the bottom of the ladder, the end with the rubber feet, on the floor near the location the ladder is to be used. One person must stand at the feet of the ladder and keep them from lifting up or sliding while the other two people walk the other end of the ladder up, moving hand-over-hand until the ladder is completely vertical.

2. When the ladder is standing straight up and down, the people who walked it up must balance the ladder in place while the third person pulls on the rope on the back of the ladder; this will cause the extension to rise out of the top of the ladder. The people balancing the ladder can help the extension rise by pushing up on its rungs. As the ladder extends it will become more difficult to keep balanced and also more difficult to continue to raise the extension. A fourth person may be needed to push the bottom of the extension up with a board or by standing on another short ladder to reach it. As the ladder gets taller, it might be easier to rest the top end against a wall that is free of obstructions. This will allow the ladder to continue to rise to the needed height with the added support provided by the wall.

3. Once the appropriate height is achieved, both brackets must be firmly hooked over the supporting rung. To do this, the extension is lifted just high enough to cause the top of the brackets to clear the supporting rung and hook onto it as the extension is lowered until both brackets are solidly engaged on it.

4. Rest the top of the ladder firmly and squarely against a solid surface such as a brick wall. The sides of the ladder a foot or two down from the top may be rested against a solid surface such as a thick, *rigid* pipe or a beam. The ladder should be at an angle of approximately 60° to 75°. Anything steeper may cause the person climbing it to fall backward; anything shallower may cause the bottom of the ladder to slide backward.

5. A person *must* brace the bottom of each leg whenever someone is climbing or working on the ladder.

A-ladders (Figure 3–13) are available in heights ranging from 2'-0" to 16'-0" tall. They are made with or without a folding paint shelf. In most instances, it is safer *not* to use a ladder with the paint shelf, since the shelf, which is not designed to carry the weight of a person, often ends up being used as a step. These ladders can be used closed, leaning against a sturdy support in the manner of an extension ladder, or they can stand free of any supporting structure on their own four legs. When these ladders are set up they can be quite secure so long as the folding braces are opened fully and all four legs rest squarely and firmly on the floor. When working on an uneven surface, a large wooden block should be placed under any leg that is off the floor.

As many wooden and some fiberglass A-ladders age, they will begin to wiggle and sway from side to side. The sway can be reduced or eliminated by tightening the little nuts on the outside of the ladder attached to the rods that pass underneath each step. Be sure the ladder is resting firmly on a flat surface when making this adjustment.

FIGURE 3–13
An A-ladder.

A-frame extension ladders (Figure 3–14) are a combination of an A-ladder and an extension ladder. They are often used in theatres to climb to electric pipes on stage since they provide a solid base to reach significant heights. The ladder consists of an A-frame base with rungs on each side. At the top of the **A** is an extension ladder that rises

FIGURE 3–14
An A-frame extension ladder mounted on a rolling X-frame.

straight up. A-frame extension ladders that extend as high as 36'-0" are
available. The ladder may be stood up and opened like any A-frame.
Once set up, the ladder is climbed to the height of the extension, which
is simply lifted through the center of the ladder until the desired height
is reached. A metal bracket hinges underneath a rung of the extension
to keep it at the proper height. A pair of guides that are usually part of
the hinge-brace for the A-frame also brace the bottom of the extension
portion of the ladder.

The ladder is designed so that a technician will sit on the very top
of it to work. Once the worker reaches the top of the ladder, he or she
turns sideways and throws one leg over the top rung and hooks a toe
behind the second or third rung down while the heel or toe of the
other foot is also hooked behind a rung on the opposite side of the
ladder. In this way, the technician can have both hands free while
securely seated on top of the ladder. A-frame extension ladders provide
a very sturdy base, but until the worker is settled at the top of the ladder
the extension will shift a short distance from side to side or may shift
unexpectedly as the person on top adjusts his or her center of gravity.
This shifting can be startling and takes some getting used to.

A unique ladder that is very handy for working on scenery and to
use to solve occasional problems when working on lights is a **stair-
climbing ladder** (Figure 3–15). These ladders are designed to be
placed on a stairway or some other grossly uneven surface and allow
someone to climb 5'-0" or 6'-0" up. The ladders are fairly sturdy and
are handy to have around. Unfortunately, all stair-climbing ladders are
made from aluminum.

FIGURE 3–15
A stair-climbing ladder.

An A-frame extension ladder or any regular A-ladder can be made especially convenient if it is attached to a rolling base. A standard stage wagon can be used for this purpose by bolting a loose pin hinge or angle iron to the bottom of each leg of the ladder and also to the platform lid. The ladder can be taken off the rolling base by removing the bolts. An X-frame is a way to provide a demountable, rolling base that folds up for storage. This is especially handy for A-frame extension ladders since they take up a great deal of floor space when they are set up.

To Build a Rolling X-Frame

Materials List	*Equipment List*
Ladder	Saw
2 2 × 6 × (as needed)	Hammer
4 2 × 6 × 8"	Drill
12d common nails	2 crescent wrenches
White glue	
4 4" rubber covered ball-bearing swivel casters	
16 ¼" × 4" flathead stove bolts, nuts, and lock washers	
12 $^3/_{16}$" × 4" hex-head machine bolts, nuts, and lock washers	
12 $^3/_{16}$" × 1" hex-head machine bolts, nuts, and lock washers	
4 2" backflap loose-pin hinges	
1 ½" × 4" hex-head machine bolt, nut, and 2 washers	
Pin Wire	

1. Set up the ladder and measure the diagonal distance between two opposite legs. Cut both 2 × 6s the length of the diagonal plus 8". Drill a ½" diameter hole in the very center of each board. Glue and nail one of the 8" blocks on top at each end of both boards.

2. Using the ¼" × 4" bolts, lock washers, and nuts, attach a caster to the top of the 2 × 6 × 8" blocks at each end of only one board. The bolt heads should be on the side of the board opposite the caster. Attach a caster at each end of the other 2 × 6 on the side opposite the blocks with the bolt heads on the side of the board opposite the caster. Each board will have a caster at each end. The casters on one board will be on top of the blocks and the casters on the other board on the side opposite the blocks.

3. With all four casters facing down, slip the ½" × 4" bolt through (1) a washer and then through (2) the holes at the center of the two boards, (3) another washer, and finally (4) fasten the nut onto it.

4. Open the frame to form a wide X and place the opened ladder on top of it. The ladder should rest on a 2 × 6 or 2 × 6 block close to

a caster at each corner. Attach a loose-pin hinge to the outside at the bottom of each ladder leg using the $^3/_{16}$" × 1" bolts. Attach the hinges to the top of the X-frame as well, using the $^3/_{16}$" × 4" bolts. If the bolts are going to conflict with the caster plates, adjust the frame so at least one bolt may be used and replace the conflicting bolts with 1½" × 8 flathead wood screws.

The ladder can remain attached to the X-frame or the pin wires can be removed from the hinges and both the ladder and the frame folded for storage.

CONCLUSION

Established performance spaces usually are equipped with a variety of fixed lighting positions. These positions meet a range of needs for a production from the most minimal illumination to the most elaborate lighting design. Sophisticated facilities include amenities such as cat-walks and lighting bridges that make it especially convenient to reach the equipment to hang, focus, and maintain the lights. Less well equipped facilities increase the amount of time the work on lighting requires by necessitating creation of mounting positions and making access to hang and focus the lighting instruments difficult. Since almost any kind of space or facility is used to stage a play, opera, ballet, musical, or variety show, it is often challenging to find ways to install lighting equipment for a production in these nontraditional performance spaces. Equally challenging is finding a means to provide sufficient electrical power to the lights once they are installed. Certain basic understandings about how electricity functions and the equipment that distributes it are important. The establishment of lighting positions affects and is affected by how electrical power is brought to the lights.

CHAPTER 4

Lighting Instruments

INTRODUCTION

The development of theatrical lighting instruments has evolved throughout the twentieth century. Spotlights and floodlights are used in the theatre because they produce efficient, controlled illumination that can be directed and modified in artful ways. This equipment has been designed to do specific lighting tasks that yield predictable results. Newer stage lighting fixtures have been designed to increase efficiency, control, and ease of handling. Still, all of the equipment has a single purpose: to put controlled light on stage.

THE TYPICAL LIGHTING INSTRUMENT

The typical theatrical lighting fixture (Figure 4–1) consists of nine standard parts: the hood or housing, color holder, socket, lamp, pigtail, connector, yoke, and mounting device, including safety cable.

The Housing

The **hood** is the outer housing of the lighting instrument. In addition to providing a means to hold all of the parts of the fixture together, the hood limits the pattern of the light projected by cutting off portions of the beam of light created by the lamp. In so doing, the hood absorbs light energy and transforms it into heat energy so that it becomes extremely hot while the light is operating. The metal forming the hood must be sufficiently durable to withstand these temperatures as well as the rough handling that is often imposed on stage lights. The housings are usually made from thin steel or cast aluminum because these materials are strong and can dissipate the heat. Usually both the inside and the outside of the instruments are painted black. The inside is black to absorb stray beams of light; the outside is black so the fixture will not be very noticeable when mounted above the audience or stage.

To help deal with the high temperatures that are built up within the lighting instruments, all fixtures are designed to allow free passage of air through them. Convection currents carry air over the lens (when present) and past the lamp and socket without letting light leak out of the housing at undesired angles. This ventilation is often provided by a series of holes or slotted openings near the back of commercially manufactured equipment. At the front of the hood on almost all lighting fixtures is a **color-holder slot** to mount special accessories or frames designed to carry coloring media.

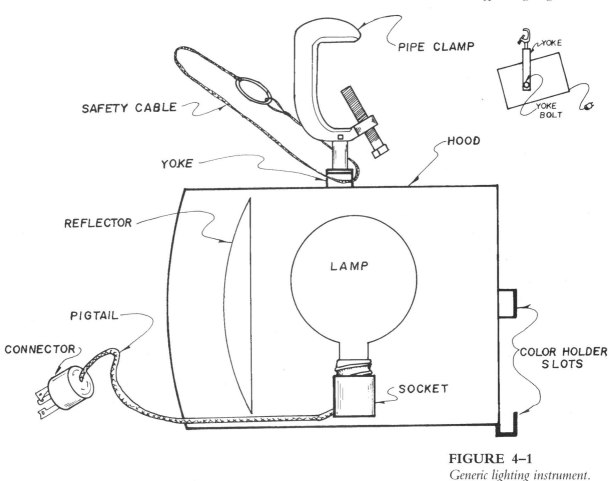

FIGURE 4–1
Generic lighting instrument.

The Reflector

The **reflector** is one of the most important parts of any theatrical lighting instrument. It serves two functions: (1) to increase the efficiency of the lighting instrument by redirecting what would otherwise be unused rays of light and (2) to create specific patterns and qualities of light as part of the redirection process. **Reflection** is the technical term for redirecting rays of light by bouncing them off a surface. The kind of reflection with which most people are familiar is called **mirror reflection**, which occurs when an image strikes a surface and is reflected in exactly the same pattern. This kind of reflection is used in spotlights to create a hard, tightly controlled beam of light. The opposite of mirrored reflection is **diffuse reflection**, in which the image is completely broken up and reflected in no specific pattern. A variation of this kind of reflection is often used in floodlights to create a soft nondirectional beam of light. The reflector in a lighting instrument may simply be the interior of the housing or it might be a completely separate piece of metal or glass. Proper alignment of the reflector, lamp, and lens (when used) is critical to the operation of most lights.

The Socket

The **socket** is the part of the fixture that holds the lamp (light bulb) in place and conducts power to it. Sockets for theatrical lighting instruments must be able to withstand the extreme heat built up within the fixture because of the very powerful lamps used, but in spotlights they also must provide a way to properly align the filament of the lamp they carry with the reflector and lens of the lighting instrument. There are many different kinds of sockets used in theatrical fixtures from a simple screw base to a prefocus socket; they vary not only in shape but also in size and must match the base of the lamps used in them.

Although sockets are a fairly permanent part of most lighting instruments, they will wear out with age. The interiors of the sockets of very old lights may be corroded or become damaged because of an improperly seated lamp or as a result of incorrect procedures when trying to remove a lamp. Damaged sockets can be replaced. This is a fairly simple and inexpensive process with most of the older lighting instruments. However, replacing sockets in some of the newer spotlights can be tricky. If that becomes necessary, the manufacturer or dealer should be contacted for instructions.

Lamps

Lamps, or light bulbs, are designed to fit specific equipment based on the design of the socket, reflector, lens (when used), and the overall size of the lighting instrument. Lamps are described by a number of characteristics: shape, size, base, wattage, voltage, color temperature, average life, means of incandescence, and filament design. All of these characteristics are summarized in a three-letter code called the **ANSI lamp designation**. The letters of the code have no specific meaning individually; they are simply a group of letters that have been selected to identify a particular lamp. The three-letter designation is being used to identify almost all stage and studio lamps. Often lamps of three or four different designations may be used in a single lighting instrument. However, sometimes only one type of lamp will fit and properly function in a light.

Figure 4–2 shows some of the more common **bulb shapes**. The names of the shapes tend to be literally descriptive, so that a long skinny lamp is called a *tube* and a large round ball is called a *globe*. Each shape bulb is available in various sizes. The sizes are described as the maximum diameter of the bulb in eighths of an inch, so that there is a T12 lamp, meaning the lamp is tube shaped and twelve eighths (1½") of an inch in diameter, and a PS52 lamp, which is pear shaped with a diameter measuring fifty-two eighths (6½") of an inch.

The **base** (Figure 4–3) is the portion of the lamp that fits into the socket. There are several different base shapes and sizes manufactured to correspond with the sockets in lighting instruments.

Although **wattage** specifically refers to the rate at which a lamp uses electricity, it also indicates the quantity of light created by the lamp. A 75 watt lamp is adequate reading light at home. However, most stage lighting instruments use 250 to 1,000 watt lamps, and some equipment even uses 5,000 watt lamps! Voltage affects the intensity of lamps, no matter what the wattage. **Voltage** is a fixed value of the

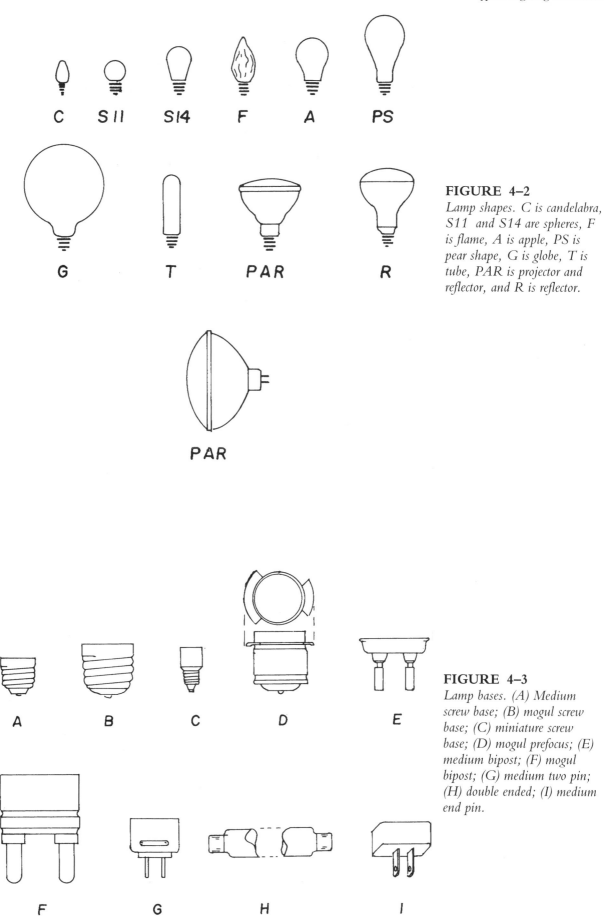

FIGURE 4–2
Lamp shapes. C is candelabra, S11 and S14 are spheres, F is flame, A is apple, PS is pear shape, G is globe, T is tube, PAR is projector and reflector, and R is reflector.

FIGURE 4–3
Lamp bases. (A) Medium screw base; (B) mogul screw base; (C) miniature screw base; (D) mogul prefocus; (E) medium bipost; (F) mogul bipost; (G) medium two pin; (H) double ended; (I) medium end pin.

electricity provided from the electric company. Most lamps used in the United States are made for operation at 120 volts; however, a few are made for use at 130 volts. The higher voltage lamps have a greater life when operated at 120 volts but yield reduced illumination. The actual brightness of a lamp is described as **candela, lumens, footcandles**, or **candle power**. These are relative terms that simply indicate the intensity of the light created by the lamp.

All light has color. The color may be some shade of white or it might be a deeper tone. Lamps are made with a particular degree of whiteness built in, which is referred to as **color temperature**, measured in **degrees Kelvin**. The equivalent of balanced daylight is considered to be a color temperature of 3,200 Kelvin in the theatre. In the movie and television industries, daylight is considered to be 5,500 to 6,500 Kelvin. The light emitted from lamps with higher color temperatures tends to be bluer in color; the light from lamps with lower color temperatures tends to be redder in color. Most lamps used on stage are in the 2,800 to 3,400 Kelvin range.

Average life is a means by which to determine the value of a lamp. Most lamps for theatrical lighting instruments have an average life of between 100 and 2,000 hours. A few lamps have an average life of only 10 to 25 hours, and other lamps have an average life as long as 4,000 hours. This rating is an approximation based on laboratory tests. Some lamps will outlast their rated average life significantly, and others will fall short of their average life. Generally, as color temperature (degrees Kelvin) increases, lamp life diminishes. The life expectancy of a lamp is affected not only by how long it burns but also by how the lamp is handled and used. Cost has little effect on and is no indication of the life of spotlight lamps.

When a material is heated until it glows, it produces light. Light produced by glowing materials is called **incandescence**. A **standard incandescent lamp** creates light by causing a tungsten filament wire to heat until it glows. It is placed in a gaseous atmosphere to extend the life of the filament wire. As the filament glows, it slowly burns away. The minute particles that are burned off are deposited on the interior of the glass bulb as black soot. In high-wattage lights as used on stage, this burning process will quickly cause the inside of the bulb to turn black and reduce the amount of light projected from the bulb. A standard incandescent spotlight lamp begins to lose brightness within the first few hours of operation and may project less than 40% of its rated output before it actually burns out. Another kind of incandescent lamp has been developed that virtually solves this blackening problem: these are **tungsten-halogen lamps (T-H lamps)** or **quartz lamps**—the names are used interchangeably (Figure 4–4). Because of the way this lamp is constructed, the burning cycle does not deposit black particles on the inside of the bulb but allows the lamp to operate at virtually full brightness until it finally burns out at the end of its normal life. These lamps usually do not have a greater life cycle than standard incandescent lamps, but they project their total luminance throughout their entire life. This results in consistent illumination when lamps are replaced and makes better use of existing lighting instruments since all of the light available is projected on stage rather than absorbed inside the light bulb.

Many lighting instruments designed for use with standard incandescent lamps can use **retrofit tungsten-halogen** lamps. All lamp

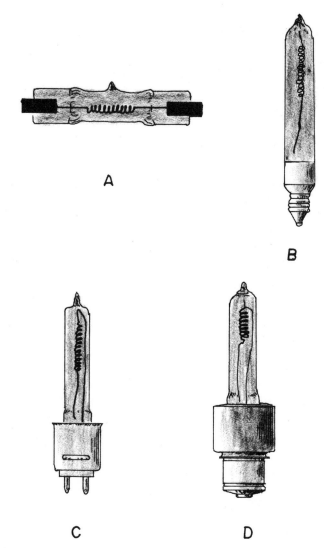

FIGURE 4–4
T-H lamp types. (A) Double ended; (B) mini-can screw; (C) medium two pin; and (D) medium prefocus.

manufacturers and many theatrical supply catalogs provide charts that indicate retrofit lamps for these instruments. Often, retrofit T-H lamps are less expensive than standard incandescent lamps for the same instruments. Professional lighting designers do not like to mix lighting instruments with standard incandescent lamps and T-H lamps on the same production.

The way lamps are handled is very important. Lamps are expensive materials that can easily be damaged as a result of carelessness.

1. Always store lamps in a safe place. Whenever possible, keep them protected in their original wrapping.
2. **Never touch the glass part of a lamp**. The deposit of skin oils will decrease the life of a standard incandescent lamp by leaving impurities on the surface where heat will collect. Skin oils deposited on a tungsten-halogen lamp will cause the bulb to explode or burn out as soon as the lamp is turned on.
3. When inserting or removing a lamp from an instrument, always handle it from the base so as not to twist off the glass bulb.

4. Whenever possible do not relocate a hot light. If possible, wait about 20 minutes before moving a recently used lighting instrument. This will permit the filament to cool and become more rigid, allowing it to withstand the shock of handling.

Pigtail and Connector

The **pigtail** is the wire that comes out of the lighting instrument and terminates in a plug. On commercial lighting instruments the pigtail is usually made of three individual wires each coated with Teflon insulation and encased in a silicone/fiberglass sleeve. Older lighting instruments may have two or three wire pigtails covered with a white, fuzzy material, which is heat-resistant asbestos insulation. Due to recent health concerns about asbestos, asbestos-covered wiring should be replaced with heat-resistant asbestos-free pigtails. Pigtails are usually 24" to 36" long.

The plug at the end of the pigtail is designed to make a firm, gap-free connection to allow electricity to flow into the light with the least amount of electrical resistance. The plug on the fixture is a **male plug** (also called **cord cap**) and inserts into a **female connector** (also called **cord body** or a **receptacle** when it is in the wall). When the connection is made or broken, a well-designed plug will not allow fingers to contact metal that is carrying electricity. Some older equipment has plugs that may expose current-carrying metal while the connectors are being joined. These plugs should be removed from service whenever possible.

There are many different styles of connectors used in the theatre. The most common are straight-blade two-pole-plus-ground plugs (Figure 4–5C) which are sometimes referred to as "Edison plugs"; pin connectors with (Figure 4–5D) or without (Figure 4–5E) a grounding pin or lock (Figure 4–5F); and 15 and 20 amp twistlock connectors (Figure 4–5A and B). All plugs are rated in amps and volts for a maximum electrical load; for the stage, they are usually 15 or 20 amps at 115/220 volts. Pin connectors and twistlock connectors will only mate with plugs of exactly the same blade configuration and amperage rating. It is impossible to plug a 15 amp male twistlock connector into a 20 amp female twistlock even of the same design. The pattern of the pins or blades on plugs has been standardized in a national code, called the

FIGURE 4–5

Stage connectors. (A and B) Twistlock; (C) parallel blade u-ground; (D) two pole plus ground pin connector; (E) two pole pin connector; (F) HARJ pin connector (note locking hook on grounding pin).

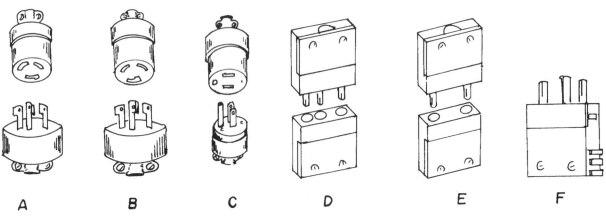

A   B   C   D   E   F

NEMA designation. The most commonly used twistlock connectors for the theatre are NEMA L5–15 and NEMA L5–20.

Mounting Hardware

All lighting fixtures have either a yoke or hanging irons from which they are suspended. A **yoke** (Figure 4–6A) is a metal band that makes a loop around the lighting instrument and bolts to it at each side. The yoke is attached to the fixture with handwheels or bolts that can be loosened to allow the instrument to tip up and down and then retightened to hold the instrument firmly in place. These bolts often become very stiff and difficult to loosen. If that happens, it is sometimes possible to attain a mechanical advantage by tipping the entire lighting instrument up or down until the bolt is freed. Yokes are a standard part of almost all lighting instruments. **Hanging irons** are short metal straps used to carry the mounting hardware of long, slender lighting instruments such as border and strip lights. Rather than making a loop over the entire instrument, a short metal strap is attached to each end of the lighting fixture and clamps are inserted in the ends of the straps.

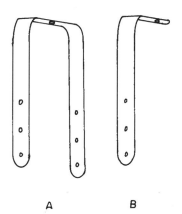

FIGURE 4–6
Mounting hardware. (A) Yoke; (B) hanger iron.

At the top center of the yoke is a hole through which a **pipe clamp** (Figure 4–7) may be attached. A bolt is passed through the hole and into a threaded stem in the clamp. The only function this bolt serves is to attach the pipe clamp to the yoke—it must be kept tightly fastened at all times! The stem to which the bolt is connected passes into the bottom of the pipe clamp. There is a small bolt on the side of the pipe clamp that allows the lighting instrument to swivel on the stem or to be locked rigidly in place. This bolt is used to control side-to-side rotation of the light when it is being focused, and it must be securely fastened to hold the instrument in place. Finally, another bolt sticks out of the other side of the pipe clamp opposite the stem. This bolt fastens the clamp to the pipe when the instrument is hung in place. The clamp and bolt should be very solid without chewing into the pipe.

There are two other kinds of pipe clamps available. One is a very light-weight clamp (Figure 4–7B) that is used to hang small lighting instruments. It is simply a shaped metal strap with a small bolt to attach to the yoke and a long slender thumbscrew to attach the clamp to a pipe or board. The third clamp available is called a **sure-clamp** (Figure 4–7C). This is a fairly expensive device that automatically closes and grips a pipe as soon as the clamp is hooked over it. The jaw of the clamp is tightened down with a smooth operating ring that requires no tools to fasten the clamp to the pipe.

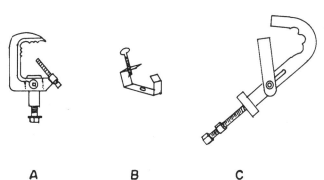

FIGURE 4–7
Pipe clamps. (A) Standard pipe clamp; (B) light-weight pipe clamp; (C) Sure-Grip clamp.

Because accidents happen, people err, and equipment fails, **safety cables** or **safety chains** are used with all lights (see Figure 4–8). Although not required by law, most theatres and production companies require safety cables or chains by policy. A safety chain is an extra piece of light-weight cable or chain that is wrapped over the pipe on which the lighting instrument is hung and through the yoke of the instrument attaching to some part of the fixture housing and making a complete loop as it hooks back to itself. Should a light start to fall, it will be caught by the safety cable or chain. Whenever lighting instruments are hung above the audience or performers, safety cables should be used. They should also be threaded through accessories such as top hats, barn doors, and color holders to prevent these accessories from falling.

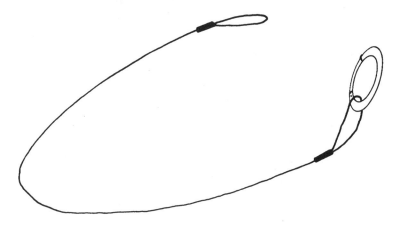

FIGURE 4–8
Safety cable.

STAGE LIGHTING INSTRUMENTS

Floodlights and spotlights are the two general classifications of theatrical lighting instruments. They are distinguished in purpose and design. **Floodlights** provide general illumination; they are made to wash the stage with a flood of nonspecific light that may be clear or colored. **Spotlights** are designed to illuminate a specific location—a spot—on the stage. The light may be hard, crisp, and cut off from areas or it might be soft and blend into other spots of light. In terms of construction, floodlights utilize a diffuse reflector and usually no lens, whereas spotlights usually are distinguished by the presence of a lens and a mirror-like reflector. There are several different kinds of floodlights and spotlights. Each is designed to produce a distinctive quality or shape of light for a specific purpose.

Floodlights

Scoops

Scoops, also called **ellipsoidal reflector floods (ERF)** (Figure 4–9), are the most common floodlights in the modern theatre. These are fairly simple instruments consisting of a metal hood that has been formed into half an ellipse. The interior of the hood is coated with a grainy-looking light-reflective material and the outside is usually painted flat black. A large lamp is screwed into a socket at the top rear of the hood, although some scoops use a double-ended or medium prefocus lamp. The equipment is designed so that the socket points up and the round end of the bulb points down when the instrument is properly mounted. At the front of the light there is usually a square color-holder slot, which should be able to rotate 360°. Some larger scoops use a round color holder that is attached to the front of the fixture with bolts that tighten behind a lip on the front edge of the instrument. A standard yoke, clamp, and pigtail complete the fixture. Scoops are manufactured in sizes as small as a 10" diameter opening at the front of the instrument to as great as a 24" diameter opening for the theatre (larger sizes are used in television and film). These instruments produce a wide, even wash of light shaped in a broad oval. The edges of the beam are easy to distinguish near the instrument, but at greater distances the edges of the beam of light fade away. Scoops are used to wash a somewhat directional flood of light over a drop or over a large area of the stage. Many smaller stages have been equipped with numerous 10" scoops to provide general illumination.

Border and Strip Lights

A long narrow trough that contains several lights in a row is called a borderlight, strip light, or x-ray. Although these terms are interchangeable, **borderlight** tends to refer to permanently installed continuous troughs that cross the entire stage, while **strip lights** are usually individual 6'-0" to 8'-0" sections of lights that are portable. Used on the floor at the front of the stage, the instruments are called **footlights**, and on the floor at the rear of the stage where they illuminate the bottom of a drop they are referred to as an **electric ground row (EGR)**. These fixtures produce a soft wash of a single color of light or a soft, smooth blend of up to four colors of light. They are used for general illumination and for washes of color on the stage or on drops. Borderlights are usually hung in rows 8'-0" to 10'-0" apart from downstage to upstage. They may be mixed with spotlights on the same pipe. There are several different styles of strip lights, varying from a primitive hood with colored light bulbs to more sophisticated equipment with individual compartments, reflectors, and holders for separate color media (Figure 4–10). Modern instruments are designed to accommodate a variety of styles and sizes of lamps.

A.

B.

FIGURE 4–9
Scoops. (A) Round frame; (B) rotatable square color holder slot. (Courtesy Altman Lighting Company)

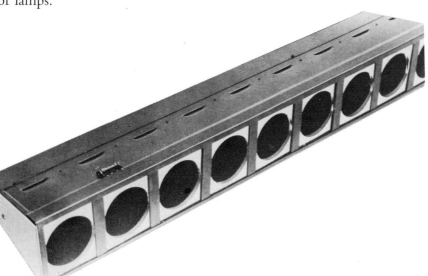

FIGURE 4–10
Borderlight. (Courtesy Altman Lighting Company)

The basic concept for strip lights is very simple. A row of lamps is wired in three or four individual circuits so that the first, fourth, seventh, and tenth lamps all come on at the same time under one control; the second, fifth, eighth, and eleventh lamps turn on together, but independently of the first group of lights, and the pattern is repeated with a third and sometimes a fourth circuit of lights. This allows each group of lights to be a different color and each color to be controlled individually. For instance, one group of lights may be red, the next blue, and the last amber. The light from each lamp washes the stage and mixes with the other light emanating from the strip to create a consistent, smooth pattern of illumination.

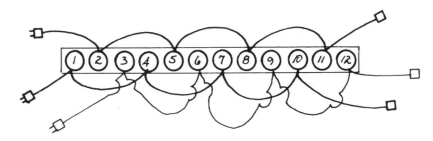

FIGURE 4–11
Circuit layout for three-circuit borderlight.

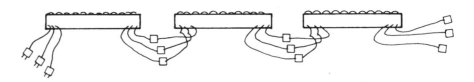

FIGURE 4–12
Interconnecting borderlights.

Since strip lights are only 6'-0" to 8'-0" long, several units must be combined to cover the entire width of most stages. Individual units may be mounted next to each other and plugged together. This is possible because pigtails with male connectors for each circuit are installed at one end of each strip and pigtails with female connectors are usually installed at the other end of the strip. These are the simplest lighting instruments to use because they require almost no focusing and color is frequently built in.

Some strip lights are hung by chains and others are mounted on hanging irons with pipe clamps. Those strip lights mounted on hanging irons can be aimed at a drop or focused straight down by loosening the handwheels or bolts that attach the strip to the hanging irons, pointing the fixture as desired, and retightening the bolts. The pipe clamps can be removed from the hanging irons and the strip lights can be placed on the floor. Whenever possible, the strips placed on the floor should be fastened down through the holes in the hanging irons where the pipe clamps were attached. It is best to attach the strip lights to the floor with stage screws, lag screws, or even nails through the holes in the hanging irons (Figure 4–13C). Those fixtures suspended by chain can also be aimed if the chain goes from the fixture, wraps 360° around the pipe, crossing over itself, and finally hooks back to the fixture (Figure 4–13B). By lifting the fixture and pulling on the chain, the instrument can be tipped to direct the beam. These chain mountings are not especially safe. Additional safety chains should be used with these fixtures to reduce the likelihood of an accident.

Most strip lights can use permanent color media made from glass or can use disposable color media, gel, which was discussed in Chapter 2. The glass color media are called **rondels** or **roundels**. These mount in frames or in rings in front of the lamps in the strip lights. The interchangeable rondels are available in five different colors. The colors produced by each manufacturer differ, so care must be taken to match colors when replacing rondels.

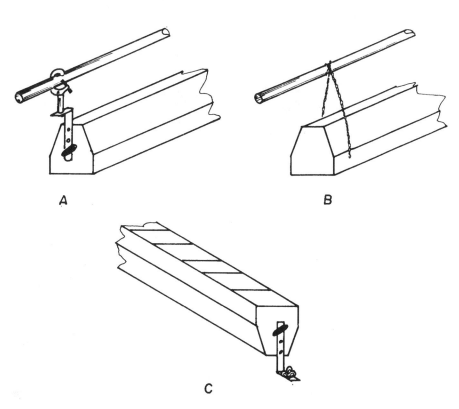

A   B   C

FIGURE 4–13
Mounting borderlights: (A) Pipe clamp and hanger iron; (B) chain over pipe (additional safety rigging strongly recommended); (C) floor mounting.

Another kind of floodlight has been designed especially to provide washes of light and color on cycloramas and drops. These instruments, called **cyc lights** (Figure 4–14), have names such as Far Cyc and Sky Cyc. They are constructed with one, two, three, or four separate compartments, each wired individually for separate color control. The fixtures use a double-ended tungsten-halogen lamp and produce a soft wash of light. These floodlights are designed to be mounted approximately 8'-0" away from a drop. At this distance, the beam of light adequately illuminates an area of the drop measuring approximately 16'-0" high × 12'-0" wide. Three fixtures could satisfactorily illuminate a 16'-0" high by 36'-0" wide drop.

FIGURE 4–14
Sky Cyc. (Courtesy Altman Lighting Company)

Beam Projector

A **beam projector** (Figure 4–15) carefully controls the projection and reflection of light to produce a very narrow beam with almost parallel rays. This fixture was created to emulate the streaming rays of the sun on a bright day. A movable plate on the bottom of the instrument carries a lamp in a socket as well as a baffle or secondary reflector; these move as a unit from the open front to the mirrored back of the instrument. The baffle forces all of the rays projected by this light to be more or less parallel. As the lamp and baffle/reflector move forward and backward, they modify the diameter of the beam produced by this light.

To Focus a Beam Projector

1. Make sure the pipe clamp is firmly fastened to the pipe and the yoke bolt is firmly fastened to the pipe clamp. Loosen the small bolt on the side of the C-clamp and the handwheels or bolts on either side of the yoke.

FIGURE 4–15
Beam projector. (Courtesy Altman Lighting Company)

2. Turn the light on. Move the lamp and baffle assembly all the way to the back of the instrument. Direct the beam of light to the desired location and tighten the handwheels or bolts on the side of the instrument. Tighten the bolt on the side of the C-clamp.

3. Adjust the beam to the proper diameter by sliding or cranking the lamp closer to the front of the light.

PAR Can

A **PAR can** is one of the most practical theatrical lighting instruments currently available. A PAR can (Figure 4–16) is a simple housing with a yoke, pipe clamp, color holder slot, and socket. The heart of the instrument is its PAR lamp, which is mounted at the back of the housing with a spring ring to hold it in place. A PAR lamp has its own lens built into a tough glass housing. Larger PAR lamps look

FIGURE 4–16
PAR can. (Courtesy Altman Lighting Company)

like car headlights. The arrangement of the filament, built-in lens, and built-in reflector causes the lamp to produce a rectangular beam of light that is either a very narrow or narrow spot or a medium or wide flood. The lamps are available from 150 to 1,000 watts in a variety of sizes and beam spreads as standard incandescent or tungsten-halogen sources of light. These lamps generally have a very long life and are almost impossible to damage; they will withstand severe shock, and it is completely safe to touch the glass portion of the lamp (when it is cool). The only focusing characteristics they have are the beam spread, which is selected when the lamp is purchased, and the angle to which the rectangular beam pattern is rotated. To focus the light, aim it at the desired location; then simply reach in the back of the fixture and rotate the lamp to the proper angle.

Low-Voltage, High-Intensity Lamps

Lamp manufacturers have developed several families of lamps for special applications that have been adopted for the theatre. One of the earliest lamps to be used for this application is the aircraft landing light, or **ACL.** These lamps produce extremely bright, extremely narrow beams of light. They are low-voltage lamps requiring voltages of 5, 6, 10, 12 or 15 volt power supplies. The lamps are normally placed in a simple housing, similar in design to those used for PAR lamps, but usually much smaller. In addition to providing a socket, housing, and mount for the lamp, these fixtures usually include a small transformer to reduce voltage to the proper level. One manufacturer calls the fixture they market for these lamps a Rainlight (Figure 4–17).

Lamp manufacturers produce another line of low-voltage, high-intensity lamps that are being used heavily in architectural applications and have been placed in special fixtures for the stage. The most common lamp is the MR16. This is a very small low-voltage tungsten-halogen lamp built into its own reflector, which is about 2" in diameter. A smaller version of the lamp is the MR11, which is only 1-3/8" in diameter (Figure 4–18). There are several other low-voltage, high-intensity miniature lamps available. These lamps are physically very small and can be placed in tiny housings; however, they operate at very high temperatures and anything that may overheat, burn, or melt must be kept quite a distance from the sides, back, and especially the front of the fixture. Standard color media cannot be used with these lamps because the high temperature either destroys the media or fades the color very quickly. Glass dichroic colors are usually required for these fixtures. These lamps have been placed in miniature strip lights and spotlights now marketed by several manufacturers.

Care must be taken whenever low-voltage fixtures are used. In addition to potential heat problems related to the lamps, the transformers in the fixtures are not compatible with many dimming systems. The current produced by some dimmers can cause the transformers to burn out on the fixtures. An interesting solution has been implemented by the manufacturers of low-voltage strip lights. Ten low-voltage lamps in these fixtures are wired in a pattern (series) that adds the voltage of each lamp together so that a transformer is not required for these fixtures.

FIGURE 4–17
Low-voltage, high-intensity (ACL) lamp in housing. (Courtesy Altman Lighting Company)

$$12 \text{ volts} \times 10 \text{ lamps wired in series} = 120 \text{ volts}$$

FIGURE 4–18
MR16 and MR11 lamps.
(Courtesy GE Lighting)

Spotlights

Spotlights are intended to illuminate a specific area of the stage with a controlled beam of light. There are several different kinds of spotlights, each fulfilling a distinctive function by creating a specific quality of light as a result of the combination of reflector, lenses, and accessories. It is the presence of one or more lenses, the degree of beam spread, and the quality of light produced that distinguishes a spotlight from a floodlight.

Lenses are essential to spotlights. These specially shaped, heat-resistant pieces of glass collect the light that strikes them and bend the rays into a concentrated beam. Spotlights use **plano-convex lenses**, which are flat on one side and curved outward on the opposite side. The effectiveness of a lens is determined by the degree of curvature on the convex side: lenses with deeper curves cause more extreme bending of the rays of light. The curvature is controlled by the thickness of the glass. Unfortunately, extremely thick lenses, which induce the greatest amount of bending, are heavy and make some lighting instruments difficult to handle. In addition, the thick glass lenses absorb a great deal of heat, which causes them to crack. As a result of these problems, a number of lens systems have been devised to maximize the concentration power of spotlights yet reduce the weight and heat problems. One of these solutions has led to the development of a special stage lighting instrument, the fresnel.

Fresnel

A **fresnel** (pronounced fruh-nell) spotlight (Figure 4–19) produces a soft-edged beam of concentrated illumination. This instrument is distinguished by its lens (Figure 4–20). Looked at from the front, the lens has a series of circles carved into it, and from the back the flat surface is textured. This relatively thin piece of glass creates the effect of a very thick plano-convex lens, which is accomplished by reproducing the *shape* of a deep convex curve on a series of stepped ridges (Figure 4–21). This can be seen when the lens is cut in half to expose its constuction (Figure 4–20). These instruments are usually used to light upstage areas from mounting positions on stage.

FIGURE 4–19
A 6" fresnel. (Courtesy Altman Lighting Company)

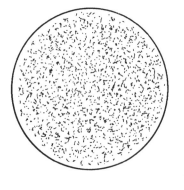 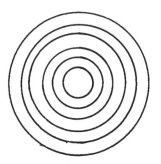

FIGURE 4–20
Fresnel lens: (A) back; (B) section; (C) front.

A   B   C

The instrument consists of a fresnel lens at the front of a housing, with the reflector and the lamp mounted in a socket on a sliding base. The base, lamp, and reflector move forward and backward as a unit to increase or decrease the diameter of the beam of light (Figure 4–22). The movement of the lamp/reflector unit may be controlled with a crank at the back of the instrument, a knob on the side of the fixture, or by sliding a bolt or thumbscrew forward and backward on the bottom of the housing. The crank, knob, or bolt that moves the lamp and reflector must always be oriented toward the bottom of the instrument. As the lamp and reflector move closer to the lens, the

FIGURE 4–21
A fresnel lens reproduces the curves of a plano-convex lens but eliminates the parallel planes of glass to produce a thinner lens with the same light bending power as the thicker lens.

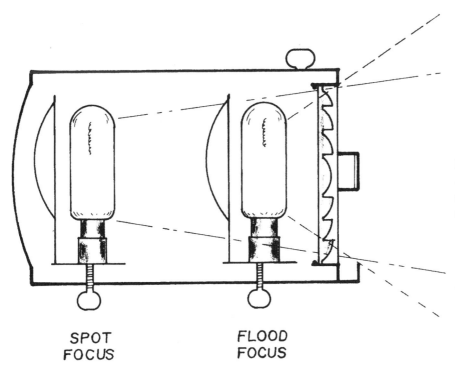

SPOT
FOCUS

FLOOD
FOCUS

FIGURE 4–22
Fresnel spotlight. The lamp and reflector move from flood to spot focus.

107

beam becomes wider (flood focus); as they move toward the back of the instrument, the beam becomes narrower (spot focus) (Figure 4–23). There is a color holder slot on the front of the fixture.

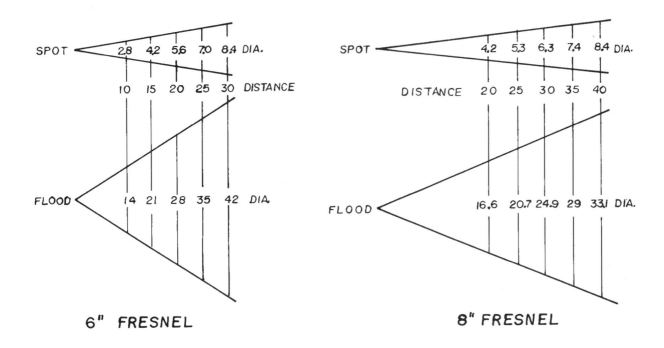

FIGURE 4–23
Beam spread for a 6" and an 8" fresnel spotlight at both flood and spot focus. Both diameter and distance are given in feet.

Three different style lamps are used in fresnel spotlights. The most common is a medium prefocus lamp. It is changed by grasping the bulb near the base, pressing down, and rotating it approximately 90° until the flanges on the lamp align with the openings in the socket. The lamp is then lifted out of the socket and replaced by aligning the flanges on the base of the new lamp with the proper openings in the socket, pressing down and rotating the lamp until it stops moving and is firmly seated. Many newer fresnels use either a double-ended lamp or a medium two-pin lamp. The double-ended lamp is removed by grasping the bulb near one end and pushing the lamp toward the opposite side until the end that is held may be pulled free from the socket. The lamp is then removed from the instrument. The new lamp is replaced in exactly the same way. Protecting the bulb, slip one end of the lamp into the socket on one side, and then press the lamp to that side until it is possible to engage the opposite end. Rotate and wiggle the lamp to ensure that it is firmly seated. Removing and replacing a two-pin lamp is even easier. The lamp simply pulls straight up out of the socket and is replaced by pressing the new lamp straight down into the socket. After a two-pin lamp is pressed into the socket it is almost always necessary to place a thumb on either side of the exposed base of the lamp and again to press firmly down to ensure that the lamp is fully seated.

CAUTION: **Whenever changing lamps on any fixture, always be sure that the circuit is turned off and the light is unplugged. Never touch the glass part of any bulb.** A recently burned-out lamp will be extremely hot and will cause skin burns. A new lamp will be damaged by the deposit of skin oils.

Access to change any of these lamps is fairly easy. Start by turning off and unplugging the light. Some old fresnels have a door on the top of the instrument. The door is held closed by a threaded or spring-loaded thumbscrew that sticks straight up from the top of the light. The thumbscrew is simply released or unscrewed and the door opened; normally it will hinge to one side of the light. However, most fresnels allow access to the lamp through the front of the instrument. There is usually a brass bolt, a spring-loaded pin, or some other mechanism located at the top front of the instrument or in some cases at the side front of the fixture. The knob is turned, pulled, or un-screwed to release the door that carries the lens; the door will swing open to expose the interior of the instrument and the burned-out lamp.

Sometimes it is necessary to remove the lens from a fresnel. The flat side of the lens rests against a lip behind it and is held in place by a spring ring placed in front of the lens. The **spring ring**, a metal band, is secured behind a set of dimples in the metal in front of the lens (Figure 4–24). The lens is removed by squeezing the ends of the spring ring to make it small enough to slip past the dimples and slide out of the lens opening. The lens will drop out after the ring is removed.

To Focus a Fresnel

1. Make sure the pipe clamp is firmly fastened to the pipe and the yoke bolt is firmly fastened to the pipe clamp. Loosen the small bolt on the side of the C-clamp and the handwheels or bolts on either side of the yoke.

2. Turn the light on. Move the lamp/reflector assembly to spot focus at the rear of the instrument. Aim the light at the desired location.

3. Tighten the bolts or handwheels on the sides of the yoke and then the small bolt on the C-clamp.

FIGURE 4–24
Removing the lens ring on a fresnel spotlight.

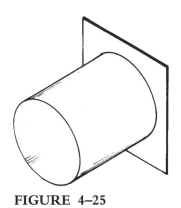

FIGURE 4–25
A top hat.

4. Using the crank, knob, or sliding bolt on the bottom of the instrument, move the lamp forward until the light fills the area to be illuminated.

The beam of light may be modified not only with the addition of color but also with two accessories: a top hat and a barn door. A **top hat** or **snoot** (Figure 4–25) is a metal tube the same diameter as the lens and about 6" to 8" long. It is mounted on a frame that looks like a color holder and fits in the color holder slot on the front of the instrument. It may be used with or without an additional color holder in the color holder slot of the instrument. The top hat cuts off **ambient light** or **spill**, stray rays from the beam of light, without reshaping the beam or creating hard edges. The longer the barrel of the top hat, the more rays of light will be cut off. Although the top hat was designed for use with fresnel spotlights, it may be used for the same purpose with ellipsoidal spotlights.

The second accessory to control the beam of a fresnel is a **barn door** (Figure 4–26). This device also fits in the color holder slot at the front of the instrument and can be used with or without an additional color holder in the slot. The unit consists of four metal flaps that can be individually opened or closed to cut off a portion of each side of the beam of light. After the barn door is in place, it can be rotated to orient the doors as needed. Barn doors are especially handy when trying to keep light off of drapes or from spilling into the audience. There are three problems with barn doors. First, as each flap is closed to cut off a portion of the beam of light, the barn door actually diminishes the quantity of light projected from the instrument so the overall intensity of illumination is reduced as the flaps are closed. The second problem is that sometimes as the barn doors close they cut off a portion of the light

FIGURE 4–26
A barn door.

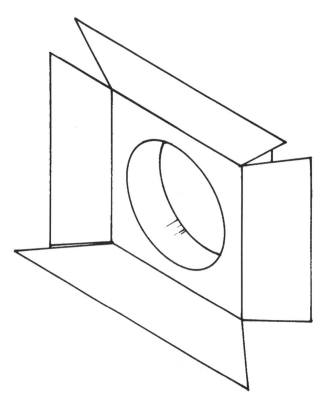

on one side of the beam but reflect that light to the opposite side of the beam, creating a great deal of spill light. Finally, partially opened barn doors may get in the way of scenery or other lights.

The size of a fresnel spotlight is described by the diameter of its lens. The *greater* the diameter of the lens, the *narrower* the beam of light. Large fresnels producing narrow beams are intended for longer **throws**, the distance from the lighting instrument to the area illuminated. The most common size fresnel used in most theatre applications has a 6" diameter lens. These instruments produce an **effective circle of light**, the bright area at the center of the beam before it fades off at the edges, that is about 8'-0" in diameter at a throw of approximately 15'-0" to 20'-0". The effective circle of light will fade to diffuse, low-intensity illumination and will softly disappear or blend into other soft-edged beams of light. The 6" fresnels are usually equipped with 500 watt or 750 watt lamps, although they will accept 250 watt lamps as well. An 8" fresnel is intended to project a narrower beam of light a greater distance than a 6" fresnel. These instruments produce about an 8'-0" circle of light at a throw of about 30'-0". The 8" fresnels usually use 1,000 watt lamps, although some instruments will accept 500, 750, or 2,000 watt bulbs. Fresnels are available in additional diameters as small as 3½" to as great as 12" for the theatre.

Ellipsoidal Reflector Spots

Ellipsoidal reflector spotlights, variously known as **lekos** or **klieglights**, have become the primary lighting instrument in the modern theatre. These spotlights are used in virtually every location in the theatre and for almost every possible purpose of stage lighting. There are two "generations" of ellipsoidal reflector spotlights. The older style, which has been in existence since the 1930s, is the traditional shape (Figure 4–27A). It has a long front end, a bulbous back end, and a chimney that sticks up at an angle of approximately

A.   B.

FIGURE 4–27
Ellipsoidal reflector spotlights. (A) Traditional old-generation ellipsoidal; (B) axial ellipsoidal with the lamp mounted on the centerline axis of the lens and reflector. (Courtesy Altman Lighting Company)

111

75°; it uses a standard incandescent lamp or a retrofit T-H lamp. An axial mount ellipsoidal (Figure 4–27B), similar in appearance to the traditional ellipsoidal but the chimney sticks straight out of the back of the instrument, is also of the old generation design. These fixtures are distinguished by a true elliptically shaped reflector that is cut off on one side for the light to pass and is interrupted on the other side for the lamp to enter the reflector space. The reflectors are made of steel with a polished reflectorized coating.

The "new-generation" ellipsoidals (Figure 4–28) were developed in the late 1970s and early 1980s. These fixtures are designed to use the much smaller but hotter tungsten-halogen lamps. In contrast to the "old-generation" ellipsoidals, the reflectors in the new ellipsoidals are smaller and are usually made in compound geometric shapes that include an ellipse but also may incorporate portions of a parbola or sphere (depending on the manufacturer's specific design). The reflectors are made from either metal or glass with a coating that is designed to draw heat away from the lamp. Further refinements of these fixtures include alloy shutters, which are more resistant to heat, and lens systems that require less glass to shape the beam of light. The designs also have permitted the development of zoom focusing spotlights. These "new-generation" fixtures are distinguished in general appearance by a rectangular or circular rear lamp housing with a focusing knob on the back and the absence of the traditional chimney that distinguishes the appearance of the "old-generation" ellipsoidals. Even newer designs of ellipsoidal fixtures are under development to maximize the use of high efficiency, high output concentrated beam lamps, more complex electrical and optical theories, and new metal alloys (Figure 4–29).

Both new-generation and old-generation equipment utilize the same theory of operation to make the light function. The lamp is placed

FIGURE 4–28
New-generation ellipsoidal spotlight with completely redesigned optics and mechanics. (Courtesy Altman Lighting Company)

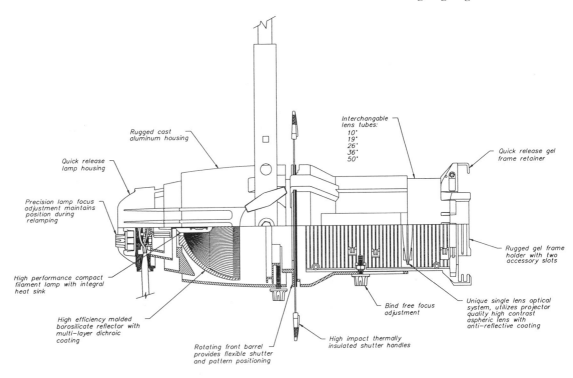

Rugged cast
aluminum housing

Quick release
lamp housing

Precision lamp focus
adjustment maintains
position during
relamping

High performance compact
filament lamp with integral
heat sink

High efficiency molded
borosilicate reflector with
multi-layer dichroic
coating

Interchangable
lens tubes:
10˚
19˚
26˚
36˚
50˚

Quick release gel
frame retainer

Rugged gel frame
holder with two
accessory slots

Unique single lens optical
system, utilizes projector
quality high contrast
aspheric lens with
anti-reflective coating

Bind free focus
adjustment

High impact thermally
insulated shutter handles

Rotating front barrel
provides flexible shutter
and pattern positioning

PATENTS PENDING

FIGURE 4–29
*Another new type of ellipsoidal
spotlight using a compact lamp
and special reflector to improve
the performance. (Courtesy
Electronic Theatre Controls,
Inc.)*

within an elliptical reflector (Figure 4–30), and by means of a carefully controlled pattern of reflection, it projects a beam of light that may be adjusted to a sharp, crisp image or to a somewhat soft-edged beam. Located near the center of the instrument are a set of **shutters**, handles that can slide in and out of the housing to cut off a portion of the light on the opposite side of the beam. (Figure 4–31) An **iris**, a device that opens and closes to increase or decrease the size circle projected by the instrument, may replace the shutters, and a **pattern** or **gobo**, a metal stencil designed to project a shadow image, may be inserted at this point. At the front of the instrument, the lens is mounted in the **lens tube** that moves a few inches front to back inside a barrel. Lens tube movement allows the beam of light to be sharply focused to a very crisp edge or permits the light to have a fuzzy quality (Figure 4–32).

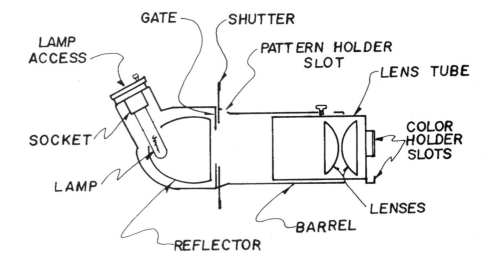

FIGURE 4–30
Anatomy of an ellipsoidal reflector spotlight.

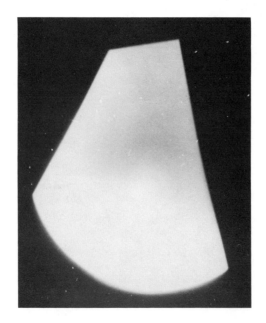

FIGURE 4–31
The beam of an ellipsoidal spotlight with the shutters pushed in on three sides.

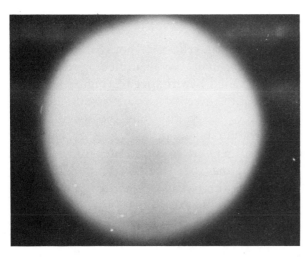

A.

B.

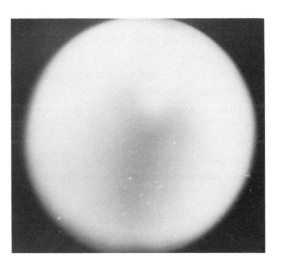

C.

FIGURE 4–32
Focusing an ellipsoidal. (A) Underfocused; (B) focused; (C) overfocused.

Old-Generation Ellipsoidals

Selecting the proper ellipsoidal reflector spotlight requires an understanding of how these instruments are identified as to intensity and the size beam they project, called **beam spread** (Figure 4–33).

The lamps (light bulbs) that fit these fixtures are usually identified on a label located on the side of the yoke. Only the specific lamps designed for an instrument should be used; with the exception of retrofit tungsten-halogen lamps, there are no substitutes for the proper lamps. If the label is missing, it may be necessary to find the *exact* instrument in a catalog to identify the instrument and lamp to be used or contact a theatrical equipment supplier to obtain this information. All old-generation 6" ellipsoidals, that is, spotlights with a 6" diameter lens, are able to accommodate lamps rated from 250 watts all the way up to 750 watts. The 8" through 12" ellipsoidals are usually rated for 1,000 to 3,000 watt lamps, and a few spotlights may be equipped with lamps as large as 5,000 watts.

In addition to accommodating lamps of various wattages, these instruments are available in a variety of beam spreads. That is, instruments are available that will produce beams that are extremely wide all the way down to very, very narrow beams of light. The size beam produced by an old-generation ellipsoidal is identified by its lens characteristics, so a spotlight will be described as a 6 × 12 or an 8 × 9. The first number on each pair describes the lens diameter and the second number identifies the focal length of the lens or lens train. **Focal length** is the distance in inches that light must travel until the rays converge after having passed through a lens. Together the numbers

FIGURE 4–33
Beam angle is the brightest portion of the beam, whereas field angle is the overall beam of a spotlight.

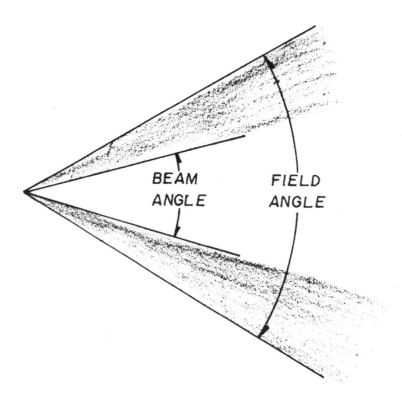

indicate the beam spread of the instrument. Unfortunately, this information is pretty meaningless unless there is some way to translate that data into the dimensions of effective pools of light. Table 4–1 provides some guidance as to the size beam probably projected by some of the popular-size, old-generation instruments.

If instruments on hand are not identified as to their size, it may be desirable to measure the lens. To do this, the lens must be removed from the fixture. The entire lens tube can be taken out of the barrel by removing the thumbscrew, bolt, or knob on the top front of the instrument and then sliding the lens tube all the way forward until it is free of the barrel. The entire lens assembly may be measured or the lens or lenses may be removed from the tube. There may be one or two plano-convex lenses (flat on one side, curved out on the other) or a single step lens (Figure 4–34) inside the lens tube. Many fixtures require disassembling the lens tube to remove the lens, while in other instruments the lens is held in place with a spring ring in the same way the lens is mounted in a fresnel. To identify the lens, first measure its diameter. Then project light through it onto a surface up to 2'-0" away. Move the lens back and forth until a concentrated point of light appears where the rays converge. Measure the distance in inches from the lens to the point at which the rays of light converge (Figure 4–35). The dimensions should be similar to a set of numbers in Table 4–1, although they will probably not match the numbers exactly.

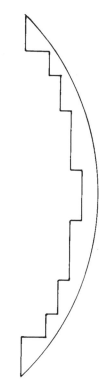

FIGURE 4–34
Step lens. Used in ellipsoidals, the parallel planes of glass are cut away on the flat side of the lens.

Lens Configuration	Beam Angle (Degrees)	Field Angle (Degrees)
Double-Lens Fixtures		
3½ × 6	21	38–40
3½ × 12	17	18–20
4½ × 6½	22	55–60
6 × 9	15–18	35–40
6 × 12	11	26–30
6 × 16	9	19–20
6 × 22	8	11–12
Single-/Step-Lens Fixtures		
6 × 8	11	21
6 × 6	12	24
8 × 8	10	18
8 × 11	9	14

Table 4–1
Beam spread of ellipsoidal reflector spotlights.

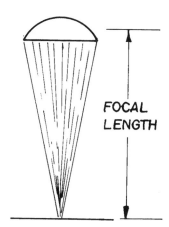

FIGURE 4–35
Measuring the focal length. The distance from·the center of the lens or lens train to the point at which light projected through the lens converges on a point.

117

To Focus an Ellipsoidal Reflector Spotlight

1. Make sure that the yoke bolt and the bolt that holds the pipe clamp to the pipe are tight. Pull all four shutter handles out until they stop. Loosen the small bolt on the side of the C-clamp, which will allow the light to turn from side to side, and loosen the handwheels or bolts on the sides of the instrument to allow the light to tip up and down.

2. Turn the instrument on and point the light at the area to be illuminated. Tighten the bolts or handwheels at the sides of the instrument to prevent it from tipping down. Tighten the small bolt on the side of the C-clamp to prevent the instrument from rotating side to side. The instrument should be held rigidly in place and all of these bolts must be secure.

3. Adjust the lens tube to the quality of light desired by loosening the knob at the top front of the instrument (do *not* remove this knob or the lens tube will fall out of the barrel) and moving the lens tube forward or backward. Sharp focus is at the approximate center of the travel available to the lens tube; this will result in a crisp, defined beam of light. The lens also may be moved ahead or behind the focus point, resulting in a softer beam that blends more easily with other pools of light and casts softer shadows.

4. If a portion of the beam of light spills into the audience or somewhere else not desirable, slide in the shutter on the *opposite side* of the instrument to cut off the undesirable portion of the beam. The shutter may be rotated several degrees to adjust the cutting line to match an angle.

To Change the Lamp in an Ellipsoidal Spotlight

1. Turn off and unplug the instrument; then remove the cap on the chimney. One of three different kinds of devices holds this cap in place: (a) a large brass bolt with a slot on the top and knurls on the sides, which unscrews to lift off the cap; (b) a spring-mounted butterfly knob located on top of the cap, which must be pressed down and turned 90° to release the cap; or (c) a spring-loaded clip on the back of the chimney, which must be pushed in to release the cap. The cap, with the lamp mounted in its socket, is withdrawn from the instrument.

2. The lamp usually has just burned out and is very hot when it is being replaced, so gloves or some kind of hand protection is required. If the lamp is a *medium prefocus base*, it is grasped near the base, pressed down about ⅛" into the socket, and rotated approximately 90° clockwise to align the flanges of the lamp base with the flange openings in the socket. The lamp is then lifted straight out of the socket and thrown away. If the lamp is a *medium bipost*, it is removed by pressing down and rotating the lamp until the collars on the posts are released from the retainers and the lamp is slipped out of the socket and discarded.

3. The new medium prefocus or medium bipost lamp is inserted in reverse order. Without allowing skin to touch the glass part of the bulb (clean white cotton work gloves solve this problem), firmly grasp

the new lamp near the base, align the flanges or posts of the base with the matching openings in the socket, press down, and rotate the lamp until it stops moving. The lamp should be firmly seated.

4. Reinsert the lamp and chimney cap in the spotlight and, making sure all parts are properly aligned, fasten the chimney cap in place.

Effective operation of the ellipsoidal spotlight requires that the source of light is properly positioned within the reflector. This is accomplished by using a specific lamp placed in a properly aligned socket. With age and handling, sockets will shift out of alignment, resulting in unfiltered light that appears very blue or red or has a dark shadow in the beam or a badly off-centered beam. The lamp can be realigned in the reflector through a process called **bench focusing**.

To Bench Focus an Ellipsoidal Reflector Spotlight

1. Mount the spotlight in a comfortable working position so the beam of light can be projected onto an even, light-colored surface such as a cyclorama. Turn the light on and adjust the lens to get as crisp a beam of light as possible.

2. Evaluate the color of the light. If it appears quite blue, red, or dim, the lamp is not at the proper depth in the reflector. There are three screws or bolts located on top of the chimney to adjust the position of the lamp (Figure 4–36). The screw at the center moves the lamp in and out of the reflector without changing the angle at which it is mounted. This will adjust the color and brightness of the light. This screw or bolt often sticks out above the top of the chimney. Slowly turn the screw clockwise—if the quality of light begins to improve, continue rotating the screw in the same direction. If no change occurs or the quality of light gets worse, slowly turn the screw in the opposite direction until the intensity is as high as possible and the light as white as possible.

3. Near the right edge and at the center back of the chimney are two additional screws that will turn with some ease. These screws are

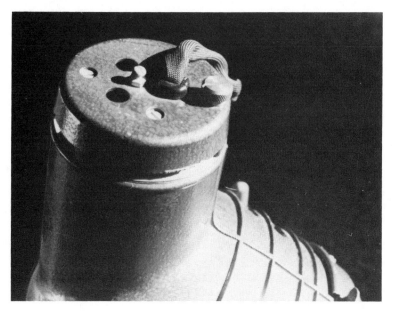

FIGURE 4–36
Screws used when bench focusing an ellipsoidal spotlight. The screw at the back tips the lamp forward and backwards, the one at the side tips the lamp right or left to center it in the reflector. The center screw adjusts the depth of the lamp in the reflector to modify the color and intensity of the beam of light.

119

wrapped with springs that press against the plate supporting the socket. The screw at the side of the chimney tilts the lamp right and left, and the screw at the back tilts the lamp forward and backward. Adjust these screws no more than a quarter-turn at a time to center the **hot spot**, the brightest area within the beam of light.

4. After centering the hot spot, slowly adjust the center screw again so that the hot spot flattens out to as even a light as possible without changing the color of the beam of light, reducing intensity, or creating a dark shadow at center.

These are minute adjustments that take time and patience. Fortunately, it is not necessary to bench focus an ellipsoidal spotlight very often.

Another version of the old-generation ellipsoidals places the lamp and chimney at the center rear of the reflector (Figure 4–27B). These are called **axially mounted ellipsoidals** because the lamp is on the centerline axis of the reflector and lens. This design reduces the cutaway area needed to insert the lamp into the reflector. Operation and adjustment of these instruments are almost exactly the same as for the traditional ellipsoidal reflector spotlights with the chimney sticking up at the rear.

New-Generation Axial Ellipsoidals

New-generation axial ellipsoidal reflector spotlights (Figure 4–28) utilize (essentially) the same theory of reflection, beam control, and beam shaping as the old-generation equipment but maximize the advantages of the physically smaller and more efficient tungsten-halogen lamps. In addition, these instruments are sturdier, brighter, more efficient, and easier to focus because of other changes in design. The lens tube has been made easier to adjust with the addition of Teflon strips that allow it to move more easily. More recent fixture designs move the lens in the barrel rather than move the lens tube. Lenses can be rearranged in the tube to change the beam spread of the instrument. Shutters have been redesigned to allow them to be sturdier and to adjust to more severe angles. All new-generation axial ellipsoidals are designed with a slot for pattern or gobo holders, which are supplied with the instruments. Only tungsten-halogen lamps are used in these various instruments, and the lamp may be easily aligned with a single knob.

These new-style instruments do not have a chimney. The socket and lamp are mounted on a plate at the back of the instrument on the centerline of the reflector and lens. This mounting system has introduced **joystick focusing**, which is a simple means to align the lamp in the reflector. On the back of the new-generation fixtures there is a knob, the **joystick** (Figure 4–37), that slides from side to side and top to bottom to change the position of the lamp in the reflector. On some new-generation axial ellipsoidals, the joystick controls the depth of the lamp in the reflector as it rotates to the right or left. Other new-generation instruments mount this knob on a plate that slides in and out of the back of the light. The depth of insertion of this plate controls the brightness and smoothness of the beam of light. If the plate is too deep

FIGURE 4–37
A joystick knob on the back of many new generation ellipsoidal spotlights replaces all three focusing screws found on the old generation ellipsoidals.

in the instrument, the beam will be dim and blue; if the plate is not deep enough, the beam will be dim and red. Due to the ease of access and operation, adjustment of the joystick allows additional control of the beam of light during focusing. The light could be adjusted to a completely smooth, even field or with a hot spot that can be placed near the top, bottom, or side of the beam simply by moving one or two knobs.

Access to change lamps in these fixtures is achieved by removing a section of the rear of the instrument. This may be a plate that slides in and out of the back of the instrument, an entire housing that is attached to the back of the fixture, or a small insert that slips into the back of the light. When the plate or insert is replaced in the fixture with the new lamp, it must be aligned to locate the lamp at the correct depth in the reflector to obtain the proper color (not bluish or reddish) and intensity. As usual, the instrument should be turned off and the fixture unplugged when changing lamps. Most of these instruments use medium two-pin lamps rated from 500 watts up to 1,000 watts.

New-generation axial ellipsoidals are identified by approximate degree of beam spread rather than by lens characteristics, so that an instrument is not classified as a 6 × 9 but is called a 30°. These more descriptive identifications provide information about the actual beam produced by the instrument. Table 4–1 compares some old-generation ellipsoidals with the beam spread of some of the new-generation equipment.

The new-generation instruments are capable of producing up to 50% more illumination than old-generation fixtures with lamps of equal wattage. Most of the new fixtures tend to be quite heavy but are better made. They have improved cooling capabilities, which increases lamp life, and they maximize the use of modern metals and plastics. In general, these new-generation axial ellipsoidals make it quicker and easier to focus lights for a show, and, due to their increased efficiency, they make it possible to provide more illumination with fewer instruments. Development of the new-generation axial ellipsoidals has lead to creation of two new fixtures, zoom ellipsoidal reflector spotlights, called zoom ellipses, and mini-ellipses.

Zoom Ellipse

A **zoom ellipse** (Figure 4–38) is a new-generation axial ellipsoidal reflector spotlight with an adjustable beam spread. In addition to the usual knob on the top front of the instrument to adjust focus, zoom ellipses have a second nob and lens in the barrel area that permits the size of the beam to be increased or decreased within fixed boundaries without cutting off any part of the light. By loosening and sliding the rear knob, the size of the beam is increased or decreased; by adjusting the front knob, the beam may be adjusted from a hard to a soft focus.

Combined with shutters and lamp adjustments, these fixtures offer maximum flexibility. Typical beam spreads for 6" zoom ellipses are 14° to 24°, and 20° to 40°. While these instruments are somewhat more expensive to purchase than a standard new-generation axial ellipsoidal reflector spotlight, they are especially practical for a program with limited funds that requires maximum flexibility and utilization of equipment.

FIGURE 4–38
A zoom ellipse. The knobs on the bottom of the instrument, just ahead of the shutters, and just behind the lens adjust the beam spread and the focus of this light. (Courtesy Altman Lighting Company)

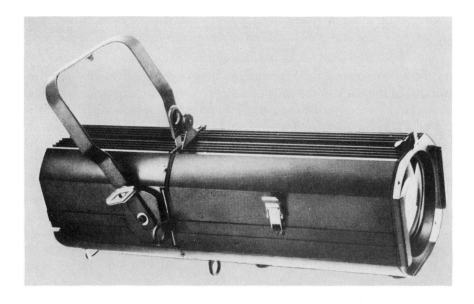

Mini-Ellipse

Mini-ellipses (Figure 4–39) are similar to new-generation axial ellipsoidal reflector spotlights and have many of the same features. They use lower-wattage lamps (250 watts to 600 watts) and are intended for use in smaller theatres. They are available as zoom ellipses as well as with fixed beam spreads.

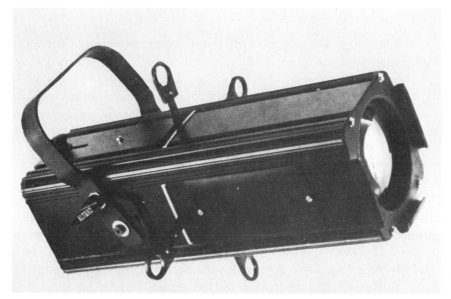

FIGURE 4–39
A mini-ellipse. (Courtesy Altman Lighting Company)

Follow Spots

Follow spots (Figure 4–40) are theatrical lighting instruments that are placed in locations where an operator can continually reposition and change the color, size, and shape of the beam of light. Their purpose is to create a moving beam of light that follows a performer or an object around the stage. The typical follow spot consists of a long narrow tube with a powerful source of light at one end. It is located behind a series of controls and lenses. The fixture is mounted on a stand that is adjustable in height and allows the instrument to swivel and tilt easily and smoothly.

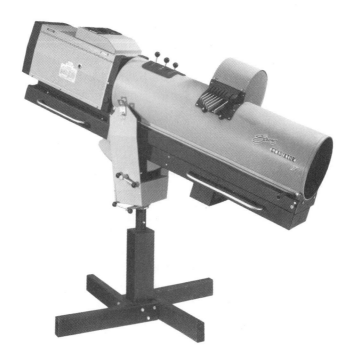

FIGURE 4–40
Professional follow spot using a high-intensity vapor lamp. (Gladiator, Courtesy Strong International)

Follow spots are designed for ranges of throw. Short-throw instruments produce a wider, less bright beam than long-throw follow spots; the range of throw varies from as short as 35'-0" up to several hundred feet. A spotlight of the appropriate size must be used or adequate control will not be possible; the beam will be too narrow, too wide, too bright, or too dim.

Most modern follow spots use either standard incadescent tungsten-halogen, or special high-output lamps. In addition, there is an entire family of follow spots that use carbon rods as the source of light. The rods actually burn up as they create an intense point of light. Rods must be replaced every 70 to 90 minutes of operation. Generally, carbon-arc follow spots are being replaced with more modern equipment. *CAUTION*: **Where carbon-arc follow spots are used, local electrical and fire codes should be examined to determine if the fixtures must be restricted to operation in an enclosed and ventilated booth.**

Better small and large follow spots have at least one fan built into them to keep the lamp from burning out prematurely and to prevent lenses from overheating and breaking. *CAUTION*: **Any follow spot with a fan should be used only if the fan functions when the instrument is turned on.**

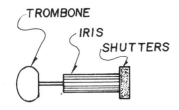

FIGURE 4–41
Typical follow spot control handles at the back of the instrument.

There are two styles of follow-spot controls. The first has most of the controls located on a multi-part handle on the back of the instrument (Figure 4–41). At the end of a long slender handle there is a knob on the end of a rod that may be pulled out from the back of the hood. This knob moves a lens at the front of the instrument and allows the operator to focus the light from a fuzzy to a sharp-edged beam. The knob is called the **trombone** because of the way it slides in and out of the fixture. The long slender handle in front of the knob is meant to be the primary operating handle of the fixture. In addition to providing a good grip for following performers, the handle rotates to control the iris. The **iris** adjusts the diameter of the circle of light projected by the follow spot. By adjusting the trombone and the iris, a great deal of variation can be obtained to shift from a very large, wide circle of light to a very small, tight pattern of illumination. In front of the trombone, next to the back of the hood, is a wide knurled ring. This handle controls a pair of blades that can be used to cut off the top and bottom edges of a beam to make it into a narrow band or strip of light. These blades are called the **shutters**, **choppers**, or **strippers**—the terms are interchangeable. By opening the iris as wide as possible and partially closing the shutters, it is often possible to light the entire width of the stage without spilling excess illumination into the audience or overhead.

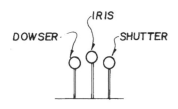

FIGURE 4–42
Typical follow spot control handles on the top of the instrument.

The second control system (Figure 4–42) places the handles on top and toward the side of the instrument. The trombone is a handle that sticks out of the right side of the fixture near the bottom front of the housing. It slides forward and backward to adjust the focus of the beam of light. A small knurled knob at the very front of the instrument, in line with the trombone, is used to make fine-tuning adjustments to the trombone. Once set, the trombone is locked in place by tightening the large handle in place. The remainder of the controls are located at the top center of the instrument. There may be two or three levers sticking up. The lever located closest to the front of the light is the chopper or shutters and behind that is the iris. The handles are simply moved from side to side to open or close the shutters and iris. On some follow spots there is a third handle, a **dowser**, which fades the beam of light on and off; this is also operated by moving the handle from side to side (Figure 4–42).

Most follow spots have some kind of built-in color changer. The color changer may be controlled by a group of small handles protruding from the right side of the instrument or there may be a metal basket with color holders that slide up and down at the front of the instrument. The color changer is called the **boomerang**, or **color boom**. Some boomerangs automatically drop out the previous color when a new frame is slipped into position, but it is also possible to hold two or even three colors in the beam of light at one time. The colors used in the booms are replaceable gel (see Chapter 2). Most follow spots are designed to have six colors in the boom. Many users replace the last color with a piece of tin or dense cardboard that can be used as a dowser to fade the beam of light on and off rather than to suddenly open the iris or choppers.

To operate a follow spot with the controls at the back, the operator stands in a comfortable position at the rear of the fixture, body turned toward the stage. The left hand controls the iris/chopper and the right hand operates the color boom. Both hands will help direct the light. To operate follow spots with the controls at the top center of the fixture, the operator stands at the side of the light near the front of the fixture, body turned toward the spotlight and eyes facing the stage. The dowser, iris, and chopper are operated with the left hand and the color boom with either the left or right hand. The operator aims the light by holding the trombone or handles on the color boom in the right hand. When possible, the top of the fixture is no more than armpit or shoulder height. Height is adjusted by raising the instrument in its stand and tightening a thumbscrew or lever-like handle that locks the stem of the follow spot in position but allows it to rotate freely. The handwheels on each side of the instrument should be adjusted so that the follow spot tilts up and down easily but will not freely tilt down and bang when the operator lets go of the light.

Operating a follow spot well requires some practice to develop the necessary hand-eye coordination. When following a performer on stage, there are a few guidelines to keep the performer well illuminated.

1. Never let the performer move out of the light.

2. When full body shots are used, keep the performer in the center of the beam of light with about one foot of light above the head and six inches of light in front of the toes.

3. When the performer moves, always lead the performer in the direction in which he or she is moving. Do not let the light get too far ahead of the performer and never allow it to be behind either.

4. Hold the light steady. Do not allow it to jiggle.

5. Move only when the performer moves—including adjusting the size of the circle of light. The circle of light must be modified as the performer moves closer and further from the instrument. Make

adjustments as the performer moves, not after he or she has stopped moving.

6. Bring the appropriate-size circle of light up on the performer in the proper location. This may require "peaking" with a tiny circle of light. To "peak," close the iris as small as possible and slightly open the dowser to see where the light is; close the dowser and reaim the light and peak again. Repeat this process until the light is aimed. Do not drag the "peaking light" across the stage because it is very noticeable. After hitting the proper location, close the dowser and open the iris an estimated (but never too large) amount. When working behind a window, targets can be marked on the glass with a china marker. When a follow spot must come on in a certain location at the beginning of a show, the light can be preset in that position before the audience arrives and simply turned on when needed.

Follow spots are wonderful problem solvers for all kinds of lighting needs. When they are not available, ellipsoidal spotlights can be mounted for this use. Some ellipsoidals have been adapted with an iris in place of the shutters, and they might also have a wooden "follow handle" on the instrument to help the operator. Whether or not they have the follow handle, ellipsoidals get extremely hot so operators using ellipsoidal reflector spotlights as follow spots should wear long-sleeved shirts and welder's leather gloves for protection.

The movie industry regularly uses a family of fixtures constructed around **HMI lamps**. These are high-voltage, high-intensity lamps that are filled with metallic gases under extreme pressure. In operation, the gases are heated to incandescence to efficiently produce very bright beams of light in the 5,500 to 6,500 Kelvin color temperature range. The color and quality of this light is making HMI fixtures popular for use in grand-scale productions such as classical opera and large-scale rock concerts.

HMI fixtures have several characteristics that make them difficult to use for the stage. (1) The fixtures require a ballast. The ballast is large, heavy, and includes a fan that can create distracting noises during a performance. (2) The ballast operates on 220 volt power, which is not commonly available where lighting fixtures are mounted; however, the ballast can be located at a distance somewhat remote from the fixture. (3) As of yet, there is no practical way to dim a ballasted light source, so fading of HMI lights must be accomplished with a mechanical dowser, similar to the dowser used with follow spots. Manually operated and remotely operated dowsers are available. (4) The beam of light produced by HMI fixtures is extremely hot (in excess of 300 degrees Centigrade in some fixtures). As a result, any coloring medium other than heat-resistant dichroic glass will not survive in a front of one of these fixtures for more than a few moments. This is a very expensive coloring medium. (5) HMI lamps have an average life of 300 to 750 hours and the lamps are very expensive to replace.

Even with all of these problems, HMI fixtures are being used in various theatre situations. HMI PARS with 1,500 to 4,000 watt lamps are used with interchangeable lenses that permit modifying the beam of light from a very narrow rectangle as small as 5 degrees by 10 degrees to a large flood of light 25 degrees by 60 degrees. HMI fresnel fixtures are available with lenses as small as 12" to as large as 30" in diameter using lamps from 2,500 watts to 20,000 watts. The fixtures are large, heavy, awkward, and expensive, but the quality of light is sometimes the perfect choice for a production.

Care must be taken when using HMI fixtures. The pressure in the lamp may cause the globe to explode. Fixture manufacturers have designed HMI fixtures so they can only be ignited with the protective lens in place. No effort should ever be made to defeat this protection system.

ALTERNATIVE LIGHTING EQUIPMENT

Although most people doing stage lighting would prefer to work with commercially manufactured theatrical lighting instruments, budget may prohibit availability of this equipment. There are a variety of alternatives that can be used for stage lighting. A few of these solutions are highly practical and very inexpensive. Usually the equipment is available from local hardware stores or electrical suppliers.

Alternative 1: Garage Lights

R40 flood lamps or PAR 36 spot or flood lamps can be screwed into the sockets of swivel-based garage lights (Figure 4–43). These simple fixtures mount on square or octagonal conduit boxes. The conduit boxes can be screwed to a board or can be rigged with a standard theatrical pipe clamp. When placed on stage, these simple fixtures can be used for a general wash of illumination or, if narrow spot lamps are used, can be restricted to special lighting effects. Metal rings are available from some theatrical sources to attach color media to these lamps.

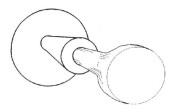

FIGURE 4–43
Garage light with 150 watt PAR lamp.

Alternative 2: Yard Lights

Some very practical and inexpensive yard lights are available. These are enclosed fixtures with a clear-glass lens intended to protect the lamp from exposure to rain or snow. Many of these fixtures have yokes that permit them to be easily attached to standard theatrical pipe clamps (Figure 4–44). The fixtures are manufactured in a variety of rectangular beam spreads from a fairly narrow pattern to very wide patterns of light. The fixtures use a long-life tungsten-halogen lamp and make excellent floodlights. Color media may be clipped to the glass lens in front of the light.

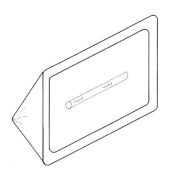

FIGURE 4–44
Yard light.

LIGHTING FIXTURES IN PRODUCTION: THE HANG AND FOCUS

A practical system in preparation for a crew installing the lights is to use chalk to mark each location where the lights are to be placed with an indication of the kind of light to be installed and the circuit or dimmer to which the instrument is to be connected. If the light shares a circuit with another instrument, that might be noted as well. Another approach can also be used. Rather than marking on the pipe, a roll of adding machine paper can be marked with the same information and taped to the pipe. Either approach requires some advanced preparation by the person running the crew, but both reduce paper handling and the likelihood of error when the work is performed.

The instruments should be mounted firmly to the pipe. The C-clamp bolt and the bolt that attaches the yoke of the instrument to the C-clamp must be secure. After each instrument is hung in place, the bolts or handwheels on the sides of each light should be tested to make sure they are no more than hand tight. If it is difficult to loosen these bolts, they should be worked on during this period rather than when the lights are being focused. In the case of extremely tight side bolts, it sometimes seems impossible to get the bolts or handwheels loosened. Since the lighting instrument can give some extra leverage, a way to initiate loosening these stubborn bolts is to tip the instrument up or down until the bolt starts to give, then loosen the bolt and tilt in the opposite direction until the bolt on the other side of the instrument also works free. The shutters on ellipsoidal spotlights should be pulled out as soon as an instrument is hung in place (they should be pushed all the way in just before dismounting an ellipsoidal). This will minimize the likelihood of the shutters getting badly bent. It is usually most practical to allow each instrument to hang with its lens pointing straight down until it is time to focus the lights. In this way the lights will not shine randomly about the stage while awaiting focusing. This also avoids the potential fire hazard of lights close to scenery or drapes overheating the materials before they are aimed.

After the instruments have been properly mounted, they must be hooked up to power. This often requires the use of extension cable and may or may not require two-fers. In most production situations, it is a good idea to tie a piece of thin rope, a **tieline**, such as No. 6 sash cord, around the connectors to make sure they do not come apart. Another way to keep the connectors together is to make giant rubber bands out of inner tubes. The best size tube to use for this is a 3.70 diameter tube. Extension cords should *not* be wrapped around the pipe on which the lighting instruments are mounted. Wrapping takes a lot of time, makes it difficult to get to the pipe clamp of instruments, and makes it almost impossible to trace a cable when checking connections. The extension cables should be tied to the pipe with No. 6 sash cord or some other kind of rope or string. When tying cable to the pipe, it is best to use regular bow knots (as on shoelaces) since they are strong but can be easily untied when taking the lights down. This also permits saving tielines from one show to the next. Another way to connect cable to a pipe is to use plastic electrical ties. These are long, narrow plastic strips that are wrapped around the cable and the mounting pipe and then the end of the strip is slipped into a little fastener built into the strip and pulled tight. These are not reusable and must be cut from the pipe when it is necessary to remove a cable. Finally, velcro bands can be used to hold cable to the pipe. Strips of black velcro fabric are commercially available for this purpose or they can be homemade. These are reusable and repositionable fasteners that are quick and secure. When tied to the pipe, a loop of cable about 18" long should be left at each instrument. This loop allows the instrument to be tilted up and down and rotated from side to side. If the cable is pulled too tight without leaving the loop, it will be impossible to focus the lights.

After all of the lighting instruments have been mounted in position and hooked up to power, it is a good idea to turn each fixture on to make sure it is functioning and connected to the proper circuit.

The final step in preparing the lights for focus is to cut the gel. Each piece of gel should be cut to the appropriate size and marked with the color number in a corner so that it can easily be identified. The gel is then placed in a color holder. After the gel is readied, it may be (1) placed in each instrument—removed during focus and then replaced; (2) put in stacks of the appropriate color and distributed as each instrument is focused; (3) placed at the base of each instrument and inserted as each light is focused; or (4) handled in some other manner that minimizes confusion.

Focusing the lights for a show usually requires a minimum of three people: one person to actually determine where the light should fall; a second person to manipulate the lighting instrument—actually focus it; and a third person to turn the lights on and off. Working with fewer than this number of people makes the work very time consuming even when just a few lights must be focused. The person focusing the lights should be positioned safely and comfortably while working on each instrument. In facilities that require climbing ladders to access the lights (some are found in almost all production situations), one person should be stationed at each leg of the ladder to keep it stable. When an A-frame ladder is used, this will require four people just to hold the ladder. The person focusing the lights will need an 8" crescent wrench to adjust the various bolts that tighten most lighting instruments in place. It is a good idea to connect the wrench to a rope that is also tied to the belt of the crew member so that when the wrench slips it will not fall and injure someone on the ground.

The lighting designer usually stands on stage and directs the focus of each light, one instrument at a time.

To Focus an Old-Generation Ellipsoidal Spotlight

1. With the light turned on, stand at the center of the focus area. There are two approaches to this focusing: facing the light and turned away from the light. While looking into the beam of light, have the instrument tipped up and moved around until the **hot spot**, the brightest part of the beam, shines directly into your eyes. Have the lighting instrument locked into that position. Alternatively, face away from the light and watch its pattern on the floor. When you see the hot spot surrounding the shadow of your head on the floor, have the instrument locked into position (this is much easier on the eyes.)

2. While watching the edge of the light as the beam strikes the floor or scenery, adjust the lens forward or backward to get the appropriate beam quality. A sharply focused hard-edged beam of light will appear when the lens tube is near the middle of its travel distance in the snoot, a narrower softened beam will appear as the lens tube is moved forward, and a wider soft-edged beam will appear as the lens tube is moved back from the point of sharp focus.

3. After the lens tube has been adjusted to project the quality of light desired, adjust the shutters. The shutters cut off light on the opposite side of the beam so that the shutter located on the bottom of the instrument will cut off the top edge of the beam of light.

4. Slip the color holder into the light.

To Focus a New-Generation Ellipsoidal Spotlight

1. With the light turned on, adjust the joystick or focus plate at the back of the instrument to get the smoothest and whitest beam of light.

2. Stand at the center of the focus area with your back toward the light. Have the instrument adjusted up, down, and sideways until the beam covers the area desired. Be sure to watch your shadow and make sure that it does not disappear as you move around the area the instrument is supposed to illuminate.

3. Adjust the joystick to a smooth beam of light or, if there is a hot spot, so it falls on your face at the center of the focus area.

4. While watching the edge of the light as the beam strikes the floor or scenery, adjust the lens forward or backward to get the appropriate beam quality. A sharply focused hard-edged beam of light will appear when the lens tube is near the middle of its travel distance in the snoot, a narrower softened beam will appear as the lens tube is moved forward, and a wider soft-edged beam will appear as the lens tube is moved back from the point of sharp focus.

5. After the lens tube has been adjusted to project the quality of light desired, adjust the shutters. The shutters cut off light on the opposite side of the beam so that the shutter located on the bottom of the instrument will cut off the top edge of the beam of light.

6. Slip the color holder into the light.

To Focus a Fresnel Spotlight or Beam Projector

1. With the light turned on, stand at the center of the focus area and have the beam adjusted to **spot focus**. In spot focus, the lamp is located all the way to the back of the instrument and the beam becomes very narrow.

2. Facing away from the light and watching the floor and scenery behind you, have the hot spot adjusted so it falls on the back of your head and have the instrument locked into place.

3. Step out of the focus area and watch the edges of the beam, staying conscious of the quality of light at the center of the beam; have the lamp slowly moved forward to flood the light into a larger pool. When the light covers the entire area desired, lock the lamp in place.

4. If the focused light spills on drapes, scenery, or other undesirable locations, insert a **barn door** in the color holder slots. Open all of the flaps of the barn door and then close them only as far as necessary to cut off the unwanted portions of the beam of light.

5. Slip the color holder into the slot (behind the barn door).

To Focus a Scoop or Strip Light

1. Stand away from the stage and watch the beam of light.

2. Have the instrument tipped and twisted until it covers the desired area, and lock the instrument in place.

To Focus a PAR

1. Stand away from the stage and watch the beam of light.

2. When the instrument is turned on, have a crew member reach inside the back of the can and rotate the ceramic socket to orient the projected beam in the desired direction.

3. Have the instrument tipped and turned until it covers the desired area; then stand in the light to make sure it will properly illuminate the performer as planned. Have the instrument locked in place.

4. If the focused light spills on drapes, scenery, or other undesirable locations, insert a barn door in the color holder slots. Open all of the flaps of the barn door and then close them only as far as necessary to cut off the unwanted portions of the beam of light.

5. Slip the color holder into the slot (behind the barn door).

CONCLUSION

Every type of lighting instrument has its own characteristics that distinguish its purpose and application. Selection of the equipment for a show should be determined on that basis. However, all of the equipment necessary (or desirable) often is not available. In these situations, substitutions of other kinds of equipment, when available, or manufacture of homemade lighting instruments is necessary, sometimes just to provide sufficient illumination to make the performance visible. Adapting to these restrictions often produces some wonderfully creative solutions to the problems of production.

CHAPTER 5

Projections and Special Effects

INTRODUCTION

A simple beam of light can illuminate a production and contribute to the ever-changing mood of the performance. This light can be modified with the addition of color media or diffusion materials to enhance its effectiveness, but the light can also be treated in a pictorial way. Beams of light can be used to project patterns, photographs, or drawings or to create abstract compositions that enhance the psychological effects of the performance. In some circumstances, projections can even create the actual setting. These treatments of light as projected textures and images can greatly enrich a production and have become an expected part of concert lighting as moving images. The theatre is increasingly adopting moving light as part of the performance as well.

BEAM OF LIGHT AS A PROJECTION

A beam of white or colored light is the most basic kind of projection. It can be treated simply as a visible shaft of light in the air or beams can be projected on scenery and drapes in planned patterns. Usually, concentrated beams from ellipsoidal reflector spotlights, PARs, ACLs, or other low-voltage, high-intensity sources of light are used in this compositional way.

A visible shaft of light in the air can serve as an arrow to focus attention sharply on a single performer or area of the stage, or several shafts of light or a shaft of light broken up into individual parallel shafts can create a pattern or a texture in the air (Figure 5–1). Projecting an evenly spaced row of concentrated beams of light angled from one or both sides of the stage makes a very dramatic visual statement, whether projected from above toward the floor or from floor-mounted fixtures pointing up.

When creating patterns of light in the air, the rays must reflect off vapor or dust to be visible. This is most easily accomplished by using a chemical fog machine to spray a fine mist in the acting area before and during the performance. The foggy mist will make the beams of light especially apparent against dark backgrounds so that visible shafts of light become almost palpable. Only a small amount of fog is needed to achieve this dramatic effect.

A spotlight may be placed next to a curtain or drop, with the beam intentionally aimed to cast a cone of light on the scenery. A single spotlight can cast a narrow incisive shaft of light, or several spotlights can be arranged in a design such as a sunburst of individual shafts of light at the base of a drop or curtain. An interesting pattern of light can be created by locating instruments at the top or bottom of drapes to project vertical stripes of light on the fabric. Each light may be colored or left white (Figure 5–2).

Rather than mounting lights so their beams are seen as long shafts on the scenery, any spotlight can be placed squarely in front of or behind a translucent drop to cast a circle of light on it. This image can be used to suggest the sun or moon in the sky or assembled as a pattern of white or colored circles. To create movement, a fixture can be rigged to the carriers on a traveler track and the light can be drawn across the stage, perhaps to create a moving sun, moon, or headlights from a car. When a beam of light is aimed directly at scenery or

FIGURE 5–1
Visible shafts of light in the air as a scenic effect.

FIGURE 5–2
Shafts of light falling on scenery to paint a pattern with light. (Courtesy Theatre UNI, University of Northern Iowa)

curtains, there should be a minimum of four feet of space between the lens and any fabric to prevent scorching or burning the fabric; the distance must be increased if the light is on for a great length of time. In this situation, scenery should be checked frequently for any indication of damage due to heat.

Those same circles of light can be aimed straight down at the floor in sharp or softly focused patterns. Each circle or pool of light might be used to isolate characters on stage or to paint the floor with patterns of individual or overlapping circles of light. When ellipsoidal spotlights are used for these projections, the shutters may be adjusted to other geometric shapes (Figure 5–3).

FIGURE 5–3

Patterns of light projected on the drop and floor. (Courtesy Theatre UNI, University of Northern Iowa)

A single beam of light can be used to cast a silhouette through translucent scenery such as a muslin cyclorama. The object that is to appear in silhouette is placed behind the drop with an intense light behind it aimed toward the drop (Figure 5–4). The pattern of the beam of light as well as the shadow of the object or person will be projected on the drop.

The quality of the cast image can be modified several different ways. The size of the image can be changed by adjusting the distance between the source of light, the object or person, and the surface on which the projection is to appear. As the distance between the projected object or person and the source of light increases, the size of the image will diminish (Figure 5–4A); as the distance between the source of light and the projection surface increases, the image will become larger (Figure 5–4B). The position of the source of light will also make a difference. A spotlight placed directly behind the figure will project an undistorted, although slightly enlarged, image, but if the source of light is placed above or below the figure, the size of the cast image will be modified. A spotlight placed at the floor pointing up at a severe angle will enlarge the projection and cause the top of the image to expand in a distorted pattern, whereas a spotlight placed at a steep high angle overhead will cause the figure to shrink (Figure 5–4C). The projected image may appear sharp and distinctly defined

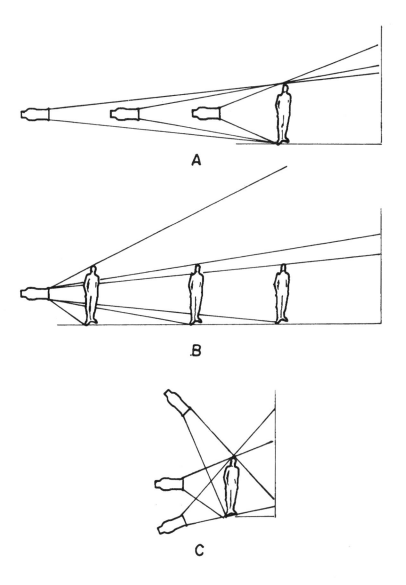

FIGURE 5–4
(A) A silhouette will diminish in size as the source of light is moved further from the figure. (B) A silhouette will enlarge as the figure is brought closer to the source of light. (C) The angle of projection will distort the size of the projected silhouette. A high angle will diminish the size of the projection and a low angle will increase the size of the projection.

in a crisp circle of light when backlit with an ellipsoidal reflector spotlight, but it will be somewhat fuzzy and in a less distinct pattern of light when a fresnel or even a scoop is used as the source of illumination.

If the drop is bathed with colored light from the front and the same color of light is used to project the silhouette, the shadow will blend into the background, especially when a fresnel or scoop is used to project the image. This can be especially effective for subtle or ghost-like apparitions. To give more distinction to the cast image, the light projecting the shadow may be a different color than the light washing the drop from the front. In that case, the light behind the figure will project a pattern of colored light in which the silhouette appears. The silhouette will be the color of light that is on the front of the drop. For instance, if the drop is washed in blue light from the front, and the light casting the silhouette is red, a circle of red light containing a blue silhouette will appear on the drop. Depending on the brightness of the instruments, the rear projected light may be so intense it washes out the color of the front light, or it may be sufficiently controlled as to blend with the color of the front light, which will result in a new hue.

When a silhouette is projected through a translucent drop, the source of light should be located so that it is not visible to the audience. If the lens of the instrument is in direct line with a member of the audience, the flare from the lamp will be clearly apparent and will blind or distract viewers. Placing the above or below the figure will solve the problem but distort the image. To avoid both distortion and blinding the audience, the source of light should be placed directly behind the person or object that casts the shadow so that direct view of the lens is blocked by the figure.

PATTERNS

Gobos and Patterns

A beam of light projected from an ellipsoidal spotlight, in addition to projecting hard and soft edged circles or geometric shapes formed by the shutters, can be used to cast shadows that are textures, symbols, or pictorial images. This is accomplished by interrupting the beam with a pattern or a gobo. A **pattern** or **gobo** is a very thin piece of stainless steel with a design etched through it or heat-resistant glass with a pattern painted on it. Stainless steel and glass patterns are commercially manufactured in hundreds of designs. The metal patterns will warp and burn as a result of the heat produced within the light fixture. The glass patterns permit a great deal more detail and do not distort as they heat. A pattern is temporarily installed just ahead of the shutters in an ellipsoidal reflector spotlight.

Usually gobos are inserted upside-down in a **pattern holder.** The size of pattern holders and pattern-holder slots in ellipsoidal spotlights is not standardized so pattern holders are not necessarily interchangeable among spotlights. A pattern holder that is designed both for the gobo and for the spotlight must be used. There are two styles of pattern holders (Figure 5–5): a double-flap holder for patterns etched in rectangular plates and a single blade holder with tabs for patterns etched in round plates. Rectangular patterns can be trimmed with scissors to fit any holder; they may be pared down in height or width or cut to fit a round holder. The pattern holder is inserted in a slot just ahead of the shutter handle on top of an ellipsoidal spotlight (Figure 5–6).

Some older ellipsoidal spotlights may not have a pattern-holder slot; although it is inconvenient, patterns may still be used in these instruments. To install a gobo, the ellipsoidal must be disassembled where the reflector portion joins the barrel that carries the lens tube

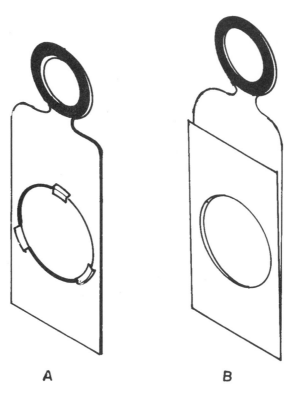

FIGURE 5–5
(A) Round pattern holder; (B) double flap pattern holder.

A   B

FIGURE 5–6
Pattern slot in an ellipsoidal spotlight just ahead of the top shutter.

(Figure 5–7). The gobo is placed against the shutter assembly and then the instrument is reassembled. If it becomes necessary to make an adjustment to the gobo, the instrument must be taken apart to attain access to the pattern.

Several hundred patterns are available from theatrical supply companies. A small sample of these is shown in Figure 5–8. One manufacturer makes sets of gobos to assemble complex multicolored patterns such as a stained-glass window (Figure 5–9). This particular set requires

FIGURE 5–7
A gobo may be inserted at the gate of an ellipsoidal without a pattern slot by disassembling the fixture.

the use of five spotlights, each of which has a different color and pattern and constitutes a portion of the stained-glass window. The same manufacturer also sells mesh gobos (Figure 5–10). These patterns are made with a fine screen to create the effect of shading a part of an image.

FIGURE 5–8
An assortment of gobo designs. (Courtesy The Great American Market, Inc.)

FIGURE 5–9
A composite gobo requiring five fixtures to project the pattern. (Courtesy Rosco Laboratories, Inc.)

A sophisticated application of gobos utilizes a **gobo rotator** (Figure 5–11). This is a motorized device that fits in the pattern slot of new-generation ellipsoidals. A pattern is placed in the pattern holder of the gobo rotator. When power is supplied, the device rotates the gobo at a preset speed. It is possible to have two gobos rotating in the same fixture so that the patterns interfere and interrelate with each other in highly complex ways.

Commercial manufacturers of gobos will make custom patterns from any design that is desired. To order a custom pattern, such as a gobo containing the name of a theatre or a performance group or some other special image, the design must be prepared in dark black ink on white paper or illustration board. The design should be as close to the actual size of the gobo as possible. The ink represents the portion of the pattern through which light is projected. The artwork is sent to a laboratory, where the gobo is produced by means of a metal-etching process.

Gobos are moderately inexpensive accessories for lights. The heat of the instruments will cause the metal to warp, distort, and eventually burn away. Thus, they are consumables, not a life-long investment.

After a pattern has been placed in a light, the instrument must be focused by adjusting the lens tube. The pattern may be sharply focused to get a precise image, or a slightly softened effect can be

A.

B.

FIGURE 5–10
(A) A mesh gobo to project a shaded image; (B) an anti-keystone gobo. (Courtesy Rosco Laboratories, Inc.)

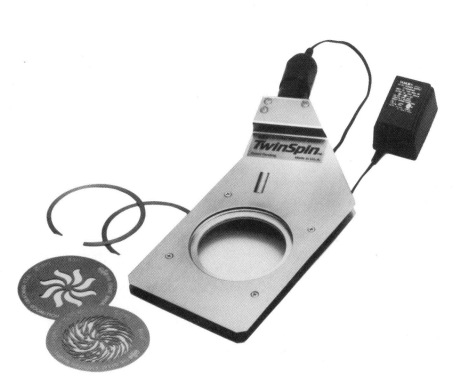

FIGURE 5–11
A gobo spinner. This device mounts in the pattern slot and rotates two gobos in opposing directions. (Courtesy The Great American Market)

created by moving the lens ahead or behind sharp focus. Often the effectiveness of an image is improved when it is slightly out of focus.

When the light from an instrument strikes a surface at an angle, part of the beam will be closer to the light and a portion of the beam will be more distant. In those very common situations, it will be impossible to focus the entire image sharply. Also, the image will **keystone**, that is, the part of the image closest to the light will be narrower than the portion furthest from the instrument. Some patterns such as the distorted window in Figure 5–10B have been designed to compensate for keystoning.

When a pattern is inserted in an ellipsoidal, it cuts off a portion of the beam of light. The light that is cut off is reflected in unaccountable ways inside the spotlight; some of that light will come out the lens as stray rays, **spill**. This is usually minimal but may be sufficient to wash out the effect of a lighting moment. The problem can be reduced by inserting a **donut** in the color-holder slot of the spotlight. This accessory looks like a color holder with a single flap and an undersized opening. The effect of a donut can be achieved by cutting a 3" diameter hole in a piece of Rolux gel or other opaque nonreflective heat-resistant material that can be placed in a color holder in front of the lens. The perimeter of the opening cuts off the stray light.

Gobos may be used to project pictorial images in shadow, such as city skylines, bridges, trees, clouds, buildings, or fire escapes; images in nature, such as stars, clouds, and trees; or symbols, such as a dollar sign, American eagle, heraldic lion, musical notes, valentine hearts, or witches. There is also a broad assortment of geometric designs, including squares, circles, and moiré effects. One of the most consistent uses of gobos is for making textural patterns. Webs, leaves, and sharp and soft "break-up" patterns can be inserted in acting area light simply to create a texture of shadows in the illumination or to establish a variety of effects from filtered sunlight in the woods to shadowy basements at night. Usually when texture-gobos are used, several are needed to create a complete effect. Several patterns might also be used concurrently to paint a sky with clouds or to paint a background with a cityscape that might combine clouds, trees, and buildings. Each pattern, of course, must be in a separate lighting instrument (Figure 5–12).

Alternative Method to Create Patterns

Another means to project shadows makes use of a fresnel spotlight. The lens is removed from the instrument and an aluminum foil or cardboard cutout of a pattern is inserted in the color-holder slot. Without the lens, the instrument projects a soft image of the cutout. It is not possible to achieve a sharply focused pattern, but a soft shadowed image of a landscape can be projected on a background with just a small investment of time to cut the pattern out of cardboard. The distance from the lighting instrument to the projection surface greatly affects the clarity of the image.

FIGURE 5–12
Four individual gobos used to project patterns of a stained glass window. (Courtesy Theatre UNI, University of Northern Iowa)

PICTORIAL IMAGES

Photographic Slides

Photographs can be projected using a standard slide projector with the brightest lamp available. Kodak Ektagraphic projectors are especially practical for these applications. They use powerful lamps and have exceptional lens systems that allow both short and long throws of images. Any slide that fits the tray of the projector can be used. The slide may be a photograph of an actual scene or might be something that has been painted on heat-resistant glass using lamp dip, Dr. Martin's watercolors, or dilute acrylic artist's colors. It is always difficult to compensate for keystoning when using slide projectors: whenever possible, the projector should be placed on a line at the center and perfectly square to the projection surface.

Built-in cooling fans are installed in all slide projectors to reduce operating temperature. *Whenever a slide projector is in operation, its fan must be on to prevent destruction of the lamp, lenses, operating motor, and slides.* To ensure this, the fan is usually wired directly to the power switch so the fan will always come on when the projector is turned on. It is only possible to fade up the image from a slide projector using a dimmer if the fan and the lamp are operated under separate controls. To dim the output of a projector, the equipment must be rewired to separate the power supply to the lamp from the power supply to the fan. In this way, the fan can function at full speed even when the lamp is partially dimmed.

No matter how the projector is wired, fan noise can often be a problem since the fan always must be on during operation. There is no adequate way to muffle this sound without diminishing the flow of air through the projector. The best solution is to locate the projector so that fan noise will not be heard by the audience. This can be accomplished by putting the projector in an enclosed control booth or by placing the instrument backstage. Either of these locations also improves access to the projector in case something goes wrong, such as a lamp burning out or a slide jamming.

Front projections of pictorial images can be very effective. They tend to be bright and clear when projected on a surface that allows sufficient nonglaring reflection. However, there are several disadvantages with front projections.

1. Although projectors located above or within the audience provide a good front angle for projection and are usually accessible to a crew member for operation, the fan noise will be a problem.

2. Projectors located in a booth behind the audience provide easy access for a crew member and also reduce or eliminate the fan noise problem. However, they are a long distance from the stage, often causing the intensity of the image to be reduced beyond acceptable limits.

3. Projectors used on stage are usually placed on the first lighting pipe, where they are inaccessible during performance and cannot be repaired in the event of a failure. Images projected from this position are usually severely keystoned.

4. The greatest problem with front projections is that unless the projector is located very close to the projection surface and the image is cast at a severe angle (resulting in extensive keystoning), actors will walk through the projections. This may be used as a stylistic device for some productions, but is usually annoying to an audience.

Most of these problems can be solved by using rear projections. A projector can be set up behind a translucent surface on which the image will appear. Muslin cycloramas are satisfactory for this purpose, however, they absorb quite a bit of light and cause images to become somewhat fuzzy as they pass through the fabric. When possible, a **rear projection screen** made from a special plastic material should be used since it is designed to project a sharp, brilliant image. Screens may be rented or purchased, or projection material may be obtained and stretched on a homemade frame. When screens are used, some means must be found to incorporate the screen in the stage picture when no image is being projected. Hiding the screen behind drapes may be one solution; another is to keep the screen constantly illuminated with projections or a wash of light from the projector by placing gel in a slide.

No matter what surface is used, there are almost always two problems associated with rear projection. First, it is difficult to get enough depth on most stages to project a very large image from behind the scenery. Second, should a projector be placed behind a translucent plane and aimed through the surface toward the audience, a number of people in the audience will be distracted by the bright flare of the lamp, which is visible when looking in the lens. This tends to have a riveting and blinding effect on the members of the audience who catch sight of the lens. Both problems, lamp flare and throw distance, can be solved with a single solution, Rather than projecting an image directly at the translucent surface, the projector is placed to the side of the stage, perhaps in one wing, and aimed across the stage at a mirror that redirects the image to the translucent surface (Figure 5–13). A high-quality mirror must be securely mounted at exactly the correct position to redirect this beam. Now that the projector can be placed offstage as far as necessary from the mirror, a greater throw distance can be obtained to get a larger image on the projection surface. Since the projector is no longer in-line with anyone in the audience, it will not be possible to look through the translucent surface into the lens of the projector.

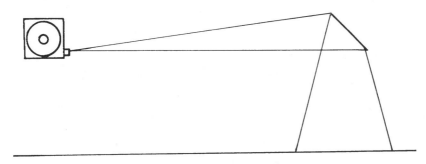

FIGURE 5–13
The rear projection image from a slide projector redirected with a mirror.

A major problem with projections is making the transition from one image to the next. The sharp click of the projector is usually more distracting than helpful. A **dissolve unit**, available from audiovisual sources, permits cross-fading from one slide image to another without the abruptness usually associated with a slide presentation. The device uses two different projectors, fading out the image from the first as the image from the second is faded up. In this way, there is no abrupt change in the slides but the images seem more or less to dissolve into each other.

Moving Projections

Moving pictorial images, films, can be projected on stage by replacing slide projectors with film projectors. Once again, machine noise, keystoning, lamp flare, lens size, and throw distance must be taken into consideration.

Other kinds of moving projections as well as static images and slides can be projected on stage with an **effects projector** (Figure 5–14). This is a powerful source of light usually with interchangeable lenses and a number of attachments to carry slides, gobos, swirling patterns, or film loops. As with slide projectors, effects projectors are equipped with a fan to keep the system cool. Since this equipment is usually made for the stage, the fan is usually wired separately from the lamp so that the projector can be dimmed. These are often large, heavy, expensive pieces of equipment.

FIGURE 5–14
An effects projector, The Great American Scene Machine. (Photo courtesy The Great American Market)

USES OF PROJECTIONS

Many different kinds of effects can be achieved with effects projector systems.

1. They can be used as a powerful source of light to project a shadow image in the same manner as a gobo in an ellipsoidal reflector spotlight.

2. Usually the quality of lenses in the effects projector is significantly better than in spotlights, so greater detail and sharper images can be achieved. Painted or photographic slides can be used in these

projectors in the same manner as in a carousel slide projector. However, an effects projector usually requires slides in larger formats such as 4 × 5 or 8 × 10. The slides must be protected with heat-resistant glass. A slide carrier that will hold a single slide or a magazine or tray that will carry up to six or ten of the large-format slides can be used with these devices.

3. The slide carrier can be replaced with a machine that will cause a disc to rotate, projecting swirling patterns.

4. A film loop can be mounted on the machine to project images that move continuously in a linear pattern, such as clouds passing across the stage or flame or snow moving in a vertical line. Both speed and direction of movement can be controlled.

The use of projections on stage is only limited by imagination, the availability of equipment, and time to experiment and perfect the images. Here are some ideas for the use of projections.

1. Project a distant scene on a neutral background. When a three-dimensional set stands in front of a cyclorama, a cityscape, landscape, mountains, forest, or any other distant scene can be projected on the background. If a play takes place in New York City, the Statue of Liberty or the skyline around the Chrysler Building or the Empire State Building may be visible through a window. If a play occurs in a room in Italy, perhaps the Vatican or Coliseum can be seen. These images may be photographic slides of the actual locales or patterns in ellipsoidal spotlights.

2. Project the sun, moon, or stars on a sky. Stars or a crescent moon can be projected using gobos. The images may be white or colored. Stars projected from a gobo are more effective when the pattern is not perfectly focused. A wonderfully romantic sky of deep night blue scattered with bursts of stars can be part of the background as Romeo calls to Juliet or Curly woos Laura in *Oklahoma*.

3. Project the image of moonlight or sunlight through a window. The window may or may not be present. Simply cast the shadow of the window on the walls or floor of the setting by placing a pattern and an appropriately colored gel in an ellipsoidal spotlight. This could be an effective way to create the setting for a play such as *Hello, Out There*, which takes place in a lonely jail cell. The acting area can be defined by a square of cool blue light. The image of a barred window can be projected on the floor with rays of sunlight or moonlight from an ellipsoidal spotlight equipped with a gobo. A bench and this lighting could serve as the setting. In other productions wonderfully effective romantic or tragic stage pictures can be created by casting the image of light through a window on the performers.

4. The sense of a forest can be created by casting the glow of moonlight or sunlight through the trees. The acting area could be illuminated with a variety of green lights while ellipsoidal spotlights with breakup gobos project golden sunlight streaming through the trees. The atmosphere of a forest can create a sense of a hot summer day or a romantic evening in the woods. A fearsome night in a dark lonely forest of mystery can be created by placing sharp breakup gobos

in the green forest light so that the performers are constantly moving in and out of shadows (Figure 5–15).

  5. A sense of texture that is patterns of shadow, can begin to creep into the lighting as the tension of a drama increases or the complexity of a plot becomes more entangling. A web, bars, or some other image can

FIGURE 5–15
Forest shadows created with several gobos.

wash the stage with a literal or impressionistic texture that suggests the coming crisis in the action.

  6. Project a complete set. Using slides of actual rooms, landscapes, townscapes, or other places, project the slides onto a cyclorama. As the locale for the action changes, change the slides. Using a dissolve unit or projectors that have been rewired to allow dimming, the slides can fade from one locale to another or the shift of scenes could be accomplished with a blackout followed by a fade-up of a new projection. This technique can be used for productions with a lot of different settings. Although the slides alone can be used to create a new locale, this technique is most effective when slide changes are accompanied by changes of furniture and platforms as well.

  7. Project symbols or a logo. Using photographic slides or standard or custom gobos, any kind of symbolic image may be projected. For instance, a Halloween show might have gobo patterns of flying witches, carved pumpkins, scared cats, and ghosts projected on the background to help establish the mood of the show. A band might project a pattern with the name of the group. A special event, such as an honors assembly, may be given additional prestige by projecting the title of the event or an image of the award. In dramatic produc-

tions, a symbol, such as a heraldic lion for *Camelot*, could be projected on the act curtain before the performance, during intermission, or during a scene to help set the mood.

8. Slides can be used in an expository way. Some dramatic productions are enriched and clarified in purpose by projecting images that help tell the story. Slides that provide background information about the characters or historical period can help the audience understand the action, historical period, location, or mood of the performance. This device is often used in movies with the opening of a book to begin to tell the story. A similar effect could be created on stage by projecting an image of a book while a narrator begins to read the story, "Once upon a time...."

9. Slides can be used as an editorial comment about characters or action. For instance, a character in a play might be charming and highly charismatic, but there is an underlying evil that must be clearly communicated to the audience. A powerful suggestion of this evil could be made by flashing images of Adolf Hitler on the background each time that character appears. In the same way, impending doom could be suggested by images of a nuclear explosion. To help an audience understand the timeliness of a historical drama, slides of contemporary newspaper headlines could be projected before or during the performance to help the audience make the connection between the historical event in the drama and contemporary conditions in the world.

10. For those persons adopting the Epic style of Brecht, the placards so often described in his scripts can be slide projections.

Obviously, there are numerous ways to use projections for a production. This list barely scrapes the surface of what is possible.

MOVING LIGHT

Lighting has increasingly become a scenic element in the concert industry and has also become an element of decor in nightclubs and discos. The excitement generated by flashing lights and changing colors has been enhanced further by making the beams of light move—individually or in groups. There are two types of equipment designed to make beams of light move automatically: moving light fixtures and scanning light fixtures.

The Vari-Light Company manufacturers several different versions of **moving lights** (Figure 5–16). These are very specialized fixtures designed to rotate, change intensity, beam size, and beam quality (hard/soft), as well as change color and even insert gobos or patterns in the beam of light. The company markets fixtures for long and short throws in narrow, medium, and wide beam spreads. To direct the movement of fixtures, Vari-Light provides a dedicated control system to program and record the cues for the fixtures. Managed in this way, one, two, or even several hundred lighting fixtures can be cued at the same time. Vari-Light systems are leased, not sold. There is a minimum order requirement, including a minimum quantity of fixtures, the control system, and at least one operator who is responsible for programming as well as maintenance of the equipment. Normally this equipment is obtained directly from Vari-Light.

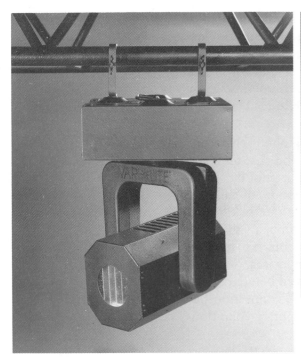

A.

B.

FIGURE 5–16
Moving lights. (A) Vari-Lite VL4™ Wash luminaire; (B) Vari-Lite VL2C™ Spot luminaire; (C) Vari-lite Artisan® Control Console. (Courtesy Vari-Lite, Inc.)

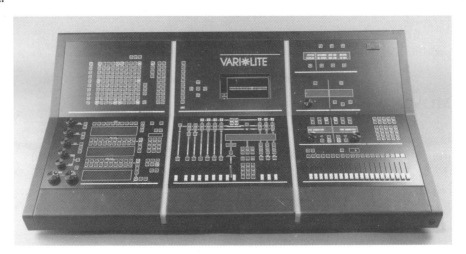

C.

An alternative to moving lights are **scanners**. These light fixtures incorporate a moving mirror located near the face of the lighting fixture. It rotates and tilts to redirect the beam of light. The more sophisticated scanners incorporate a means to change color, adjust beam size and beam quality, and insert patterns in the beam of light. There are several manufacturers of scanners. Some require dedicated control systems to operate the equipment; others can be operated on personal computers or even with signals generated by modern lighting control boards. The scanning lights are generally available for sale as well as rental. Although the control of these fixtures can be complex, some systems can be operated by a minimally trained stage electrician rather than requiring a highly skilled and specially trained operator.

SPECIAL EFFECTS

Projection of abstract and pictorial images has been treated as a way to "paint the stage" as well as a means to create special effects with light. Other kinds of special effects can be achieved utilizing both standard and specialized equipment.

A **wall of light** can be created by focusing a number of ellipsoidal spotlights, rainlights, or beam projectors in a row straight down at the floor or up in the air. If the light is sufficiently bright and the area behind it is backed with a black drape, it will appear that a wall of light has been created. The effect can be strengthened by adding fog to the atmosphere. A chemical fog machine is most effective for this purpose. The intense beams of light become strongly apparent as they strike the mist in the air.

Flashes may be created a number of ways on stage. Whether the audience is to perceive the effect as lightning, explosions, or fireworks is mostly dependent on sound effects and the situation in the performance.

One source of flashes available is a **strobe light**. This is a lighting instrument that is designed to flash a very bright white light rapidly and repeatedly. The frequency of flashes can be adjusted from a moderately slow rate of 1 flash per second to as high as 12 flashes per second. Better strobes have a built-in fan to keep the lamp cool and require a protective lens in case the lamp should shatter. When used to simulate lightning or an explosion, the most effective results are achieved by placing the strobe light a few feet in front of the bottom of a cyclorama and directing the flash at the drop. This will appear as a bright flash of lightning or an explosion at a distance.

It is the law in some states and a courtesy everywhere to notify the audience that a strobe light will be used during the performance because *the repeating flash of a strobe light can trigger an epileptic seizure.*

The simplest way to get the sense of an offstage explosion is to set off a camera flashbulb. Disposable flashbulbs work best because the flash lingers a little longer than more modern electronic flash units for cameras. A flashbulb that is shot from the wing toward the stage creates a good effect as well as a flash that is set off behind a platform or other scenic unit on stage. Any explosion is more credible when accompanied by appropriate sound effects.

Flash paper is a chemical-impregnated tissue that has a low ignition point and will instantly burst into flame. The 12" square sheets will burn in the air for a moment and then disappear. They can be ignited with a match, cigarette, or any other brief spark. The paper burns rapidly and at a relatively cool temperature so it usually will not ignite anything else. *CAUTION*: **Flash paper and any other fire effects should not be used in the vicinity of explosives or highly flammable materials.**

Flash powder is a combination of black powder and gun powder that is ignited in a **flash pot** by means of an electric spark. *CAUTION*: **Only a commercially manufactured flash pot system should be used. Operation of the system should be strictly according to the directions that come with the equipment. Be sure that the flash pot is disconnected and the system is turned off whenever loading it.**

The better flash systems use a key-operated switch that sends current through the flash circuit for just a moment to cause a spark in the igniter wire, which explodes the flash powder. The flash powder will shoot out of the container in the direction the top of the container is facing. *CAUTION*: **No one within 20 feet should be in direct line with the opening of the flash pot when it is exploded.**

A different but still exciting visual effect can be created with a **mirror ball**. (Figure 5–17). This is a globe covered with small squares of mirrored glass. It is suspended from a motor that causes the ball to rotate at a moderate speed. Very narrow beams of light must be focused on the ball from at least two sides. Each light may be white or colored. The light striking the ball will be reflected in a bright pattern of moving sparkles of light. Most motors used with mirror balls have a single speed. However, if a motor can be adapted with a controllable rate of speed, almost dizzying effects can be created.

A **chase light** is another moving-light effect. A chase-light system consists of a row of lights and a controller. The lights turn on and off in sequence to give the effect of a moving row of lights. This effect often appears on the signs outside movie theatres or on arrow signs attracting customers to special sales. A chase system consists of interplugging sections of track or flexible ropes of lights that are connected to a controller. Depending on the sophistication of the controller, the lights may be set to turn on in sequence, called **light chase,** or turn off in sequence, called **dark chase,** at a fixed rate of speed or a random speed or to seem to move in response to music or other sounds, even an amplified human voice.

Ultraviolet light (UV) is normally seen as an intense purple beam of light. When UV light falls on a white shirt or on certain colors, whatever is illuminated seems to glow. The glowing effect is created by sensitive particles reflecting the ultraviolet spectrum of light failing on them. UV is present in most light but when projected from a concentrated UV source it can create exciting glow-in-the-dark effects. There are several different kinds of UV equipment available, including fluorescent tube lights and specialized UV filters for other sources of light. In general, these fixtures are effective only when the surface illuminated has been recently treated with UV paints or dyes and is clean, close to the source of UV light, and the general atmosphere is fairly dark around the glowing items. One company has developed a very intense UV light that can be used at long distances of throw and effectively produce strong glowing colors. This equipment projects ultraviolet light with such great intensity that the company has created billboards for daytime use that effectively produce an ultraviolet effect (Figure C–15 and 5–18).

FIGURE 5–17
A mirror ball.

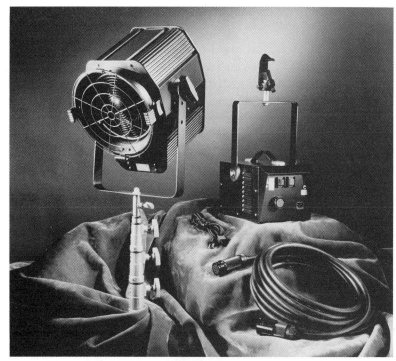

A.

FIGURE 5–18
(A) Ultraviolet spot/flood lighting fixture (WF-400S/ F); (B) ultraviolet floodlight (WF-400F). (Courtesy Wildfire, Inc.)

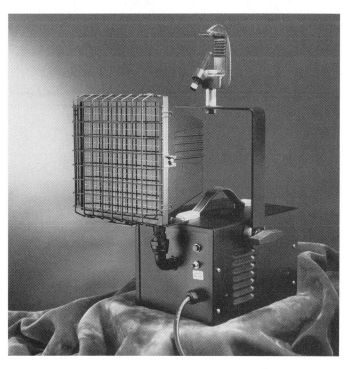

B.

CONCLUSION

Whether projections are used to create special effects or to "paint the stage with light," they can contribute greatly to the overall effect of the performance. The use of any kind of projection demands extra time in the production schedule for experimentation and to make modifications. When the time is available, projections and special effects can greatly enliven a performance.

CHAPTER 6

Electricity

INTRODUCTION

Stage lighting depends on electrical power. Although electricity is a complex physical phenomenon, for most theatre applications it is not necessary to have an extensive knowledge of how power is created or delivered to a facility. It is important, however, to be familiar with a few terms, significant safety precautions, and one simple mathematical formula.

ELECTRICAL TERMS

Electricity flows along a wire under pressure, just as water flows from a faucet with force. The *pressure* that causes electricity to flow is called **volts**. The level of this pressure is established and maintained at a consistent value by the electric company. There are three levels at which voltage is utilized in most U.S. installations. They may be thought of as "super-industrial strength," which is 220 volts—3 phase; "industrial strength," which is 220 volts—single phase; and "household strength," which is 120 volts. Power may be supplied to the theatre at any one of these strengths, but it is used by the equipment at the "household strength" of 120 volts.

The amount or *quantity* of electricity that is used by a piece of equipment is its **wattage**, measured in **watts**. This rating is commonly seen when changing light bulbs at home. Any light bulb is identified by its wattage, such as 60, 75, or 100 watts. This not only indicates the quantity of electricity consumed, it also gives a relative indication of the brightness of the bulb.

The amount of power used is directly related to the *rate* or speed at which the power is used; this value is identified as **amperage**, rated in **amps**. Most small appliances, such as a toaster, and all electrical hardware, such as plugs, fuses, wire, and switches, are rated by the maximum amps they can safely conduct.

Each of these values of electricity—*pressure*, **volts**; *quantity*, **watts**; and *rate*, **amps**—are interrelated. Together they provide essential information about the amount of power available and the size and quantity of equipment that may be used at an individual outlet or throughout a building.

Kinds of Service

Although it is much more complex than this analogy, the transportation of electricity may be thought of as a freight-delivery service. There is a multilane highway that extends from the electrical generator to each device that uses electrical power. At the generator, trucks are loaded with power. The trucks travel down one, two, or three highway lanes that are any color other than white or green to where their load is needed. The electrical power is unloaded from the truck for consumption by the electrical device, and the empty truck returns to the generator down a white highway lane. In the event of a break in the colored highway lanes, the trucks will detour down the nearest green lane of the highway to avoid an accident. Although this analogy is very simplistic, it describes the way electrical service works in that positively charged electrons travel along the colored wire of an electrical circuit to the equipment utilizing the electricity, where they give up their positive charge and then return to the generator along the white wire to receive a revitalized charge.

Power is delivered to the theatre from the electric company on transmission wires. There will always be at least two wires connecting the power to the building. The way current flows, one wire, the **hot line**, which is always some color *other than white or green*, brings the power to the building, and the other wire, called the **neutral**, which is *always colored white*, delivers an electrical charge back to the power source. When connected through equipment, this pair of wires is called a **circuit**. The power may be brought into the building on three wires, one white neutral wire, and two hot lines, to deliver **220 volt single-phase service**, or it may come to the building on four wires, three hot lines, and one white neutral line, which constitutes **220 volt three-phase service**.

An additional wire, which is either bare or covered with green insulation, is also incorporated into any modern electrical wiring. This is the **ground** wire. All electrical equipment and systems are supposed to be **grounded**, which means that one wire, which is *always bare or colored green*, will connect the equipment to the earth. In the event of an electrical overload surging through the equipment, the excess power will be drawn away from the equipment and deposited in the earth. Each of the wires that are *not* white or green will be connected to a fuse at some point. *The white (neutral) and green (ground) wires are* **never** *connected to a fuse.*

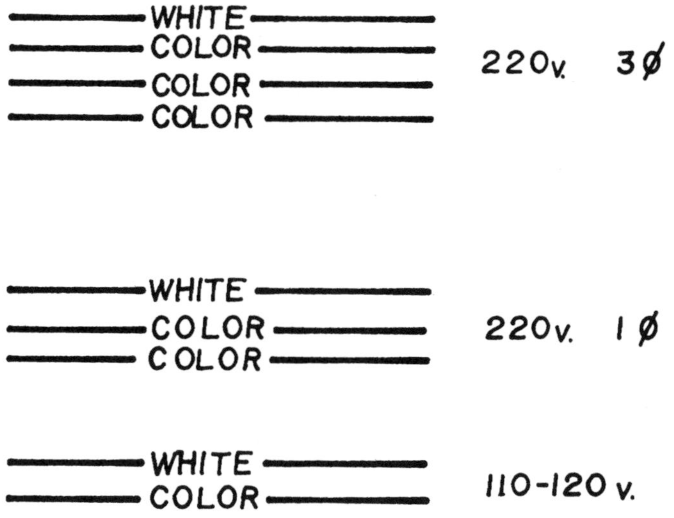

WHITE
COLOR
COLOR
COLOR   220v. 3∅

WHITE
COLOR
COLOR   220v. 1∅

WHITE
COLOR   110-120 v.

FIGURE 6–1
Standard wiring patterns. The wires indicated as "color" will be any color except white or green. A green ground wire should accompany each type of electrical service The symbol ∅ means "phase."

157

To determine how much power is needed to operate equipment or the capacity of equipment being used, it is necessary to apply the **West Virginia (W. Va.) formula** to the known information:

$$W = VA$$

$$\text{Watts} = \text{Volts} \times \text{Amps}$$

Since almost all stage lighting equipment utilizes 120 volt current, that value is usually known and constant.

To Determine the Number of Watts When *Amps* and *Volts* Are *Known*

Formula: **Watts = Volts × Amps**

If volts = 120 and amps = 20, then

$$120 \times 20 = 2400 \text{ watts}$$

If volts = 120 and amps = 12, then

$$120 \times 12 = 1440 \text{ watts}$$

To Determine the Number of Amps When *Watts* and *Volts* Are *Known*

Formula: Amps = Watts ÷ Volts

If volts = 120 and watts = 2400, then

$$2400 \div 120 = 20 \text{ amps}$$

If volts = 120 and watts = 7500, then

$$7500 \div 120 = 62.5 \text{ amps}$$

If volts = 120 and watts = 150, then

$$150 \div 120 = 1.25 \text{ amps}$$

There are times when it is necessary to understand the application of the West Virginia formula with other voltages.

To Determine *Watts* When Volts Are *220* Single-Phase

Formula: Watts = Volts × Amps

If volts = 220 1ϕ and amps = 20, then

$$220 \times 20 = 4400 \text{ watts}$$

If volts = 220 1ϕ and amps = 50, then

$$220 \times 50 = 11,000 \text{ watts}$$

To Determine *Watts* When *Volts Are 220 Three-Phase*

Formula: Watts = (Volts × Amps) × 3

If volts = 220 3ϕ and amps = 20, then

(220 × 20) × 3 = 13,200 watts

If volts = 220 3ϕ and amps = 100, then

(220 × 100) × 3 = 66,000 watts

To Determine *Amps* When *Volts Are 220 Single-Phase*

Formula: Amps = Watts ÷ Volts

If volts = 220 1ϕ and watts = 44,000, then

44,000 ÷ 220 = 200 amps

If volts = 220 1ϕ and watts = 2400, then

2400 ÷ 220 = 10.9 amps

To Determine *Amps* When *Volts Are 220 Three-Phase*

Formula: Amps = (Watts ÷ Volts) ÷ 3

If volts = 220 3ϕ and watts = 44,000, then

(44,000 ÷ 220) ÷ 3 = 66.6 amps

If volts = 220 3ϕ and watts = 2400, then

(2400 ÷ 220) ÷ 3 = 3.63 amps

With the ability to determine the quantity of power needed or carried by equipment, it is possible to determine the size wiring, electrical service, or lamps that may be used.

CURRENT LIMITING AND CIRCUIT PROTECTION

Any point in an electrical system is capable of drawing 100% of the power generated by the electric company. However, each part of the system has a maximum capacity of power it can safely handle. This is determined by a number of factors, especially the physical size of the equipment. The amount of electricity allowed into any portion of an electrical system is restricted by fuses and circuit breakers that limit the flow of current and protect the circuits. Either device is designed to fail, blow out, or shut off if it is asked to carry an excess amount of electrical current. These devices are intentionally the weakest links in any electrical system. By being the first part of the system to fail due to an overload of electrical demand, a fuse or circuit breaker protects all of the other equipment drawing power on the line it protects. A fuse or circuit breaker will fail when too much equipment is connected to a circuit at one time, power attempts to take a shortcut outside of actual wiring, or when two bare wires cross, thus demanding more power to flow through the fuse or circuit breaker than it is designed to carry.

Fuses

Fuses are available in two styles: plug fuses and cartridge fuses. A **plug fuse** (Figure 6–2A) is a small metal and glass or metal, glass, and fiber device that screws into a base in the same way a household light bulb screws into a socket. Inside the fuse there is either a narrow metal band or a spring-loaded wire visible through the top. When the fuse is in good condition, the metal band is solid or the spring is stretched tight. When the fuse "blows," the metal band literally burns away, leaving a gap in the middle of the fuse, or the spring contracts, also breaking the flow of electricity. When a fuse blows, the cause of the electrical failure must be found and removed, and only then should the fuse be replaced. A fuse cannot be repaired. A good supply of spare fuses of the appropriate size should always be kept on hand. When a fuse is replaced, one of exactly the same type and capacity must be used. A plug fuse is rated by the maximum amps it may carry; this is printed on the top of the fuse. One variety of plug fuse, called *Fusestats*, screws into special nonremovable inserts that restrict the size fuse that may be used to ensure that the proper circuit protection is consistently provided.

A **cartridge fuse** (Figure 6–2B) looks like a cardboard tube with a metal band or blade at each end. These devices fulfill exactly the same function as plug fuses but are primarily used to protect high-capacity circuits. The maximum load of these devices may be printed on the tube but is usually stamped into the metal bands at the top and bottom. The interior of a cartridge fuse is not visible, so the only way to tell if one is blown is to test it in a circuit or with a meter. Cartridge fuses should only be handled with a fuse-puller, a special tool used by electricians to remove and replace these devices, or when the fuse is mounted in a protected block that must be withdrawn from the circuit to permit access to the fuse.

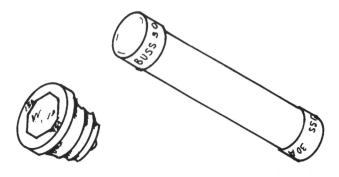

FIGURE 6–2
(A) Plug Fuse; (B) cartridge fuse.

A.   B.

There is a family of smaller cartridge fuses that are made of either ceramic or glass with a metal band at the top and bottom. These devices, found in automobiles or under round or square caps on electrical and electronic equipment, are generally designed to protect low-capacity circuits. Each of these fuses is slightly different in design, purpose, and capacity, and each type is designed for a special purpose. The fuse may be slow-blow or extremely quick-blow or carry minute levels of current. *It is imperative that these fuses are replaced* **only** *with* **exact matches** *of their designation and amp rating, which is stamped in the metal band at the ends.* Simply matching the appearance of the fuse is not adequate and may end up destroying equipment.

Some fuses are designed to meet special protection requirements. One type is used on circuits with electric motors. These require a **slow-blow fuse**, which allows a brief surge of extra power to pass through it to start the motor without blowing out the fuse. Another type of fuse is used on circuits with electronic equipment, such as computers, which require extremely fast response to protect the equipment from damage.

Circuit Breaker

A circuit breaker serves the same function as a fuse but is not disposable. One of these devices looks like a sturdy switch. It may be mounted as part of a group in a panel or electric box, or a circuit breaker might be installed on an individual piece of equipment such as a dimmer. A circuit breaker protects a circuit by **tripping**, that is, automatically turning off when excess power is passed through it. After the cause for the circuit to trip has been eliminated, the switch can be reset. As a result, these devices are more convenient than fuses because they do not have to be replaced each time there is a failure. When a circuit breaker is turned on or off, it will feel very firm and rigid in its position. When it is tripped, the switch will either snap to the "off" position or to a "tripped" position halfway between on and off; the switch will not align with any other breakers that are definitely on or definitely off and it will feel springy in its position. To reset the breaker it must be switched fully to the off position and then switched back on. Like fuses, circuit breakers are available in various sizes and are rated by amps stamped on the end of the switch. These devices are designed to protect circuits—they are not intended to be used as an on–off switch like a wall switch. Used regularly in this manner, a circuit breaker will wear out and require replacement.

DISTRIBUTION OF ELECTRICAL POWER

Wire

Electricity is distributed in a building through wires that may be within walls or in pipes or metal moldings attached to the walls. There are numerous kinds of wire that may be used. Some are intended for permanent installation to be kept entirely within walls, and others are intended for portable use as extension cords.

All wire consists of two components, the conductor and the insulation, which determine how it may be used. The **conductor** is the part that carries the electrical current. It is usually made from copper or a copper alloy that may be a single, solid wire or a bundle of fine, flexible strands. No matter the composition, the diameter of wire is identified as its "gauge." The smaller the gauge number, the thicker the wire down to gauge 0, and there is even wire as large as 0000. **Insulation** encases the conductor to prevent electrical current from flowing out of it and to protect the wire from physical damage. The insulation is colored to make it easier to identify a single wire at each end of a bundle of cables or in a cord without having to trace the wire its entire length. The use of two colors of wire insulation is strictly regulated in the United States. **Wire with *green* insulation may only be used as a *grounding* wire; wire with *white* insulation must be used on the *neutral* line.**

A broad array of insulations is available for permanent wiring as well as for portable cords. One insulation is a Teflon material for high-temperature use, another is oil resistant, and yet others have different characteristics. Wire used inside walls has different insulation than the wire used to make extension cords. Wire is identified by the (1) size of the conductor, (2) the number of conductors, (3) whether it is solid or stranded, and (4) the kind of insulation that it has. Table 6–1 lists several wire sizes and the maximum load each may carry.

TABLE 6-1

Wire gauges and capacities for portable cable (S, So, and SJ cable).

Wire Gauge	Capacity in Amps
18	7
16	10
14	15
12	20
10	25
8	30

Distribution Equipment

In commercial buildings such as theatres, permanent wiring is installed in metal pipes called **conduit**. These pipes provide a protected path for the wires in or on walls, ceilings, and floors. The wiring connects with theatrical distribution equipment of various types. Often, **connector strips** (Figure 6–3A) are mounted on light pipes over the stage and audience seating. These are long metal troughs about 4" × 4" with either female sockets mounted in them or **pigtails**, short electrical cords with plugs at the end, hanging from them. A connector strip might be supplemented by or replaced with a floor or wall pocket. A **wall pocket** is a metal box either in or on the wall that has outlets in it, and a **floor pocket** (Figure 6–3C) is a covered metal box recessed in the floor that also has outlets in it. Another device for distributing power is a **borderlight cable**. This is a large cable composed of several individually insulated wires that may have as many as 24 or more different circuits wired through it. The thick, heavy wire may terminate in either a mass of plugs or a box with flush connectors or pigtails (Figure 6–3B).

Many facilities avoid the cost of theatrical connector strips by installing conduit with outlets at frequent intervals to distribute power around the stage. This system is adequate when only a small number of circuits are involved. However, an excessive amount of pipe, wire, and labor may be needed, so it is usually more practical to use connector strips for larger installations. Other performance spaces have no permanent wiring. Often plays are produced in spaces other than

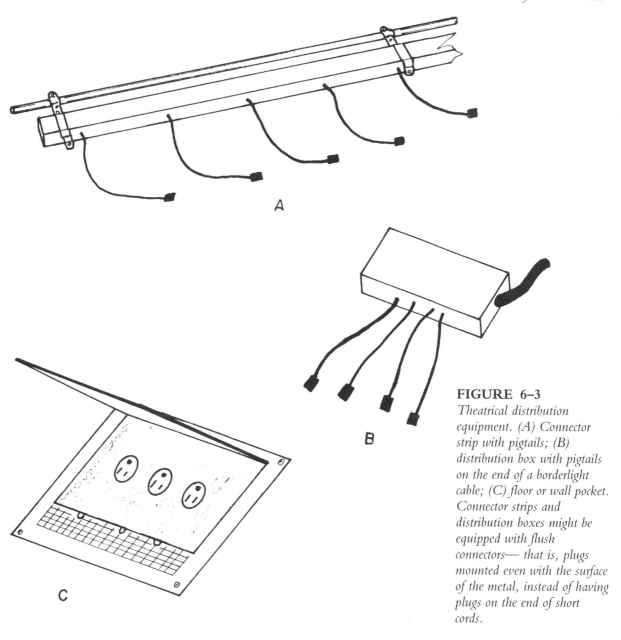

FIGURE 6–3
Theatrical distribution equipment. (A) Connector strip with pigtails; (B) distribution box with pigtails on the end of a borderlight cable; (C) floor or wall pocket. Connector strips and distribution boxes might be equipped with flush connectors— that is, plugs mounted even with the surface of the metal, instead of having plugs on the end of short cords.

theatres so there is no means to distribute power from dimmers or even from wall outlets. In that case, flexible extension cords must be run from the lighting instruments to the point of control, whether it is a bank of dimmers or a wall switch. When extension cords are used they must be the proper size wire to carry the load. If the wire must travel a long distance (100 feet or more), an oversized gauge of wire should be used. Extension cords terminate with plugs that permit temporary connection to lighting instruments and other equipment. The plugs should match the connectors on the lighting fixtures, as discussed in Chapter 4.

Whether or not a built-in electrical distribution system is available, extension cords are almost always necessary to install the lighting for a show. Although it is possible to purchase extension cords from the hardware store, these usually are made from #16 SJ wire, which is only rated to carry 10 amps; SJ insulation is *not* rated for use on the floor, abrades badly, and may be cut easily. Sometimes it is possible to find better extension cords at the hardware store. Hardware store extension cords are acceptable so long as their capacity is not exceeded, the wire is protected as much as possible from physical damage, and it is inspected regularly. It is usually preferable to build extension cords or have them made from 14/3 or 12/3 S or SO cable. This is 14 gauge or 12 gauge stranded wire with three conductors and rubber insulation. The SO cable is also resistant to damage or penetration by oil. **Always check state and local codes and ordinances for restrictions on the size and type of cable that may be used for portable cords in the theatre.**

WIRING PORTABLE EQUIPMENT

To Make an Extension Cord

Materials List	*Equipment List*
25'-0" #12/3 S cable	Matte knife
1 male parallel blade u-ground plug	Wire stripper
1 female parallel blade u-ground connector	Screwdriver

1. Draw a line on the insulation 2" from each end of the cable. Wrap one end of the cable over the index finger of your left hand and bend the cable into a tight U (Figure 6–4). Press the blade of the matte

FIGURE 6–4
Safely stripping the insulation off of a rubber cord.

knife against the black rubber insulation until the rubber splits and it is possible to see the colored insulation inside the cable. Keeping the wire in a tight U, rotate the cable and press the knife blade down again with no more force than is necessary to cut through the black rubber. Repeat rotating the cable and pressing the blade into the insulation until the black rubber insulation has been cut all the way through all the way around its perimeter.

2. Pull the 2" chunk of rubber insulation off the end of the cable. Spread apart the three wires and paper or fabric strands inside the cable. Cut the paper or fabric strands flush with the end of the rubber insulation. Inspect the insulation of the three remaining wires to be sure that it has not been penetrated by the knife. If the inner insulation has been cut, cut off the three wires at the end of the black insulation and start over.

3. Cut each of the three remaining wires to a length of 1". Measure ½" down each of the three individual wires inside the cable. Find the groove marked "12" on the wire strippers and place it on the ½" mark on one of the wires. The beveled side of the stripper should face the end of the wire. Close the handles on the stripper and rotate it. With the stripper still closed, pull the handle toward the end of the wire to remove the short piece of insulation. Repeat on each end of each wire (Figure 6–5).

FIGURE 6–5
A stripped wire with about ⅝" of bare copper exposed.

4. Loosen the two screws on the metal band that sticks up from the back of the male plug; this is the **strain relief**. Do not remove the screws, just loosen them until there are only two or three threads exposed at its point. Discard the rubber ring that was inside the strain relief.

5. Turn the plug over (Figure 6–6). There are two or three screws that attach the top half to the bottom half of the plug. Loosen those screws until the top and bottom parts separate. It is not necessary to remove the screws from the plug. Slide the top half of the plug, the one with the strain relief, over the end of the cable. The part that joins the bottom of the plug should face the end of the cable, and the strain relief should be toward the middle of the cable.

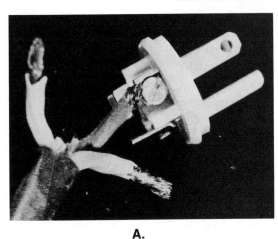

A.

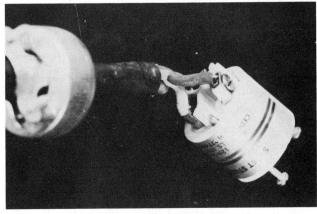

B.

FIGURE 6–6

Plugs are made with various kinds of connections inside. (A) Wire twisted into a tight bundle and then wrapped around the terminal bolt in the direction it turns to tighten; (B) wire twisted into a tight bundle and slipped between two plates that firmly grip it as they are brought together with the terminal bolt.

6. There are three screws holding little plates inside the plug; these are the **terminals** for the wire. The green screw always connects the green ground wire, the silver screw always connects the white neutral wire, and the brass screw always connects the colored hot wire. Make sure each of the screws is loosened as far as possible. Twist the end of each of the three bare wires into three individual neat solid bundles so no "wild hairs" stick out. Find the green wire and slip the bare end of it between the two metal plates of the terminal that has the green bolt. Tighten the green bolt firmly and make sure that no bare wire or wild strands of wire are exposed above the plates of the terminal. It may be necessary to cut off some of the bare wire. Now slip the bare end of the white wire between the two plates of the terminal with the silver screw. Tighten it down and check for tightness and stray strands of wire. Finally, attach the colored wire to the remaining terminal with the brass-colored screw.

The terminals on older plugs are only a single metal plate and a bolt. To make a connection to these plugs, twist the stranded wire into tight bundles and bend the bare wire into a U to hook under the bolt so that it wraps around it in the same direction the bolt turns to tighten. Tighten down the bolt. The bundle of twisted wires will crush firmly between the bolt and the metal plate. Once again, check for a firm fastening and stray strands of wire.

7. Slide the top of the plug down onto the bottom portion of the plug, aligning the bolt holes and any grounding tab. There are usually obvious notches that must be aligned. Press the connecting screws through their holes and tighten them down. The plug should be solid, secure, and free of gaps between the top and bottom sections.

8. Press the end of the cable down into the plug until the black rubber insulation is between the metal blades of the strain relief and tighten the screws that hold those bands until they just begin to compress the insulation.

9. Strip the cable and attach the female plug to the opposite end of the cable.

10. Test the cable by first plugging it into a known working outlet. If the circuit breaker or fuse does not blow, then plug a known working light into the cable. The light should come on.

If the cable is to be manufactured with twistlock connectors, the same process is followed, except disassembly and reassembly of the plug and design of the strain relief may be somewhat different. When pin connectors are used, the terminals inside the connectors are not color coded. The grounding terminal is usually identified by a "G" engraved on the cover of the plug. The 15/20-amp pin connectors use the middle pin for ground. Standard practice requires that the white neutral wire be connected to the terminal closest to the ground terminal. Larger capacity pin connectors use a different pin for the ground wire.

Often it is necessary to plug two lights into a single outlet. This is accomplished with a two-fer (as in two-for-one). A **two-fer** (Figure 6–7) is a male plug with two short pigtails coming out of it; each pigtail terminates with a female plug. A **three-fer** is the same as a two-fer but with three pigtails rather than two. Two-fers and three-fers may be purchased or can be homemade for less cost. **Check state and local codes and ordinances regarding appropriate wire sizes that may be used for portable cords.**

FIGURE 6–7
Pigtail two-fer with one male and two female plugs.

To Make a Two-Fer

Materials List

2 pieces 14/3 SJ cable
  2'-0" long

1 male parallel blade
  u-ground plug

2 female parallel blade
  u-ground plugs

Equipment List

Matte knife

Wire stripper

Screwdriver

Pliers

1. Strip both ends of each piece of cable. Be very careful because the outer rubber insulation of SJ cable cuts very easily. Draw a line on the insulation 1" from each end of the cable. Wrap one end of the cable over the index finger of your left hand and bend the cable into a tight U. Press the blade of the matte knife against the black rubber insulation until the rubber splits and it is possible to see the insulated wire and paper and fabric insulation inside the cable. Rotate the cable and press the knife blade down again with no more force than necessary to cut through the black rubber. Repeat rotating the cable and pressing the blade into the insulation until the black rubber insulation has been cut all the way through all the way around its perimeter.

2. Pull the 1" chunk of rubber insulation off the end of the cable. Spread apart the three wires and paper or fabric strands inside the cable. Cut the paper or fabric strands flush with the end of the rubber insulation.

3. Measure ⅝" down each of the three individual wires inside the cable. Find the groove marked "14" on the wire stripper and place

them on the ⅝" mark on one of the wires. The beveled side of the stripper should face the end of the wire. Close the handles on the stripper and rotate it around the wire. With the stripper still closed, pull the handle toward the end of the wire to remove the short piece of insulation. Repeat on each end of each wire.

4. Loosen the two screws on the strain relief. Do not remove the screws, just loosen them until there are only two or three threads on the screw exposed at the screw point. Slide the rubber ring that was inside the strain relief over the end of the wire onto the black rubber insulation.

5. Turn the plug over. There are two or three screws that attach the top half of the plug to the bottom half. Loosen those screws until the two halves of the plug separate. Slide the top half of the plug over the end of the cable. The part that joins the bottom of the plug should face the end of the cable.

6. Loosen the terminal screws as far as possible. Twist each end of each of the three stripped wires into a neat solid bundle with no strands sticking out. Find the green wire and slip the bare end of it between the two metal plates of the terminal that has the green bolt. Tighten the green bolt firmly and make sure that all of the strands of the bare wire are between the plates of the terminal. Now slip the bare end of the white wire between the two plates of the terminal with the silver screw. Tighten it and check for a firm connection and stray strands of wire. Finally, attach the colored wire to the remaining terminal with the brass-colored screw.

The terminals on older plugs are only a single metal plate and a bolt. To make a connection to these plugs, twist each bare wire into tight bundles and bend the bare wire into a U to hook under the bolt so that it wraps around the bolt in the same direction the bolt turns to tighten. Tighten down the bolt. The bundle of twisted wires will crush firmly between the bolt and the metal plate. Once again, check for a firm fastening and stray strands of wire.

7. Slide the top of the plug down onto the bottom portion of the plug, aligning the bolt holes and any grounding tab. There are usually obvious notches that must be aligned. Press the connecting screws through their holes and tighten them down. The plug should be solid, secure, and free of gaps between the top and bottom sections.

8. Press the end of the cable down into the plug until the black rubber insulation is between the metal blades of the strain relief and tighten the screws that hold those bands until they begin to compress the insulation.

9. Disassemble the male plug. Discard the rubber ring. Force the bare end of each cable into the top of the male plug. Wire this plug in exactly the same pattern as the female connectors, but attach *both* green, *both* white, and *both* black wires to each appropriate terminal. Check very carefully for stray threads of wire; then reassemble the plug and tighten the strain relief.

10. Test the two-fer on a known working circuit with a known working light.

When a lighting system uses parallel-blade U-ground plugs, an easier two-fer can be assembled using standard electrical hardware. **Be**

sure that this type of two-fer is acceptable to state and local codes for portable wiring of stage equipment.

To Make a Handy Box Two-Fer

Materials List

1 piece of 12/3 S cable 3'-0" long

1 duplex handy box

1 cable connector

1 duplex receptacle

1 duplex cover plate

1 male parallel-blade u-ground plug

1 piece of green insulated wire 4" long

1 spare green terminal screw

Equipment List

Matte knife

Wire stripper

Screwdriver

Pliers

FIGURE 6–8
Removing the knockout on a handy box.

1. Strip both ends of the cable. Attach one end of the cable to the male plug.

2. Firmly rap the metal knockout at one end of the handy box. It should begin to bend away from the box. Grasp the disc with the pliers and twist it off of the box (Figure 6–8).

3. Disassemble the cable connector and insert the threaded portion through the hole. Thread the ring onto the cable connector inside the box and tighten it as firmly as possible, tapping the ring with a screwdriver until it bites into the metal of the box. The cable connector protects the wire from abrasion as it enters the box and prevents the cable from being yanked out of the box. Slide the bare end of the cable through the cable connector (Figure 6–9).

4. Strip each end of the short green wire. Twist the bare end of the green wire in the cable together with the bare end of the short green wire. Attach the pair of wires to the green terminal at the top of the duplex plug.

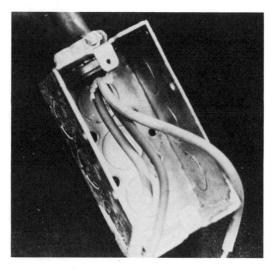

FIGURE 6–9
Stripped cable inserted through the cable connector in one end of the handy box.

Electricity

5. Twist the end of each remaining wire into a firm bundle. Then attach the white wire to one of the silver terminals and the black wire to one of the brass terminals. To make the connection to the terminal, bend the bare wire into a U and hook it under the bolt so that it wraps around the bolt in the same direction the bolt turns to tighten. Tighten down the bolt. The bundle of twisted wires will crush firmly between the bolt and the metal plate. Check for a firm fastening and stray strands of wire (Figure 6–10).

6. One of the small holes on the back of the handy box is threaded. Start the extra green grounding screw into that hole, and then wrap the free end of the short green wire around the terminal screw and tighten it firmly.

7. There are two little metal wings with holes in them on either side of the plates at the top and bottom of the plug. Using pliers, twist these wings up and down until they break off. Press the duplex plug

A.

B.

C.

FIGURE 6–10
(A) Wired duplex plug; (B) duplex plug installed in handy box; (C) cover on duplex plug.

170

into the handy box and fasten the screws at the top and bottom into the threaded holes at the top and bottom of the handy box. The duplex outlet should be firmly fastened in the box.

8. Pull all but 1" of slack cable out of the box and tighten the screws on the cable connector until it begins to compress the insulation on the cable.

9. Test the two-fer by plugging it into a known working outlet and then plugging a known working light into it. If the light does not come on, disconnect the two-fer, disassemble the plug, and check all connections. Then retest it.

10. Place the outlet cover over the plugs, insert the little screw in the hole at the center of the cover, and tighten it down.

Sometimes it is necessary to add a switch to an extension cord. In fact, it is even possible to control lights by putting switches into extension cord lines. It might also be valuable to build two-fers with a switch in the same box as the outlets. A switch is a fairly simple device. It cuts off power by disconnecting the flow of electricity through the *colored* (*not white or green*) wire in a circuit. ***CAUTION***: **Be sure that this equipment meets state and local codes for portable wiring on stage.**

To Build an In-Line Switch

Materials List	*Equipment List*
1 switch	Matte knife
1 handy box	Wire stripper
2 cable connectors	Screwdriver
1 switch plate	Pliers
1 12/3 S cable 6'-0" long	
1 male plug	
1 female plug	

1. Strip each end of the cable in preparation for attachment to the plugs.

2. At the middle of the cable, strip the rubber insulation off an area 4" long. To do this, make two cuts all the way around the perimeter of the rubber insulation; then carefully start a cut in the long direction between the two circular cuts. Grab an edge of the flap that has been formed and tear the rubber insulation off the wire. If this demands too much strength, then *very, very carefully* cut through the rubber insulation between the two circular cuts and peel off the section of insulation. Cut away any additional paper and fabric insulating materials.

3. Cut the colored wire at the middle of the open space and strip ⅝" of insulation off each new end of the wire.

4. Remove the knockouts at the top and bottom of the handy box and insert a cable connector in each hole. Firmly tighten the threaded ring of each cable connector until it bites into the metal of the box. Slide the wire through both holes, locating the stripped center section at the handy box (Figure 6–11).

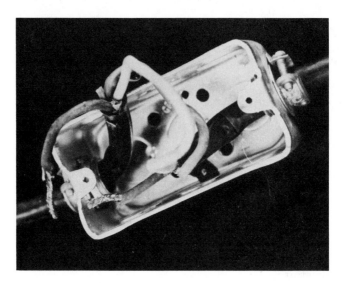

FIGURE 6–11
Stripped cable in handy box ready for connection to a switch.

5. Attach one end of the colored wire to the top screw and the other end of the colored wire to the bottom screw on the side of the switch. To make the connection to the terminal, bend the bare wire into a U and hook it under the bolt so that it wraps around the bolt in the same direction the bolt turns to tighten. Tighten down the bolt. The bundle of twisted wires will crush firmly between the bolt and the metal plate. Make sure that the connections are firm and tight and there are no threads of wire sticking out (Figure 6–12).

6. Break off the two little circle-wings at each side of the plates at the top and bottom of the switch. Press the switch into the handy box and fasten the screws at the top and bottom to the threaded hole with which they align in the box.

7. Pull most of the slack out of each end of the wire coming out of the box and tighten the cable connectors until they begin to compress the black rubber insulation.

8. Attach the male plug to the wire coming out of the "off" side of the box and the female plug to the end of the wire coming out of the "on" side of the box.

9. Test the switch by plugging it into a known working outlet and then plugging a known working light into the other end. Turn the switch on. If the light does not come on, turn the switch off, disconnect the unit, and check all of the connections.

10. Place the switch plate over the switch, insert the two little screws in the holes in the cover, and tighten it in place.

Sometimes it is necessary to construct a special light or simply attach a cable to a socket. This process is similar to wiring a plug.

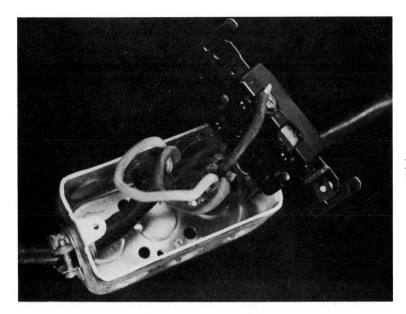

FIGURE 6–12
Wired switch.

To Wire Cable to a Ceramic Socket on an Octagonal Box (Figure 6–13)

Materials List

1 ceramic socket
1 octagonal box to fit
   the socket (an appropriately
   sized square box may
   be used instead)
1 cable connector
1 14/3 S cable 10'-0" long
1 male plug
1 piece of green insulated
   wire 4" long
1 green terminal screw

Equipment List

Matte knife
Wire stripper
Screwdriver
Pliers

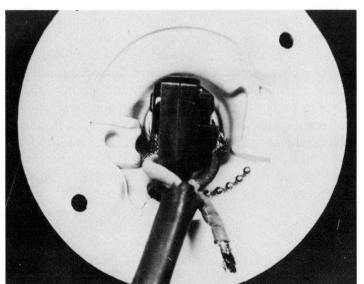

FIGURE 6–13
Rear view of ceramic socket wired for installation in a handy box.

1. Strip 4" of rubber insulation off one end of the cable. Then strip ⅝" of insulation off each individual wire in the cable. Twist the end of each wire into a neat tight bundle.

2. Remove a knockout on one side of the octagonal box and insert the cable connector, tightening the knurled ring down firmly until it begins to bite into the metal of the box. Slide the stripped end of the cable through the hole.

3. Strip ⅝" insulation off each end of the short green wire. Twist the bare end of the green wire on the cable together with one end of the short green wire and attach both to the green bolt on the socket.

4. Attach the white wire to the silver terminal and the black wire to the brass terminal of the socket. To make the connection to the terminal, bend the bare wire into a U and hook it under the bolt so that it wraps around the bolt in the same direction the bolt turns to tighten. Tighten down the bolt. The bundle of twisted wires will crush firmly between the bolt and the metal plate. Make sure that the connections are firm and tight and there are no threads of wire sticking out.

5. Find the small threaded hole in the back of the octagonal box and start the green terminal screw into that hole. Wrap the remaining end of the green wire around the screw and tighten it in place.

6. Press the ceramic socket in place on top of the octagonal box and insert the long screws that came with the socket into the appropriate holes. Tighten the screws down firmly but not so tight as to crack the ceramic socket.

7. Pull most of the slack out of the octagonal box and tighten the screws on the cable connector until it begins to compress the rubber insulation.

8. Strip the other end of the wire and attach the male plug.

9. Screw a known working light bulb into the socket, plug it in, and test it.

CONCLUSION

The lights in a theatre will not work without electrical power. This essential source of energy can be wonderfully helpful to create the appropriate mood for a production, but it must be understood and respected. It is imperative that anyone working with lighting equipment stay conscious not only of its contribution to the production but also of its potential dangers to people, equipment, and buildings. If the proper equipment is used, wiring is done with care, and safe procedures applied when handling the equipment, the work and workers should be safe. Once lights have been mounted and focused in the appropriate locations and power brought to them, it is necessary to control the lights.

CHAPTER 7

Lighting Control

INTRODUCTION

Electricity is distributed by means of wiring to each lighting instrument. Whether the wiring is temporary or permanent, the electrical power passes through some kind of device to control the lights. Lighting control can be as simple as turning on a wall switch or plugging an extension cord into an outlet, or the control can allow subtle changes in hundreds of individual lights and circuits by means of automatic devices that regulate not only the intensity of the light but the time that it takes to change from one lighting moment to another.

The technical elements of lighting control—that is, the construction of dimmers, wiring of control circuits, and so forth—is extremely complex and in general is left to the profession of engineers. However, understanding the operation of lighting control boards is essential to the theatre practitioner and is exciting once a few fundamental concepts about lighting control systems are understood.

There are two basic parts to a lighting control system: (1) the control board and (2) the dimmers. These may be a single integrated unit or two separate devices connected by wires. Each device—that is, the control board and the dimmers—might be permanently installed in a facility or may be portable equipment that is temporarily connected to the lights. An operator, by means of the control board, instructs the dimmers what to do. Based on the information received from the control board, the dimmers modify the electrical current sent to each individual light.

Lights are connected to the dimmers in one of three ways: (1) lighting circuits may be permanently wired to each of the dimmers, (2) extension cords may be plugged directly into each dimmer for a temporary set-up, or (3) circuits built into a theatre can be temporarily connected to the dimmers by means of a patch panel.

PATCH PANELS

When a lamp in a bedroom is plugged in, the nearest available outlet is usually selected so that it is unnecessary to use an extension cord to make the light work. Some bedrooms have an outlet that is controlled by a switch. In those rooms it is preferable to plug the lamp into the outlet that is controlled by the switch, even if it is not the nearest available outlet, and plug a clock, for instance, into the outlet that is not controlled by a switch. To do this it may be necessary to use an extension cord for both the clock and the lamp so they may be put in the most convenient locations but plugged to the appropriate outlet. If it were possible to make any outlet in this room controlled or not controlled by the switch, the extension cords would not be necessary. If the wiring from both wall outlets in the room ended at a panel where they could be selectively connected to a switched or nonswitched circuit, the lamp and clock could be plugged in anywhere and the circuit could be assigned to a switch or not, as desired. This is the concept of patching.

In some theatres, theatrical lighting circuits are distributed throughout the production space, in the beams, box booms on the electrical pipes on stage, and even in the floor of the stage. There may be only 12 or 18 circuits or there might be several hundred theatrical lighting circuits. The stage lighting instruments plug into these circuits. The individual circuits may be **hard wired**—that is, permanently connected to individual dimmers—or the circuits may end up at a patch panel where they may be plugged into any dimmer as desired.

A **patch panel** allows any theatrical circuit to be temporarily plugged into any dimmer. The **patching**—the temporary connection of circuit to dimmer—may always be the same for a facility or for a show, may change from show to show, or may change from scene to scene during a show. This system allows the theatrical lighting circuits to be arranged in the most convenient groups for control-board operation and to allow the use of more lights for a show than there are dimmers to control them.

For example, a show might use all blue side lights for act one and red side lights for act two, but only have enough dimmers to control one group of these lights at a time. This problem can be solved either by hooking up only the blue lights for the first act, climbing above the audience and stage during intermission to disconnect them, and then connect the red lights to the same circuits for the second act, or by attaching the blue and red lights to their own individual circuits that are replugged to dimmers at the patch panel during intermission.

Since patching can be done at a central panel backstage or in the control booth, it is not necessary to climb ladders and replug lighting instruments above the audience or stage during the show. The only limit on the amount of equipment that may be connected to an individual dimmer through the patch panel is the capacity of the dimmers. The capacity must be strictly observed to prevent overloaded circuits. With some patch panels, the number of patching positions available is also limited (Figure 7–1).

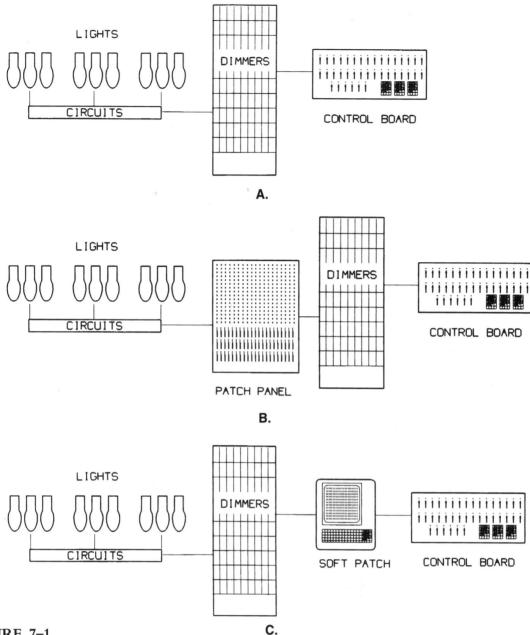

LIGHTS

CIRCUITS

DIMMERS

CONTROL BOARD

A.

LIGHTS

CIRCUITS

PATCH PANEL

DIMMERS

CONTROL BOARD

B.

LIGHTS

CIRCUITS

DIMMERS

SOFT PATCH

CONTROL BOARD

C.

FIGURE 7–1
*Traditional patching systems.
(A) Dimmer per circuit–no
patching; (B) line voltage
patching by which 110 volt
circuits are connected to
dimmers; (C) low voltage soft
patching by which dimmers are
connected to channels of the
control board.*

Direct Plugging

The simplest means of patching is also the most primitive. When
portable equipment is used, power is carried through extension cords
between the dimmers and the lights. The extension cords must plug
in—that is, patch—at the dimmers (Figure 7–2). Once again, if there
are more lights and more circuits than dimmers, the lights may be
selectively patched by connecting one extension cord and then another
to any one dimmer. In this way, the control capacity of the board can
be extended by selecting which lights any dimmer may control at any

FIGURE 7–2
Rear view of a 12-channel dimmer pack with plugs that not only attach circuits to dimmers but may also be used for repatching circuits during a production. (Courtesy Lighting Methods, Inc.)

time and changing that arrangement throughout the course of a production. In this system, the extension cords become **patch cords** and the outlets on the dimmers become the patch panel.

Telephone-Cord Patch

A common patching system is the **telephone-cord patch panel** (Figure 7–3). With this and all other line voltage patch systems, only the hot line (colored wire) of a lighting circuit is patched. The neutral (white) and ground (green) wires bypass the patch panel, so only a single wire is connected between the dimmer and the circuit. A

FIGURE 7–3
Telephone-cord patch panel. (Courtesy Kliegl Bros. Stage Lighting, Inc.)

telephone-cord patch system looks like the old telephone operator (PBX) switchboards. A single-post plug is attached to each colored wire coming from a circuit somewhere in the theatre. These plugs are mounted in a patch panel in an orderly fashion. The plugs may rest flush with the surface (retractable cord) or may simply hang down over the edge of the patch panel (hanging cord). Each of these plugs is attached to a circuit that is permanently wired into the theatre. The circuit number is engraved on the patch plug. Elsewhere a series of holes is arranged on the panel in numbered sections. Each numbered section is connected to a dimmer. A circuit is connected to a dimmer by sliding one of the numbered plugs into one of the holes on the panel. For instance, circuit 17 may be attached to dimmer 24 by sliding the single-pole plug numbered 17 into one of the holes in the section numbered 24. Dimmer number 24 will now control circuit 17. Circuit 39 might also be patched to dimmer 24, and if the dimmer has sufficient capacity, circuit 6 may be plugged as well. So, in this instance, dimmer 24 is controlling the lights on circuits 6, 17, and 39. For another production, circuit 17 might be attached to dimmer 1 or dimmer 11 or whatever dimmer is appropriate; it may be used all by itself or circuit 17 might be joined in dimmer 1 or 11 with any other appropriate circuits.

Telephone patch systems have been manufactured in various designs. The **retractable-cord** system is the most convenient and neatest since it stores excess patch cord out of the way inside the panel. A **hanging cord** system allows the patch cords to drape over the front edge of the panel or hang down from overhead, and slack always remains in the cords. A couple of cautions must be noted when working with telephone patch systems:

1. Never touch any metal portion of a patch plug when making a connection. Should the dimmer be on, the plug will conduct electrical current that may cause electrical shock.

2. Do not **hot patch**—that is, do not plug a patch cord into a dimmer when the dimmer is turned on. This may damage the plug, the light, and the dimmer. Also, if the metal part of the plug is touched while the connection is being made, it is possible to receive an electrical shock.

3. Always hold and pull on the plug, not the cord.

4. Do not drop retractable patch cords so that the plug will slam against the panel surface as the cord retracts. This action may tear the plug off the cord.

5. Do not patch a greater load on a dimmer than the capacity of the dimmer.

Slider Patch

Slider patch systems (Figure 7–4) replace the telephone patch cords and outlets with a series of handles that may be slid from one row to another to connect circuits to dimmers. If a facility has 48 circuits,

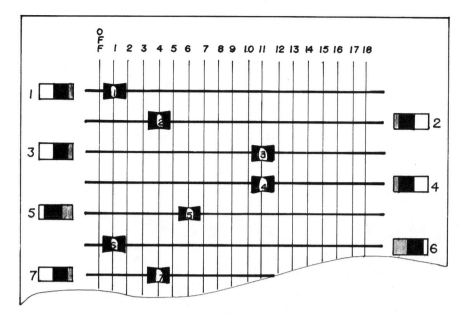

FIGURE 7–4
Slider patch panel.

there will be 48 sliders. Each slider moves to align with a row that is connected to a dimmer. If a facility has 18 dimmers, there will be 18 rows. The slider is then pressed down to make a connection with the appropriate dimmer.

These panels are simple and safe to operate. There are only two cautions that must be observed:

1. Since there is no way to limit the number of sliders that may be assigned to any dimmer, it is very easy to exceed the capacity of the dimmers. Dimmer loads must be checked carefully to prevent over-loading.

2. Any time a slider is moved, it must be fully disengaged to prevent arcing should it pass over a row connected to a dimmer that is turned on. If any dimmer is turned on, a bright spark will flash. This may damage the slider, the dimmer, or the light. Whenever possible, only patch with all of the dimmers turned off. If that is not possible because patching is occurring during a performance, be very careful not to press down on the slider as it moves across the patch panel.

Older slider patch systems that do not fully mask the conductive parts of the panel exist in many facilities. Extreme care must be taken when working with these boards. They should only be patched by an experienced person who is well aware of the danger of electrical shock.

Roto-Patch

A much simpler patch system is a **roto-patch panel** (Figure 7–5). With this system, each circuit in the theatre terminates at a dial on a panel. The dial is rotated to assign the circuit to the appropriate dimmer. This is a very safe system since no electrical parts are exposed. The only precaution that must be taken with this system is to avoid exceeding the capacity of the dimmers. Installation of these systems generally has been limited to facilities with a small quantity of dimmers and circuits.

FIGURE 7–5
Roto-patch panel.

Dimmer per Circuit

Line-voltage patch systems are designed to connect circuits to dimmers when there are fewer dimmers in a facility than there are circuits to be controlled. In some buildings, however, the red, white, and blue borderlights are permanently connected to the dimmers and some spotlight circuits may also be permanently wired to dimmers as well. These facilities do not require patch panels since the equipment is permanently connected. Following the same concept, many modern facilities are designed with a complete array of theatrical lighting circuits permanently installed in the building and each circuit is permanently wired to a dimmer. In other words, in this **dimmer-per-circuit** system, if a theatre has 48 circuits each will be permanently wired to one of 48 dimmers. These facilities do not require a line-voltage patch panel. Whether a lighting control system incorporates line-voltage patching or is dimmer-per-circuit, additional flexibility can be built into the system by utilizing soft-patching. This is a protocol incorporated into many electronic control boards that allows dimmers to be assigned to specific control board groups. Soft-patch is described in greater detail below.

Line-voltage patching increases the flexibility and ease of control of lights by permitting more lighting instruments to be used than the number of dimmers available. Lighting control, however, ultimately depends on the type of dimmers and the capabilities of the control board.

LIGHTING CONTROL SYSTEMS

A lighting control system consists of a control board, where the operator instructs the dimmers as to their output, and the dimmers, which directly modify the current flowing to the lighting circuits. The operator may control this output either by directly operating levers that are an actual part of the dimmer or by communicating with the dimmer by means of a signal sent over a wire from a remote-control board.

Mechanical Dimming and Control

Mechanical lighting control systems integrate the dimmers and the means of control in a single chassis. With these systems, the operator moves a handle that is connected directly to a rotating arm which is a part of the dimmer. The position of that rotating arm changes the electrical output of the dimmer. Either resistance or autotransformer dimmers (Figure 7–6) are used in these out of date systems. Most of these systems have been or should be replaced. Often this aging electrical equipment is worn and unsafe; it is certainly electrically inefficient. Modern electronic control systems are easier to operate, provide much more flexibility of control, and are electrically more efficient.

FIGURE 7–6
Autotransformer control board. (Courtesy Kliegl Bros Stage Lighting, Inc.)

Electronic Dimmers

Electronic technological developments have brought many changes to the way lighting is controlled on stage. Modern dimmers are sophisticated, miniature devices that electronically limit current flowing through a circuit (Figure 7–7). Contemporary dimmers are built around silicon controlled rectifiers (SCRs), thyristors (SSRs), or insulated gate bi-polar transistors (IGBT). This equipment, when instructed by an electronic signal generated by a lighting control system and interpreted by receiving devices in the dimmer rack or dimmer module, limits the voltage in a circuit and thus controls the intensity of

FIGURE 7–7
An SSR dimmer module. (Courtesy Electronic Theatre Controls, Inc.)

lighting fixtures (or power to other devices on the circuit). The dimmers are relatively small, have no moving parts, and generate modest heat output. Since the dimmers respond solely to electronic signals, the dimmers and control system can be widely separated.

In practice, dimmers can be located backstage, under the stage, in the attic, on catwalks overhead, or on a truck parked next to the performance venue—any location so long as the ambient temperature does not exceed acceptable levels. The distance between controller and dimmers is only limited by the strength of signal generated by the control system; the usual acceptable maximum length of wire between dimmers and control is 400 feet. If a greater distance of separation is required, it is sometimes possible to add a signal amplifier to the control line. This feature allows the lighting control board to be placed at the most convenient location to run the show, usually at the back of the auditorium The dimmers can be located at the most convenient location to receive and distribute electrical power, usually backstage. This concept actually allows dimmers to be placed at any convenient location for the operation of a production. Although dimmers are normally placed in portable or permanently installed racks (Figure 7–8), one manufacturer has developed dimmers to be located at the mounting positions of the lights (Figure 7–9).

FIGURE 7–8
Permanent and portable dimmer racks. (Courtesy Electronic Theatre Controls, Inc.)

FIGURE 7–9
Pipe-mounted dimmers based on IGBT technology. (Courtesy Entertainment Technology, Inc.)

Although the actual design of dimmers and dimmer racks differs from one manufacturer to another, electronic dimmers have some characteristics in common. All of the dimmers are designed to receive a signal in a specific electronic language. In the United States, the most common language used for the communication between a lighting control console and the dimmers is called **DMX 512**. This is a standard protocol developed under the auspices of the U.S. Institute for Theatre Technology. A few of the alternate languages used for this communication are **AMX 512**, **CMX 512,** and **AVAB**. Each of these communication protocols refers to the baud rate (speed), information bundle size (bits and bytes), and other details about the way information is transmitted, received, and interpreted by the electronic equipment. Special devices have been developed to allow a system to understand a "foreign" language. The dimmers must have a receiving module that interprets the incoming electronic signal. Some systems have the receiving module incorporated in the actual dimmer module, whereas other systems place the receiving module in a computer card cage located separately in the dimmer rack. Each dimmer has built-in circuit protection devices—normally, fast-acting circuit breakers. Finally, all dimmers have to be equipped with a means to move heat away from the equipment. Some systems are designed to use convection currents, others use fans mounted at the bottom or top of the rack, and some equipment actually has a small fan with each dimmer module. The fans can generate quite a bit of noise, which usually prohibits locating dimmers close to the audience.

Electronic lighting control boards fall into four categories: single-scene control, preset control, preset with memory, and memory lighting control.

Single-Scene Control

The single-scene control board (Figure 7–10) is a small, compact device consisting of **faders** or **pots** (short for **potentiometers**). A typical fader or pot is about 3" long, and ½" to 1" wide. It has a scale of dimmer settings ranging from 0 to 10 engraved in quarter steps on or next to it. There will usually be one pot on the control board for each dimmer in the system. The faders are lined up in a row to create a bank of controls. Associated with each pot is an assignment switch, usually located at the top of the fader. This three-position switch is labeled "Off-Master-Independent." It allows a control channel to be assigned to mastering or to operation independent of the master controller. The *master* is an additional pot, usually located at the left end of the bank of faders, which allows the light levels for a scene to be preset and then proportionally faded onto the stage under the control of that single pot.

The method of operation is fairly simple. Before it is time to turn the lights on and with the master pot in the down position, the board operator sets the intensity each controller shall come to once the lights are turned on. Pot 1 may be set at 5 (50% of full intensity), pot 2 at 10 (100% of full intensity), pots 3 through 5 at 8-½ (85% of full intensity), and so on. These lights will fade **proportionally.** When the master fader is moved, the lights on each pot will fade to their maximum

FIGURE 7–10
A miniature single-scene remote control board. (Courtesy Lighting Methods, Inc.)

intensity in proportion to each other. In other words, should the board operator stop the light fade with the master pot at 5 (50% of full intensity), the light from pot 1 will be projecting at 50% of the preset level, or 25% of full intensity in this case. Pot 2 will project 50%, and pots 3 through 5 at 42.5% of full intensity. If the operator moves the master pot to 7.5 (75% of full intensity), the individual outputs will be 75% of their maximum preset level (pot 1 at 37.5% of full intensity, pot 2 at 75%, and pots 3 through 5 at 63.75% of full intensity). When the master pot is taken to full intensity, the output from each dimmer assigned to the master will be at the maximum preset level. Alternatively, any pot not assigned to the master will not respond to any movement by the master pot. These pots will operate **independently,** and even when the master pot is faded out, if pot 6 is on independent and set at 10 (or 100%) it will remain at full intensity, allowing it to be faded before or after the master and at the same or a different rate of speed.

Many single-scene controllers are used in small, wall-mounted architectural dimming systems in hotels and meeting rooms. The systems often have a key-operated power switch.

Preset Lighting Control

This control board is divided into three sections: Preset 1, Preset 2, and the Master Control section (Figure 7–11).

FIGURE 7–11
A two-scene preset lighting control board with additional functions. (Courtesy Electronic Theatre Controls, Inc.)

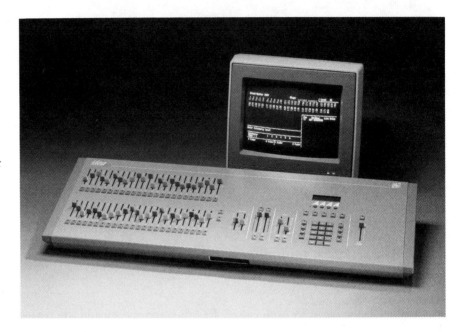

Preset 1 or **Scene 1** on this board is an exact duplication of a single-scene electronic control board. Preset 2 or Scene 2 is an exact duplication of Preset 1, with the exception of the assignment switches that are not used in the second scene. The two banks of potentiometers are located above and below each other with the pots assigned to each channel of control directly aligned to create a vertical row consisting of assignment switch, fader for Preset 1, and fader for Preset 2. Some control boards have as many as 10 Presets, each a duplication of the faders in Scene 1 (Figure 7–12).

To utilize the board, the first light cue is set up on Preset 1 by assigning each pot to Master or Independent and then presetting the fader to the level to which it is to come when the bank is energized. A different light cue with each pot, set at the same or new intensities, can be set up on Preset 2. During the performance, after Preset 1 is faded in by means of the Preset 1 Master, the lighting picture may be maintained throughout the scene, pots assigned to Independent might be added or deleted from the stage picture, or changes may be made in the intensity of individual pots or groups of dimmers, whether assigned to Independent or to Master. In addition, pots may be reassigned from Independent to Master or vice versa so long as both the Bank Master and Independent Master are at exactly the same setting. A major lighting change can be made easily since the next cue is already set up on Preset 2. The operator simply fades out Preset 1 and fades up Preset 2, using the Scene Master pots for each bank. After Preset 1 has been

on
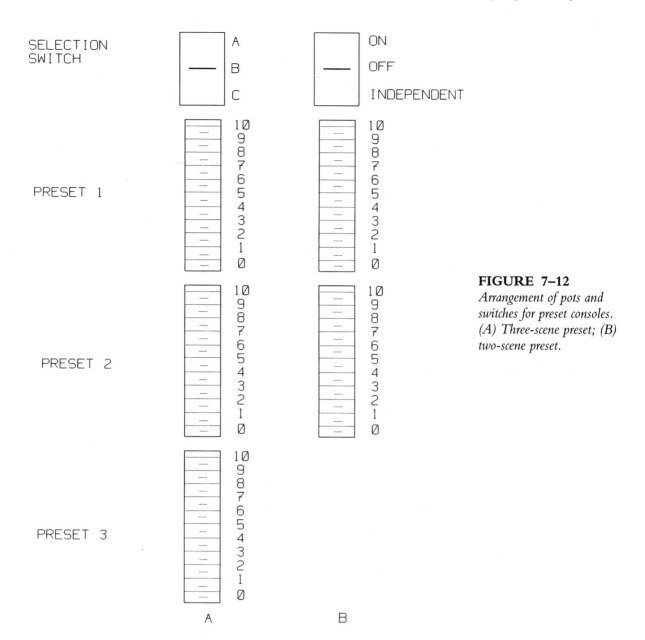

SELECTION SWITCH

A
B
C

ON
OFF
INDEPENDENT

PRESET 1

PRESET 2

PRESET 3

A   B

FIGURE 7–12
Arrangement of pots and switches for preset consoles. (A) Three-scene preset; (B) two-scene preset.

faded out, all new intensities can be preset on it for the next major change in the lighting. In the meantime, individual faders can be adjusted in Preset 2. Those pots assigned to Independent are disabled on Preset 2. After Preset 2 has been replaced with the next lighting moment that was set up on Preset 1, the pots on the lower bank can be preset for a succeeding cue. The entire show can be run in this manner. Major light changes preset on a bank and faded in to replace a previous cue as well as minor changes are made with individual pots or groups of pots in the bank of the preset pots controlling the lights currently on stage.

To facilitate the movement from Preset 1 to Preset 2, and to ensure that the transition is smooth, most boards are built with a split-handle cross fader in the master control section of the board. A **split-handle dipless cross fader** appears to be a single fader on the control board with two scales, one reading 0 to 10 from the bottom to the top and the other reading 0 to 10 from the top to the bottom. The cross fader actually consists of two handles, one assigned as a master fader for Preset 1 and the other as a master fader for Preset 2. These may replace the bank masters for each Preset but usually are in addition to the bank masters. When the handles are moved in unison, they simultaneously fade out the lights controlled by Preset 1 and replace them with the cue set up in Preset 2. This is a **cross-fade**. The handles may also be split so that one Preset fades up or out faster than the other, known as a **lead-lag fade,** or the handles can be taken to the opposite ends of their travel, leaving both Presets turned off, resulting in a **fade out** when the Independent master is also off.

At the middle of a cross-fade the dimmers receive information equally from both presets. Since many of the settings will be different between the presets, the dimmers must choose which set of instructions to follow. In all cases, when a dimmer controlled on a preset system is receiving more than one set of instructions, it will respond to the highest fader setting. This response is called **highest takes precedence** and will apply even when the masters for both Presets are at 10.

It is possible to have an entire light cue fade out with the exception of a single light or group of lights by assigning those control channels to Independent mode. On a two-scene preset board, a channel assigned to Independent operation will *only* be under control of the pots in Preset 1 and the Independent Master fader. The fader in Preset 2 for a channel assigned to Independent mode will be disabled until the channel is reassigned to Master.

Similar to the function of Independent control is submastering. A board with **submasters** replaces the Off-Master-Independent switch associated with each control channel with a switch *on each preset* that assigns each pot to a Submaster fader. A pot may be assigned to a different submaster in each scene. There may be as few as two and as many as five Submasters per scene; they are usually identified as *A, B,* and *C*. In addition to the bank master for each Preset, there will be additional Submaster pots correspondingly labeled *A, B,* and *C*. A light can only come on when (1) the pot for a control channel is set at a level above 0, (2) the Submaster to which the pot is assigned is up, (3) the bank master is up, and (4) the cross fader is set to that Preset. It is possible to control (1) individual pots up to the maximum level at which the Submaster or scene master is set, (2) a group of faders on a Submaster, and (3) an entire scene with a scene master. For further flexibility, a pot may be brought up on one Submaster and switched to another Submaster so long as both Submasters are at the same level. In this way, a pot can be brought up with one group of lights and fade out with a different group of lights. If, for instance, all the Submasters are at full intensity when the scene is brought up, any one of them could be reduced to a lower intensity or faded out. If only one Submaster is at full intensity at the beginning of the scene, then each of the other submasters could be brought up at a later time. They need not come to full intensity nor travel at a consistent rate. In addition, faders can continue to operate individually so long as the submaster to which they are assigned is up. A series of cues on this system might look like this:

Cue Number	Action
6	Cross-fade to Preset 2 with Submaster A at 10, Submaster B at 6, and Submaster C at 0
7	Fade Pot 12, which is assigned to Submaster A, from 6½ to 9
8	Fade Submaster B to 4
9	Fade Submaster C to 10
10	Switch dimmer 12 from Submaster A to Submaster C
11	Fade out Submaster A
12	Fade dimmers 14 and 19 down to 3¾
13	Cross-fade to Preset 1 with all Submasters at 10

The general illumination for a scene might be assigned to one Submaster and the lights on the sky to another; or the Submasters might be assigned to control lights in specific areas of the stage or each of the groups of colors of lights.

A preset control board often requires at least two control-board operators. The workload is divided so that one person operates the live cues, that is, fades the Presets, Submasters, and individual pots, while a second or third person presets the next cue on the bank of faders that is not active. The people presetting may be called on to help run individual pots or Submasters during very complicated cues. The system often ends up with a scramble of hands and cue sheets.

Preset Plus Memory Control

These systems look almost exactly like a two-scene preset control console and can operate in that way; however, they are capable of doing much more. When switched to **memory mode,** the system is capable of memorizing information. A light cue is set up on Preset 1 while a fader in a separate group of controls or on Preset 2 is set at full. By pressing a special function button, the levels for each fader set on Preset 1 are memorized on the identified control channel in the special group or on Preset 2. In the future, whenever the system is in memory mode and the control channel with the memorized light levels is brought up, the stage lighting picture that was memorized will reappear on stage exactly as memorized (of course, new light levels can be memorized on that channel at any time). The fader with the memorized light levels acts as a Master dimmer that proportionately raises and lowers the lights to the levels at which they were recorded. Each fader in the group that has memory capabilities can have a separate lighting moment memorized on it. In addition, some control systems have *pages of memory* for each of the fader groups. On "page one" all the memorized control channels would have one group of cues and on the "second page" the same faders could have a completely new set of lighting moments memorized. A control board with only eight memorizing control channels may have 64 or more pages of memory so that those eight channels could actually produce 512 different lighting moments.

Each lighting moment may be used independently or two, three, or all control channels with memory can be brought on stage at one time. Normally, these systems operate on a basis of highest takes precedence. In almost all circumstances, the independent faders can override the memorized light levels to increase the intensity of a channel above any of the recorded levels, but they cannot reduce the intensity below the highest active recorded level for a channel. At any time the levels memorized on a fader in the memorized group can be replaced with a revised or totally new set of light levels.

Many of these systems have additional features. When operating in two-scene mode, the fades from Preset 1 to Preset 2 can be run on a **timed cross-fader,** which automatically fades out the lighting picture on stage and replaces it with the next lighting moment—at a predetermined rate, from 0 seconds to several minutes.

Some control boards are capable of determining which dimmers are fading up and which dimmers are fading out. These systems allow the board operator to set **lead/lag** cues in which the fade up and fade out of lights happen at different rates. It is even possible to program the control boards to fade to a certain level of intensity, stop for a period, and then continue a cue, known as **step cues,** or to fade the "lead" portion of a cue, wait a predetermined period, and then fade the "lag" portion of the cue. These can be arranged with steps, as well.

In addition, the equipment may include bump/solo buttons and a chaser. A **bump** button will instantly bring the intensity of a single channel to full no matter what setting the fader is at; a **solo** button will instantly bring the selected channel of control to full intensity and black out all of the other channels of control. A **chase** is the effect of a row of lights in a moving pattern as often seen on a movie marquee. These control boards allow the operator to establish a chase sequence using any or all of the channels of lighting control. In addition, it is possible to control the rate, direction, and intensity of the chase sequence.

Another very important feature available with preset memory control and many other memory control boards is soft patch. Patching was described earlier in this chapter as a means to connect the circuits in the theatre with the dimmers, assuming that there are more circuits than dimmers to control them but there is a controller for every dimmer. Many modern facilities, however, are constructed with a dimmer for each circuit. Since every theatrical circuit is already wired to a dimmer, there is no need to patch the circuits to the dimmers. If the system is completed by having a control channel for every dimmer, then patching is totally unnecessary. However, if a system is dimmer-per-circuit but has *fewer* control channels than dimmers, it is then necessary to connect each dimmer to a controller. Because there are fewer controllers than dimmers, it will be necessary to have several dimmers controlled by one fader. A fader may control an unlimited number of dimmers. Any one or all of the dimmers on a system may be assigned to a single fader. Of course, putting all of the dimmers under the control of one pot eliminates any practical manipulation of the lights.

Assignment of dimmers to control channels is usually done through a process called **soft patch**. A keyboard with numeric and function buttons is provided to assign any dimmer or group of dimmers to any channel of control. The assignment may be maintained throughout the course of the show or changed during the performance as the needs of the production vary. In addition, the dimmers can be assigned **at level,** so that when a fader is at full intensity, the dimmer is at a reduced level of output. For instance, if two lighting instruments on two separate dimmers are assigned to the same controller, but one light is significantly brighter than the other, the brighter light can be assigned to the controller at a reduced intensity, for instance at 85%, while the duller light may be assigned at full intensity. When the fader is at any point in its travel from 0 to 10, illumination from the two lights will be proportionate to each other.

Memory Lighting Control

Memory lighting control boards differ significantly in appearance and means of operation from direct-drive systems, preset systems, or memory-preset systems. Memory lighting control boards use a keyboard to communicate the instructions of the board operator to instruct the dimmers. Each version of memory lighting control is distinct from every other version. The console may be a standard computer keyboard such as an Apple II or a console specifically designed for lighting control, with numerous buttons and levers dedicated to specific tasks (Figure 7–13). In addition to differences in console design, the display of information varies from banks of light-emitting diodes (LEDs), which look like tiny neon lights that imitate the light levels on stage, to computer terminals that maintain a constant status report of all activities of the system. Due to the variety of

FIGURE 7–13
A preset-with memory control board. (Courtesy Electronic Theatre Controls, Inc.)

system designs and rapidly changing computer technology, there is no practical way to summarize the operations of all memory lighting control boards. However, there are some points of view that characterize the use of memory lighting control and some functions that are common among these systems.

Any memory lighting control board is capable of recording every dimmer level at any moment of operation and precisely reproducing that stage lighting picture when instructed to do so. Each system is designed to allow alteration of the recorded lighting moments and to permit the board operator to override a specific dimmer or an entire cue. Additional electronics in these systems allow a cue to be faded in automatically at a predetermined rate that may be overridden by the board operator. The board operator controls initiation of the cue. Some systems permit several cues to be automatically faded simultaneously, each at its own rate, and most systems permit automatically timed lead-lag cues in which the rate of a cue fading in is different from the rate of the cue concurrently fading out. This automation allows a board operator to be in reliable control of an infinite quantity of dimmers and consistently to reproduce every lighting moment planned for a production.

The effect of memory lighting control is to simplify the task of running light cues. Any change in lighting is a **cue**. A cue may be composed of one or several dimmers. The dimmers may manage one or several lights (or other functions), changing settings at the same rate or at various rates and reaching the same level or different levels of intensity. On a manual system, such as a two-scene preset board, the cue may be run by an operator moving individual faders to adjust independent circuits of lights, by a Submaster controlling a group of dimmers, by a Bank Master to adjust the entire output of a scene, or on a Cross-fader to exchange an entire lighting picture for another complete lighting picture. Levels must be preset and one or more handles must be manipulated to accomplish these cues. With a memory lighting control system, any cue, no matter how complex, is run simply by pressing a single button or moving one pot that initiates the fade.

Most cues on a memory system are of two types: pile-ons and cross-fades. A **cross-fade** occurs when the present setting for each dimmer is replaced with a new level of output for each dimmer in the system. This means of cuing can be used when the intensity of all or most of the lights changes in a cue or when only one dimmer changes level. The electronics of the board sees the cross-fade as a complete replacement of dimmer settings, whether all of the dimmers change levels or the output of only one or two dimmers is actually changed.

Another approach to running lights on a memory system allows light cues to **pile-on**—that is, to add one cue to another cue so that two or more light cues are controlling the lights on stage at the same time. This approach will result in some dimmers receiving a signal from more than one cue at the same time. Most memory systems solve this problem by instructing the dimmers to respond to the *most recent* command; this is called ***latest takes* precedence** (in contrast to ***highest takes precedence***). In this way, no matter what the previous dimmer setting, when a cue is piled-on, the dimmers will go up or down in output as instructed by the new cue.

A show may be run using pile-on cuing by cross-fading to the first cue, which provides the basic illumination to the setting, and then slowly adding other lighting to the stage picture, for instance, the effect of a rising sun. The added cue might increase all of the amber light in the acting area, fade up bright streaks of yellow sunlight, and replace dull grey illumination on the sky by fading up bright blue daylight, and fading out green and white light on the cyc. In other words, the added cue will fade some dimmers up and other dimmers down. Later cues may add the red glow of sunset and remove the amber acting area light and bright streaks of golden sunshine.

An alternative use of pile-on cuing treats each memorized cue as a Submaster. In this way, all of the white front light for a show might be recorded as Memory #1. Each dimmer in Memory #1 is set at an appropriate level for the most effective and balanced stage lighting picture. The blue side light is recorded as Memory #2 with each dimmer set at a balanced level, the yellow sidelight as Memory #3, and so forth. A cue may be constructed by fading Memory #1 to full intensity, 100%; Memory #2 to 75%; Memory #18 to 44%; and so on. Cue 2 might be adding both Memory #7 to 91% and Memory #42 to 60%. Cue 3 might be a cross-fade that replaces everything on stage with Memory #12 at 80%, and Cue 4 might be Dimmer 19 brought to 45%. Cue 5 might change the level of Memory #12 to 55%. In other words, the memories serve the function of Submasters or Master faders, which cause a change in the lighting picture by simply adding, subtracting, or replacing memories or individual dimmers from the current stage lighting picture.

Control Board Functions

1. *Input.* The programs that organize and drive a computer are the only parts of the system that function in an automatic way. All other data, the cues, must be installed in the system for each show. Specific information is required to construct a light cue: (1) the cue number, (2) the dimmers that are used in the cue, and (3) the setting of each of the dimmers; some systems also require (4) the rate at which to fade the cue and (5) the number of the cue that follows it.

The usual process for constructing a light cue begins by calling up the cue number. After the cue is identified, the individual dimmers to be used are called up and set at levels between 1% and 100% of their output. To prevent this from becoming an extremely tedious process, some helpful keys (identified in various ways) are provided. A **Thru** key allows the operator to set a group of consecutive dimmers to the same level, for instance, dimmers 9 through 14. The **And** key allows the operator to select scattered dimmers in any order and set them to the same level, for instance, dimmers 1 And 15 And 42 And 37 And 48 And 6. Additional keys select set-up functions for timed fades and the sequence of cues. Finally, a carefully protected button records all of the light levels, fade rates, and other operational information about the cue. Most systems also include an encoder wheel or rubber strip that serves as a fader to dim up or down any dimmer or group of dimmers that is called up. The encoder may be used to set up or modify light levels when recording the show or as a fader to dim lights on stage or override a recorded level during a performance. Additional input functions may include a soft patch to be used when there are more dimmers than channels of control available in the memory system and to assign channels to manual submasters should they be present.

Some memory systems also include several manual Submaster pots that can be used to help during set-up and cue writing. They can also be used to override cues or as manual faders to supplement memorized lighting cues during playback. Often the Submasters also serve as a manual back-up system should the memory system fail.

2. *Playback.* The **playback** portion of the board may utilize the same controls that were used for cue writing or may be independent from that section of the board. It may consist of a few controls that fulfill several functions or numerous controls each dedicated to a single purpose. As a minimum, the console must include a way to name the cue that is to be brought up on stage and a way to fade it to the stage. On most systems, the cue is called up on a digital keypad similar to the one on which it was originally named. After it is called up, the cue is assigned to a manual fader, a split-handle cross-fader as on a two-scene preset board (usually labeled *A-B Fader*), or on a **timed fader** (usually identified as an *X-Y Fader*). If assigned to a manual fader, it is simply faded up by moving the pot. If the cue is assigned to the timed fader, the rate of fade may be recorded in the cue memory or might have to be set by the board operator on a pot or dial. Some boards are set up to operate in **sequence,** which automatically calls the next cue to the board in preparation for assignment to a fader. These are the basic operations of a memory system. However, many systems are significantly more complex, with single- and multi-function buttons that allow additional board operations.

Storage

Many different kinds of memory devices are used in these systems, including a few that permit library storage. **Library storage** is a way to remove the cues from the board and save them for later use. This is especially practical when a production space is used by several groups that also share the lights or in a production situation where certain events are repeated from time to time. The usual library storage devices are floppy disc and magnetic data tape recordings of cues.

All of the electronics, control board functions, and display devices of these systems are present to make movement from one lighting moment to another subtle, reliable, and consistent. The features of memory lighting control systems, the combination of simultaneous access to all of the dimmers, precise control of dimmer levels, automation of fade rates, and reliable and consistent reproduction of every lighting moment of a show contribute to a rich subtlety of lighting design and control not available on any manual system.

ALTERNATIVES TO COMMERCIAL LIGHTING CONTROL

Any lighting control board is a boon when mounting a play, musical, opera, concert, ballet, or variety show. However, many production organizations work in facilities that do not have theatrical lighting control and their budgets prohibit the purchase or even rental of commercial equipment. Nonetheless, illumination is so very important to a production that some kind of lighting control should be devised. Minimal control of lights can be established simply and inexpensively.

Plugging

When there is no lighting control in a facility, there often are no lights or positions at which to mount them, so all portable equipment must be used. This requires running extension cords from wall outlets to the lights. As an absolute minimum, spotlights can be controlled by plugging and unplugging the extension cords as needed. This approach is primitive at best, but it does allow the very minimum of lighting control. *CAUTION:* **When plugs are inserted in wall outlets, especially in older facilities, the metal portion of the plug may carry electrical current while it is exposed. Operators must be able to see what they are doing; as a minimum, they should be equipped with flashlights. Also, some electrical protection can be obtained by having anyone plugging the extension cords wear good leather work gloves.**

Switches

A significant improvement can be made in the "plugging" system described above by inserting in-line switches in the extension cords. Construction of the switches is described in Chapter 6. If the switches are combined with a two-fer or three-fer, several lights can be controlled at one time so long as the outlets used can handle the amount of power required for the lights.

Household Dimmers

If a commitment to switches has been made, they can be upgraded by replacing the switches with household dimmers. These devices are sold at discount, hardware, and electrical supply stores. Inexpensive household dimmers can be purchased for under $6.00; however, they will not offer reliable dimming nor will they withstand the extended or heavy use to which they will be subjected. Worst of all, inexpensive household dimmers will produce a loud buzz, especially when dimmed to about 50%. It is much preferable to use as good a household dimmer as budget will permit. Household dimmers are usually rated for a maximum load of 650 watts, although some are available that will handle 1000 watts. The maximum load of these dimmers must be scrupulously observed, for overloading will burn them out very quickly.

The only difference between wiring a switch and a household dimmer is that the dimmer has no terminals but will have short wires coming out of it to which the extension cord wiring must be attached with **wire nuts** (Figure 7–14). The cut ends of the black, red, or blue wire in the extension cord must be stripped back ⅝" and then twisted into a tight, neat bundle. One wire from the extension cord and one wire from the switch are placed next to each other with the ends even. A little plastic wire nut of the appropriate size is screwed onto the ends of the wires until the cap is tight and the wires are firmly seated inside. All bare wire should be covered by the wire nut. Wire nuts are available from hardware, discount, and electrical supply stores.

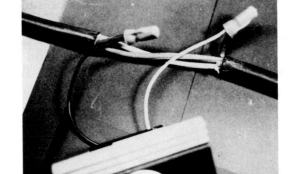

FIGURE 7–14
A household dimmer attached to cable with wire nuts.

Homemade Dimmer Board

The idea of using household dimmers may be extended to the point of constructing a small homemade dimmer board. **Before constructing this control system, check to be sure that this device meets state and local codes.**

To Construct a Homemade Dimmer Board

Materials List
6 650-watt household dimmers
8 connectable switch boxes
8 cable-to–box connectors
2 3-gang switchplates
1 1 × 6 × 1' -8"
16 ¾ × 8 roundhead wood screws
2 switchable sockets
2 20 amp plug fuses
2 duplex outlet plates
2 male plugs
6 female plugs
62'-0" #12/3 S or SJ cable

Equipment List
Screwdriver
Wire cutters
Wire stripper
Matte knife
Pliers

  6 #12 black insulated wire
       6" long, stripped ⅝" on each end
  2 #12 green insulated wire
       1'-0" long, stripped ⅝" on each end
  4 large wire nuts
  2 green grounding screws

1. Remove one side wall from four and both side walls from four of the connectable switch boxes by removing the single bolt on the side plate and twisting the side away from the hook on the other end. Assemble four boxes, two with sides, two without sides, into one long rectangle by rehooking them at one end and reinserting the bolts that hold them together at the other end. Remove the knockout on the top of one end box and on the bottom of the other three boxes. Insert a cable connector in each knockout. Place the assembled boxes at one end of the 1 × 6 and insert two roundhead screws through the back of each box. Repeat with the other four handy boxes (Figure 7–15).

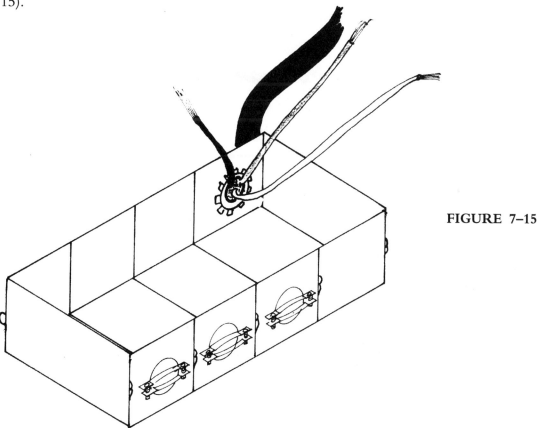

FIGURE 7–15

2. Cut the S cable into 2 pieces 25'-0" long and 6 pieces 2'-0" long. Strip one end of each piece of cable to receive a plug and strip 6" of rubber and ⅝" of interior insulation from the other end of the short cables. Strip 1'-0" of rubber from the opposite end of each long cable. Strip ⅝" of insulation from both the white and green wires. Cut the black wire so that it is only 3" long, and then strip 5/8" wire from it. Feed the long stripped end of the cable into the cable connector on the top of the assembly of switch boxes.

3. Connect the black wire in the cable to the terminal on the socket portion of the socket/switch. Connect one single black wire to the terminal on the switch. Screw the socket/switch to the switch box that the cable enters, using the flanges at the top and bottom of the assembly.

4. Slip each short cable into one of the holes on the bottom of the switch boxes. The end that has been stripped for the plug should stick out of the bottom of the box. Assemble all of the white wire ends together. There should be four ends, one from the long cable and three from the short cables. Using a wire nut, connect all four wires. Gather together the ends of the green wires and add a free 12" green wire. There should be five ends, the free green wire, three from the short cables, and one from the long cable. Using a wire nut, connect all five wires together (Figure 7–16).

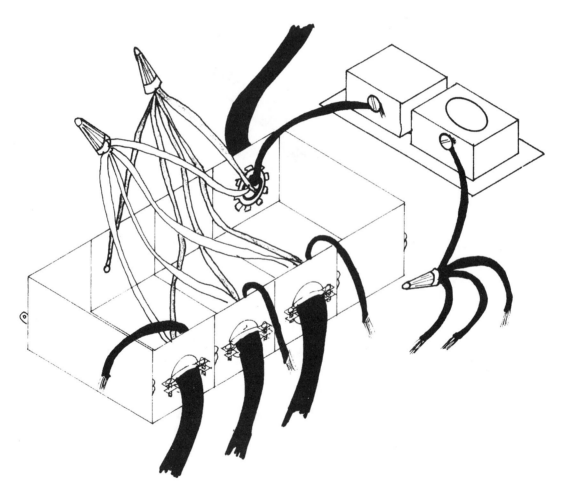

FIGURE 7–16

5. Insert a green grounding screw in a threaded hole in the back of one of the switch boxes. Wrap the free end of the short green wire around the terminal and tighten the bolt down.

6. Using a wire nut, connect the end of the black wire attached to the switch to a black wire going to the "line" side of each of the dimmers. Connect the black wire from each of the short cables to the remaining wire on each dimmer.

7. Screw each dimmer in place in a switch box. Pull the slack out of each cable and tighten the cable connectors. Connect a male plug to the end of the long cable and a female plug to the end of each of the short cables (Figure 7–17).

8. Insert a plug fuse in the socket, plug each long cord into a separate 20 amp circuit, and test the dimmers. If they all work, install the cover plates.

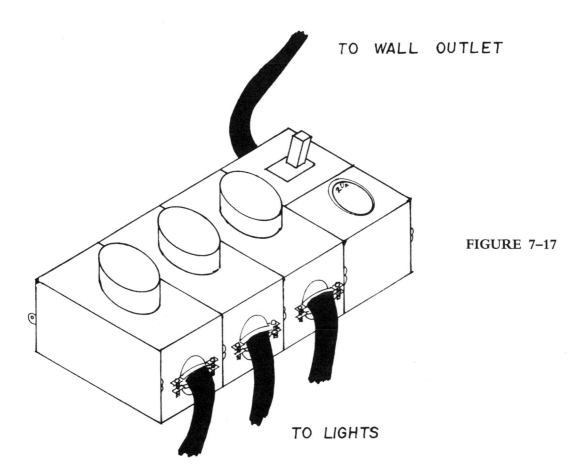

TO WALL OUTLET

TO LIGHTS

FIGURE 7–17

Each long cord bringing power to the dimmers must be plugged to a *separate* 20 amp *circuit*—not an outlet, a circuit. The maximum load is 650 watts for each dimmer and 20 amps for each half of the board.

CONCLUSION

Lighting control is perhaps the most complex technical element of theatrical lighting. However, once the operation of equipment is understood, controlling the intensity, color, distribution, and movement of light with this equipment becomes an essential part of the production. When sophisticated equipment is not available, even primitive means of control can enhance a production.

Color Media Guide

HOW TO USE THIS
COLOR FILTER GUIDE

Stage lighting is an art—not a science. So the recommendations in this guide are not hard and fast rules. Rather, they are designed to offer some general guidelines to the range of Roscolux and Roscolene colors and diffusers.

This color filter guide is organized by application. Colors used most frequently in each situation are listed and described.

Where the Roscolux and Roscolene are acceptable matches for each other, they are listed on the same line. Groups of similar colors are listed in the same box. Some colors listed together differ from each other in red, blue or green content. These differences are noted in parentheses. It should be noted that many of theses comments are the subjective opinions of the Rosco tech people who developed this guide. Opinions, therefore, may differ.

The key to success in lighting with color is experimentation. It's so simple, fast and inexpensive to change filters! If one color, or combination of colors, doesn't work for you, try another. You can assure artistic freedom by keeping on hand a full range of Roscolux and/or Roscolene filters.

For additional ideas on lighting with color and other Rosco technical literature, talk to your local Rosco dealer or your nearest Rosco office.

Courtesy Rosco Laboratories, Inc.

Special Effects

This large group of colors may be used to create such effects as fire, ghosts, water and storms. They include special color accents that add just the right note to a stage picture. By utilizing these colors and your imagination, you can create unique and startling results.

Roscolux	Roscolene	Applications
00 Clear		A durable, heat resistant polycarbonate film used in the preparation of color scrollers to allow the passage from a color to white.
10 Medium Yellow		Yellow with green. Good for special effects. Unflattering in acting areas.
11 Light Straw		Pale Yellow with slight red content. Useful for candle effects. Can be used for area lighting. For bright day feeling.
	806 Medium Yellow	Less green than 10. Unflattering in acting areas. Useful for contrast lighting, accents and hot day sunlight.
	807 Dark Lemon	Darker than 806 with higher red content.
	813 Light Amber	Dark pink amber. Sunlight. Deep sunsets.
13 Straw Tint		Suggests warm glow of candlelight, sunset or interior lighting.
19 Fire		Strong red amber. Excellent for fire effects.
	815 Golden Amber	Useful for torchlight and light from wood fires. Use with great care. Destroys most pigment values.
21 Golden Amber	817 Dark Amber	Useful as amber cyc light and late sunsets.
22 Deep Amber		Very useful as a backlight. Dramatic specials.
24 Scarlet		Very deep amber. Red with a touch of blue.
	819 Orange Amber	Provides excellent effect in Par fixtures.
25 Orange Red	818 Orange	Same as 819. Less red.
26 Light Red		Vibrant, red. Good alternate primary.
	821 Light Red	Bright red. Alternate to primary red when higher light transmission is required.
27 Medium Red	823 Medium	Cycs. Good red primary for use with three-color light primary systems in cyclorama lighting, footlights and border lights.
339 Broadway Pink		A deep, saturated pink created for musicals and "specials". Excellent for down and backlighting in Par 64 fixtures and striplights.
41 Salmon		Similar to 24, slightly more saturated.
42 Deep Salmon		Useful where red is required with pink saturation.
342 Rose Pink	832 Rose Pink	Extremely intense, hot pink. Produces strong washes of color for concert and dance. Combined with a complimentary color like turquoise, will create a dynamic, sculptured effect.
43 Deep Pink		Rich, hot pink. "Electric" in effect with rich saturation.
344 Follies Pink		A vibrant, almost fluorescent pink with a cool component. Traditionally important as a special effects color in Broadway musicals. Used in follow spot and dance applications as a modeling color.

45 Rose		Use on scenery and background effects. Adds tone and modeling to scenery.
46 Magenta	837 Medium Magenta	Similar uses as 45 where more saturation is needed.
48 Rose Purple		Pale evening color. Excellent for backlight.
	838 Dark Magenta	Greater intensity than 48.
	839 Rose Purple	Greater intensity than 838.
49 Medium Purple		Darkest of magenta purple range.
358 Rose Indigo		A warm, red purple that recalls the "Jazz Age". Useful for creating saturated color effects in live performance situations—club and musical group lighting.
59 Indigo		The original Congo Blue. A purple-blue, highly saturated, for modeling effects and non-realistic atmospheres.
	843 Medium Lavender	Excellent for nighttime scenes. Rich, vivid accents, good in backgrounds. Unrealistic.
359 Medium Violet	846 Medium Purple	Good for midnight and moonlight illusions. Useful for evening cyc wash.
370 Italian Blue		Good to create eerie mysterious effects.
76 Light Green Blue 77 Green Blue	859 Green Blue (Moonlight) 862 True Blue (bluer)	Distinctive greenish blue. Useful for romantic moonlight.
79 Bright Blue		Cool clear bright blue.
80 Primary Blue	857 Medium Blue 861 Surprise Blue	Primary blue. For use with three color light primary system in cyc lighting.
83 Medium Blue	863 Dark Medium Blue (greener)	Good for non-realistic night skies.
	866 Dark Urban Blue	Extremely dark blue. Highly saturated. Useful for cross-over lights.
86 Pea Green	878 Yellow Green	Good for dense foliage and woodland effects.
87 Pale Yellow Green 88 Light Green (darker)		Sunny spring mornings.
388 Gaslight Green		A yellow-green similar to the color emitted by gas lighting fixtures. Appropriate for period pieces: i.e. *La Boheme,* and useful for creating reflections from fields and meadows.
89 Moss Green	871 Light Green	Useful for mood, mystery and toning.
389 Chroma Green		Suggests reflected light from dense foliage. A brilliant cyc lighting color which will work for chroma-keying effects in television production.
90 Dark Yellow Green	874 Medium Green	Alternate primary where higher transmission is desired.
91 Primary Green		Primary green and mixed color.
92 Turquoise 93 Blue Green (darker)		Useful for mood of mystery and toning scenery that has been splattered in blues.
94 Kelly Green		Fantasy and unrealistic effects. Unflattering on skin tones.
95 Medium Blue Green	877 Medium Blue Green	Used on foliage in moonlight areas or for creating a mood of mystery. Good for toning scenery painted in blues, blue-greens and greens.

97 Light Grey		Neutral greys to reduce intensity without affecting color temperature.
397 Pale Grey	880 Light Grey	A half stop neutral density.
98 Medium Grey	883 Medium Grey	Helpful in balancing brightness of lamps of different wattage.
99 Chocolate	882 Light Chocolate	Warms light and reduces intensity.

Sunlight

Sunlight comes in many colors and values. Offered here are possibilities to show time of day, season, weather and mood. It is important to consider these factors when determining the color of "motivational sources" such as sunlight.

Roscolux	Roscolene	Applications
01 Light Bastard Amber	802 Bastard Amber	Enhances fair skin tones. Suggests strong sunlight.
04 Medium Bastard Amber		Especially useful when cross lit with a cool color. Excellent for natural sunlight.
	805 Light Straw	Less green than 07. Excellent realistic sunlight in a light colored show.
09 Pale Amber Gold		Deep straw. Late afternoon sunsets.
10 Medium yellow		Yellow with green. Good for special effects. Unflattering in acting areas.
11 Light Straw		Pale Yellow with slight red content. Useful for candle effects. Can be used for area lighting . For bright day feeling.
12 Straw		Greener yellow than 10. Special effects and accents. Use with caution on skin tones.
	807 Medium Lemon	Less green than 10. Unflattering in acting areas. Useful for contrasting lighting, accents and hot day sunlight.
	806 Dark Lemon	Darker than 806 with a higher red content.
13 Straw Tint		Much less green than in other straws. Suggests warm sunlight glow against ambers and blues.
14 Medium Straw		Pale amber—higher red content than 12. Sunlight, accents, area lighting with caution to skin tones.
15 Deep Straw	809 Straw	Warm golden amber with some green. Useful for special effects—candlelight, firelight.
	810 No Color Amber	Good warm glow color for fire effect.
317 Apricot	811 Flame	A rosy amber. Produces romantic sunlight effects. Useful as sidelight or backlight color.
18 Flame		Warm pinkish amber. Afternoon sunset. Good sidelight.
	813 Light Amber	Dark pink amber. Sunlight. Deep sunsets.
20 Medium Amber		Afternoon sunlight. Lamplight and candlelight. Tends to depress color pigment values.
	815 Golden Amber	Greater red content than 20. Useful for torchlight and light from wood fires. Use with great care. Destroys most pigment color values.
21 Golden Amber	817 Dark Amber	Useful as amber cyc light and late sunsets.
321 Soft Golden Amber		An amber with some green content. A good sunlight transition color that shows the progression of the sun from white or yellow to amber later in the day.

	819 Orange Amber	Provides excellent effect in Par fixtures.
25 Orange Red	818 Orange	Same as 819. Less red.
23 Orange		Provides a romantic sunlight through windows for evenings effects.
337 True Pink		A component of early morning sunrise.
96 Lime		To simulate "unnatural" sunlight after a rainstorm. Much less red than found in many straws.

Cyc Sky

This group offers suggestions for lighting cycloramas or backdrops. Cycs are generally used to set the horizon of a scene. Most exterior backdrops and sky cycs are lit by daylight which is traditionally blue in color. Special effects that can range from sunsets and sunrises to storms are achieved using virtually any color, usually deep in hue.

Roscolux	Roscolene	Applications
	815 Golden Amber	Useful for torchlight and light from wood fires. Use with great care. Destroys most pigment color values.
21 Golden Amber	817 Dark Amber	Useful as amber cyc light and late sunsets.
22 Deep Amber		Very useful as a backlight. Dramatic specials.
26 Light Red		Vibrant red. Good alternative primary.
	821 Light Red	Bright red. Alternative to primary red when higher light transmission is required.
27 Medium Red	823 Medium Red	Good red primary for use with three-color light primary systems in cyclorama lighting, footlights and border lights.
359 Medium Violet	846 Medium Purple	Midnight and moonlight illusions. Enforces mysterious mood. Useful for evening cyc wash.
357 Royal Lavender	843 Medium Lavender	Excellent for nighttime scenes. Rich, vivid accents, good in backgrounds.
64 Light Steel Blue		Useful for beams of realistic moonlight.
65 Daylight Blue		Useful for achieving depressed moods and dull skies.
67 Light Sky Blue	851 Daylight Blue	Excellent sky color. Useful for cyc and border.
68 Sky Blue		Excellent for early morning sky tones. Popular among designers for cyc and borders.
69 Brilliant Blue	856 Light Blue	Used for dramatic moonlight effects.
73 Peacock Blue	854 Steel Blue	Good for fantasy, moonlight and water effects.
	855 Azure Blue	Moonlight, natural sky on cyc. Slightly greenish.
76 Light Green Blue	859 Green Blue (Moonlight)	Distinctive greenish blues. Useful for romantic moonlight.
77 Green Blue	862 True Blue (bluer)	
80 Primary Blue	857 Light Medium blue 861 Surprise Blue	Primary Blue For use with three color light primary system in cyc lighting.
81 Urban Blue		Very cold, hard, brittle feeling.

385 Royal Blue   Excellent for nonrealistic backgrounds.

Skylight, Day and Night

Moonlight, similarly to sunlight, has many moods and colors. Whether romantic or realistic, there are many possibilities.

Roscolux	Roscolene	Applications
57 Lavender	841 Surprise Pink (redder)	Excellent backlight. Gives good visibility without destroying night illusions.
58 Deep lavender	842 Special Lavender 844 Violet	Enhances dimensionality.
64 Light Steel Blue		Useful for beams of realistic moonlight.
65 Daylight Blue		Useful for achieving depressed moods and dull skies.
67 Light Sky Blue	851 Daylight Blue	Excellent sky color. Useful for cyc and border.
68 Sky Blue		Excellent for early morning sky tones. Popular among designers for cyc and borders.
69 Brilliant Blue	856 Light Blue	Used for dramatic moonlight effects.
	848 Water Blue 849 Pale Blue (greener)	Pale greenish blue.
70 Nile Blue	850 No Color Blue	Used for very light midday skies. Occasionally used for general cool tint.
370 Italian Blue		Good to create eerie and mysterious effects.
71 Sea Blue	853 Middle Blue (greener)	Occasionally used for cool tints and nonrealistic area lighting.
72 Azure Blue		
73 Peacock Blue	854 Steel Blue	Good for fantasy, moonlight and water effects.
	855 Azure Blue	Natural sky on cyc. Slightly greenish.
74 Night Blue		Fantasy moonlight. Crisp and beautiful.
78 Trudy Blue 378 Alice Blue		A rich clean red blue that warms to lavender when dimmed.
81 Urban Blue		Very cold brittle feeling.
82 Surprise Blue		Deep rich blue with slight amount of red.
383 Sapphire		A deep romantic blue on the red side.
84 Zephyr Blue		A true blue with excellent punch for bright skies.
385 Royal Blue		Excellent for nonrealistic backgrounds.

Diffusion

A variety of filters to diffuse a light source. Helpful in controlling the shadow quality from harsh to soft or to blend sources for even illumination. Diffusion has become a legitimate design tool, giving light new form and shape, in addition to the traditional use for repair of problems after the design is conceived.

Roscolux	Characteristics	Applications
100 Frost	Slight	Changes ellipsoidal to fresnel beam pattern.
101 Light Frost	Slight	Offers softened beam.
102 Light Tough Frost	Slight	Changes ellipsoidal into flood or scoop.
103 Tough Frost	Medium	Has twin qualities of wide diffusion and warm center.
104 Tough Silk	Directional	A slash of light for stretching light along stairs, tables, cycs, etc. Diffuses while maintains compactness of beam.
105 Tough Spun	Medium	Good on scoops for cyc lighting.
106 Light Tough Spun	Medium	Removes lens shadows.
107 Cool Frost	Medium	Combines 103 and a light blue.
108 Daylight Frost	Medium	Combines 103 and a strong blue.
109 Cool Silk	Directional	Combines 104 and a light blue.
111 Tough Rolux	Heavy	Densest diffusion of the series. Spreads the light almost 180°.
112 Opal Tough Frost	Slight	Lighter than 100-103. An excellent diffuser for HMI, CID and CSI sources softening the beam slightly while maintaining excellent transmission.
113 Matte Silk	Directional	Good for striplights and specials.
114 Hamburg Frost	Slight	The lightest of the frost series; good on followspots and PAR lamps.
116 Tough White Diffusion	Heavy	A range of diffusion materials adapted from cinematography—used for softening the shadow of the beam while maintaining a relatively high color of temperature because of the use of "ultra white" pigments in the manufacturing process.
117 Tough ½ White Diffusion	Medium	
118 Tough ¼ White Diffusion	Medium	
119 Light Hamburg Frost	Slight	Lighter than 114. Recommended for followspots.
120 Red Diffusion 121 Blue Diffusion 122 Green Diffusion 123 Amber Diffusion	Medium	Combine a color with Matte Diffusion. Aids in broad, even illumination of cycs and drops.
124 Red Cyc Silk 125 Blue Cyc Silk 126 Green Silk Cyc	Directional with color	Combine a color with 104 Tough Silk. Useful in border and striplights to prevent scalloping; helps illuminate cycs and drops.
127 Amber Cyc Silk 128 Magenta Silk 129 Sky Blue Silk 130 Medium Blue Green Silk 131 Medium Amber Silk	Directional with color	The secondary colors combined with 104 Tough Silk.
150 Hamburg Rose	Slight	Combines Hamburg Frost with 05, a color flattering to skin tones.
151 Hamburg Lavender	Slight	Combines 114 Tough Silk and 52.
152 Hamburg Steel Blue	Slight	Combines 114 Tough Silk and 64.
160 Light Tough Silk	Directional	Retains the diffusion properties of 104 but with less light loss.
162 Light Opal	Slight	A lighter version of the popular 112 Opal Tough Frost.

Acting Areas/Warm

The color range here includes amber, pink, straw and salmon, with several choices in each color category. These colors are often cross-lit with those recommended for cool acting areas. More saturated colors would generally be used for dawn, late afternoon and sunset light sources.

Roscolux	Roscolene	Applications
01 Light Bastard Amber	802 Bastard Amber	Enhances fair skin tones. Suggests strong sunlight.
02 Bastard Amber		Good where a tint of color is needed. Excellent for natural skin tones.
03 Dark Bastard Amber		Most saturated Bastard Amber.
04 Medium Bastard Amber		Especially useful when cross lit with a cool color. Excellent for natural sunlight.
304 Pale Apricot		A peach amber. More yellow than 305.
05 Rose Tint		A clean pale pink; useful as a "blush" for skin tones.
305 Rose Gold		A pale blush amber for skin tones and backlight.
06 No Color Straw	804 No Color Straw	Slightly off white. Good for interiors.
07 Pale Yellow		Double saturation of 06.
	805 Light Straw	Less Green than 07. Excellent realistic sunlight in a light colored show.
08 Pale Gold		Warmer straw. Flattering to skin tones. Useful for dance.
09 Pale Amber Gold		Deep straw. Late afternoon sunsets.
16 Light Amber		Excellent area light. Light pink-amber tint. Safe for most skin tones.
17 Light flame		Heavier pink-amber tint. Useful for dance. Especially useful when balanced with a cool color. Useful for general warm tint in striplights.
317 Apricot	811 Flame	A rosy amber which produces romantic sunset color.
30 Light Salmon Pink		Excellent for general area washes. Gives overall warming effect to skin tones.
31 Salmon Pink	834 Salmon Pink	General wash. Good for follow spots. Useful in a warm and cool combination.
33 No Color Pink	825 No Color Pink	A pale almost colorless pink. A popular color among dance lighting designers.
34 Flesh Pink	826 Flesh Pink	Useful for bright musicals.
35 Light Pink		Similar to 33.
36 Medium Pink		Good for general washes and cross lighting.
37 Pale Rose Pink		Blue Pink. Use in general washes and toning.
337 True Pink		A cool pink excellent for washes and general illumination. A good follow spot color in musicals.
38 Light Rose		Greater saturation with similar uses as 37.

Acting Areas/Cool

Colors in the blue range represent a cool side of the spectrum. Numerous shades offer a wide choice.

Roscolux	Roscolene	Applications
60 No Color Blue		Helps maintain white light when dimmer is at low intensity.
61 Mist Blue (greener)		Excellent for general area washes. Very light cool tint of blue.
62 Booster Blue		Helps maintain white light when dimmer is at low intensity.
63 Pale Blue (greener)		Good for creating cloudy daylight.
64 Light Steel Blue		Useful for beams of realistic moonlight.
65 Daylight Blue		Useful for achieving depressed moods and dull skies.
66 Cool Blue	848 Water Blue	A pale, slightly green shade of blue; excellent for area or general washes.
67 Light Sky Blue	851 Daylight Blue	Excellent sky color. Useful for cyc and border lights.
	849 Pale Blue (greener)	Pale greenish blue.
70 Nile Blue	850 No Color Blue	Useful for very light midday skies.
71 Sea Blue	853 Middle Blue (greener)	Occasionally used for general cool tint and non realistic washes.
72 Azure Blue		

Acting Areas/Neutral

Lavenders work as compliments to either cool or warm acting area colors. Often used when just a hint of color is desired or to wash a scene in a tint.

Roscolux	Roscolene	Applications
51 Surprise Pink	840 Surprise Lavender	Touch of color when white light is not desirable. Good on costumes or when instruments are down on dimmer.
52 Light Lavender		Excellent for general area or border light washes. It is a basic followspot color.
53 Pale Lavender		Use when a touch of color is needed. Use when white light is not desirable.
54 Special Lavender		Same as 53.
55 Lilac (bluer)		Same as 53.
355 Pale Violet		A cool violet which acts as a neutral in a three color area lighting system. Will work well as a wash for drops or set pieces. Tones the space. Effective as moonlight shadows.
56 Gypsy Lavender		Highly saturated, good for side and back lighting and non-realistic effect.
356 Middle Lavender		A new lavender halfway between 52 and 57 in hue and value. Useful for general illumination and side-lighting.
57 Lavender	841 Surprise Pink (redder)	Gives good visibility without destroying night illusions.
357 Royal Lavender	843 Medium Lavender	A rich lavender which will enhance blue and red costumes and scenic pieces.

58 Deep Lavender	842 Special Lavender 844 Violet	Excellent backlight. Enhances dimensionally.
359 Medium Violet	846 Medium Purple	A lavender with a strong blue component, ideal for backlighting with almost ultraviolet effect.
99 Chocolate (redder)	882 Light Chocolate	Warms light and reduces intensity.
3202 Full Blue (CTB)		Converts 3200°K sources to nominal daylight.
3204 Half Blue (½ CTB)		Boosts 3200°K sources to 4100°K.
3206 Third Blue (⅓ CTB)		Boosts 3200°K sources to 3800°K.
3208 Quarter Blue (¼ CTB)		Boosts 3200°K sources to 3500°K.
3216 Eighth Blue (⅛ CTB)		Boosts 3200°K sources to 3300°K.
3401 RoscoSun 85		Converts 5500°K sources to nominal 3200°K.
3407 RoscoSun CTO		Converts 5500°K to 2900°K. Used for a warmer look or when daylight is over 6000°K.
3408 RoscoSun ½ CTO		Converts 5500°K to 3800°K.
3409 RoscoSun ¼ CTO		Converts 5500°K to 4500°K.
3410 RoscoSun ⅛ CTO		Converts 5500°K to 4900°K.

NOTE: For the complete range of correction materials, refer to the Rosco Cinegel Swatch Book and Guide. These correction materials are designed for film emulsions which are less sensitive to contrast than the human eye. Stagelighting is a visual medium, not photographic, and the degree of balance obtained between different sources on stage will vary according to background lighting, the predominant lighting hue and the sensitivity of the human eye.

Accents/Warm

These colors, which embrace a wide range of yellow, amber, pink, orange and magenta, are frequently used in sidelights, downlights and backlights. They add a warm cast while sculpting actors, scenery or props with light.

Roscolux	Roscolene	Applications
10 Medium Yellow		Yellow with green. Good for special effects. Accent unflattering in acting areas.
11 Light Straw		Pale yellow with slight red content. Useful for candle effects. Can be used for area lighting. For bright day feeling.
12 Straw		Greener tint than 10. Special effects and accents. Use with caution on skin tones.
312 Canary		Warmer than 10 and slightly greener than 11. A bright, vibrant yellow that evokes "exotic" sunlight and enhances the color of bamboo, straw and other natural scenic materials.
	806 Medium lemon	Less green than 10. Unflattering in acting areas. Useful for contrast lighting, accents, hot day sunlight.
	807 Dark lemon	Darker than 806 with a higher red content.

14 Medium Straw		Pale amber—higher red content than 12. Sunlight, accents, area lighting with caution to skin tones.
15 Deep Straw	809 Straw	Warm golden amber with some green. Useful for special effects—candle light, firelight. Tends to depress color pigment values.
	810 No Color Amber	Good warm glow color for fire effect.
18 Flame	811 Flame	Warm pinkish amber. Afternoon sunset. Good sidelight.
	813 Light Amber	Dark pink amber. Sunlight. Deep sunsets.
20 Medium Amber		Afternoon sunlight, lamplight and candlelight.
	815 Golden Amber	Greater red content than 20. Useful for torchlight and light from wood fires. Use with great care, destroys most pigment color values.
21 Golden Amber	817 Dark Amber	Useful as amber cyc light and late sunsets.
321 Soft Golden Amber		An amber with some green content. A good sunlight transition color that shows the progression of the sun from white or yellow to amber later in the day.
23 Orange		Provides a romantic sunlight through windows for evening effects.
32 Medium Salmon Pink		Deepest of the salmon pinks.
339 Broadway Pink		A deep, saturated pink created for musicals and "specials". Excellent for down and backlighting in Par 64 fixtures and striplights.
40 Light Salmon		Similar to 23 with a higher red content.
	827 Bright Pink	Basic follow spot color. Useful in live entertainment situations and strong accent.
344 Follies Pink	828 Follies Pink	A vibrant, almost fluorescent pink with a cool component. Traditionally important as a special effects color in the Broadway musical. Follow spot and dance applications as a modelling color.
44 Middle Rose		Musical pinks. Lush accents. Very versatile color.
47 Light Rose Purple		Good for eerie or dramatic effects.
48 Rose Purple		Pale evening color. Excellent for backlight.
	838 Dark Magenta	Greater intensity than 48.
	839 Rose Purple	Greater intensity than 838.
49 Medium Purple		Darkest of the magenta purple range.
50 Mauve	836 Plush Pink	Subdued sunset effect. Useful in backlights.
358 Rose Indigo		A warm, red purple that recalls the "Jazz Age". Useful for creating saturated color effects in live performance situations—club and musical group lighting.
96 Lime		To simulate "unnatural" sunlight after a rainstorm. Much less red than found in many straws.

Accents Cool

These shades of blue and green are widely used in evening or moonlight scenes where additional accents of color are needed. Like the warm accent colors, they are most frequently used in sidelights, downlights and backlights. Accent lighting can color the shadows cast by the general illumination and create realistic sources.

Roscolux	Roscolene	Applications
68 Sky Blue		Excellent for early morning sky tones. Popular among designers for cyc and borders.
69 Brilliant Blue	856 Light Blue	Used for dramatic moonlight effects.
73 Peacock Blue	854 Steel Blue	Good for fantasy, moonlight and water effects.
	855 Azure Blue	Moonlight. Natural sky on cyc. Slightly greenish.
74 Night Blue		Popular as a backlight or sidelight in contrast to area light.
76 Light Green Blue	859 Green Blue (Moonlight) (redder)	Distinctive greenish blues.
77 Green Blue	862 True Blue	Useful for romantic moonlight.
80 Primary Blue	861 Surprise Blue	Primary Blue. For use with three color light primary system in cyc lighting.
	857 Light Medium Blue	
81 Urban Blue		Very cold brittle feeling.
82 Surprise Blue		Deep rich blue with slight amount of red.
84 Zephyr Blue		Lovely contrast to pale blues; adds coldness to shadows.
85 Deep Blue		Deeply saturated blue with a hint of red.
385 Royal Blue		The most saturated blue. Pronounced red content that will shift towards purple when dimmed. Low transmission but will offer a striking contrast when used as a background with lighter accents.
86 Pea Green	878 Yellow Green	Good for dense foliage and woodland effects.
89 Moss Green	871 Light Green	Useful for mood, mystery and toning.
389 Chroma Green		Suggests reflected light from dense foliage. A brilliant cyc lighting color which will work for chroma-keying effects in television production.

APPENDIX B

A Revised Standard Graphic
Language for Lighting Design

Most lighting designers and electricians feel that standards in the nomenclature, characteristics and use of stage lighting equipment provide clear criteria for training and for professional use. However, in a large area like entertainment lighting technology, the task of creating such standards is both complicated and ongoing. There are many areas where standards can apply, from lighting equipment manufacturers' specifications to the system of communication between designers and electricians. It is also difficult to determine how much detail to include in a standards statement.

The work of a previous lighting graphics standards committee that culminated in 1985 with the publication of the current lighting graphics standards enabled USITT to offer a communication framework for lighting design information that was acceptable to the professional lighting community as a whole. However, as in all areas of technology, rapid change usually dictates a restructuring of guidelines. The current USITT lighting graphics standards committee includes professional designers and electricians from academic and commercial theatre. It became our task to update the existing lighting graphics standards by incorporating new technology, finding a method of accurate scale representation of symbols, and providing more concise drafting guidelines. Also, since it would be cumbersome to represent all manufacturers instrument profiles on lighting templates, the USITT standard symbols continue to represent generic instrument types.

A point to stress is that young designers do emulate both the professionals who train them and those whose commercial successes they adopt as role models. In terms of the training and of the clarity of our industry practice, it is important that a common means of communication exists between all professionals that does not inhibit the development of a personal style of graphic representation. The current committee endeavored to solicit the opinion of all interested lighting professionals in USITT by generating and distributing a survey at the

Source: Printed with permission of the United States Institute for Theatre Technology

1991 conference in Boston. What follows is an assemblage of the committee's work and the survey results.

THE LIGHT PLOT

A major reason for doing scale lighting drawings is to present a clear, consistent and efficient picture of the instruments and how they fit into the represented space. All electricians have tried to hang lighting instruments in places where the symbol will fit on the drawing but the real unit won't fit in the real space, or will just fit but then can't move in the desired direction for focus. Also, lighting drawings that are inconsistent or that have too much information on them just confuse the process and waste time.

The light plot is a horizontal offset section in which the cutting plane intersects the theatre at whatever level gives the most descriptive view of the instrumentation in the stage configuration. The only information clearly represented on the light plot and (usually) nowhere else is the actual position and size of the instrument. Even in a repertory situation, accurate pictorial information about instruments is critical for standard hangs and for special designs or to communicate unusual rigging ideas.

In the general description of the light plot there are several items essential to a clear understanding of the designer's intentions. These are the center line, transverse and/or longitudinal scales, a line-set index with designations, a representation of the apron, the edge of the stage or the edges of the playing area, the interior walls of the stagehouse or of the flexible theatre space, all masking, all architectural and scenic obstructions, the proscenium arch, the plaster line, the smoke pocket or other architectural details (in non-proscenium spaces) necessary to orient the lighting design, elevations of booms, torm ladders and other vertical positions, identification (name and plan location) of lighting positions, identification of critical sightlines, identification of lighting areas, the instrument key, and the titleblock.

The instrument symbols used on scale lighting plots should accurately represent the actual size of the instruments and use a standard identification mark for focal length or beam angle. Instruments require adequate spacing in layout to allow traverse during focus. Servo-operated instruments should have their rotation area indicated. The standard information on the plot that should be included with the instrument symbol consists of an instrument number as an aid to location, a symbol for attached hardware (such as templates, irises, color scrollers, top hats, barn doors, etc.), the channel, the circuit and/or dimmer number or a space for the electrician to add the circuit and/or dimmer number, the color notation, a symbol for lamp axis alignment on PAR cans, and a standard technique for showing "two-fers." Striplights should be shown actual size in scale and their notation should include the channel, the circuit and/or dimmer, a symbol for lamp axis alignment (where applicable), the color, and an indication of focus direction. The wattage and the focus notes are still included on the standard notation diagrams but for clarity should be kept only on the hook-up.

The accepted designation and numbering of hanging positions and instruments in proscenium configurations include the following conventions: Onstage electric pipes should number from downstage to upstage. Onstage booms should number from downstage to upstage. Box-boom or torm positions should number consistently within each plot. All lighting positions should designate by stage directions. Front of house (FOH) ceiling positions should number from the apron to the rear of the house as should FOH boom positions, side coves, ladders or ports. Balcony rails should number from the floor to the ceiling. Pipe grids in "black-box" type theatres should number on the "x" or "y" axis of the grid and letter on the opposing axis.

Non-conventional black-box lighting positions should identify by compass directions. Trim measuremenents should be from the stage floor or the deck to the pipe with a note on the plot . . . that designates "stage floor" or "deck." Instruments on stage electric pipes should number from stage left to stage right. Instruments on booms should number from top to bottom. Strip lights should label (using numbers or letters) from stage left to stage right. Acceptable locations for titleblocks are in the lower right-hand or left-hand corners or centered on the bottom of the plate. The instrument key is a very important source of information. It should minimally contain standard identifications of all instruments and devices shown on the plot and controlled by the lighting console, the instrument manufacturer, the wattage (if typical for instrument type), and a representation of the typical instrument notation method.

THE VERTICAL LIGHTING SECTION

Vertical lighting sections should minimally contain batten and/or grid trim heights from the stage floor or the deck, with a note that designates from "stage floor" or "deck," identification of lighting positions including configurations for trusses and bridges, a scale view of a lighting instrument in each position, an indication of where the section is cut, the apron or edge of the playing area, the back wall of the stagehouse or the walls surrounding the playing space, all masking visible in the section, all architectural and scenic obstructions including masking, vertical audience sightlines, a sectional view of the scenery, an approximate representation of the lengths between the clamp and the bottom of an instrument, a scale representation of a human figure, and the titleblock. Vertical sections should also be in the same scale as the plot. In proscenium theatres, vertical sections should include the proscenium arch and the smoke pocket.

SYMBOLS

See pages 220–222.

LINE WEIGHTS

The adopted line weight standards are, for ink, a 0.010" to 0.0125" thin line and a 0.020 " to 0.025" thick line and, for pencil, a 0.3 mm thin line and a 0.5 mm thick line. In terms of computer-aided design, these standards are well within the parameters of DM/PL and HPGL plotters. Guidelines for object emphasis in drawings are that instrument outlines should be darkest followed by architectural lines while the set lines shown for landmarks should be the lightest. Also, instrument outlines and information should take precedence over other objects in the plot. Lettering legibility, ease of use, and the allowance of rapid execution are the major attributes of good lettering. For hand lettering, the single stroke Gothic style in the upper case meets these requirements adequately. In the computerized drawing, legibility and consistency become the primary attributes in the choice of fonts.

COMPUTER–AIDED DESIGN (CAD) SYMBOLS STANDARDS

The symbols in this document are the product of a CAD program and should therefore answer the question of whether these symbols will work in a CAD environment. The ease with which more specific symbols libraries are created on a computer combined with the wish not to inhibit personal style should make the adoption and use of these guidelines more acceptable to the entertainment lighting community.

FUTURE STANDARDS

As already noted, this process is and should be ongoing. This standards document is not final and will continue to be revised as new technology and techniques are discovered. According to comments on the lighting graphics survey, it appears that the film and television area of lighting graphics will need to be considered next.

THE GRAPHICS STANDARDS BOARD, LIGHTING GRAPHICS STANDARDS COMMITTEE

Patrick Gill, IES
Neil Jampolis, USAA
Richard Nelson, USAA
Rob Shakespeare, IES
William B. Warfel, USAA
Eric Schultz, IATSE
John Tissot, USAA
Chris Watts, ABTT

Advisory members:
Dawn Chaing, USAA
Mark Stanley, USAA

Approved by the USITT Executive Committee, August 1991, Seattle, WA and recommended for adoption by the Board of Directors at the Winter Business Meetings, November 1991, Reno, NV.

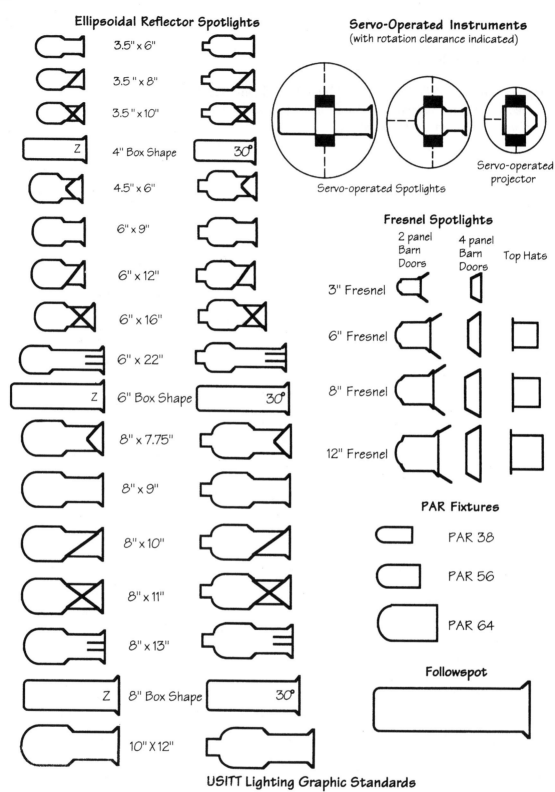

FIGURE B–1
USITT lighting graphic standards.

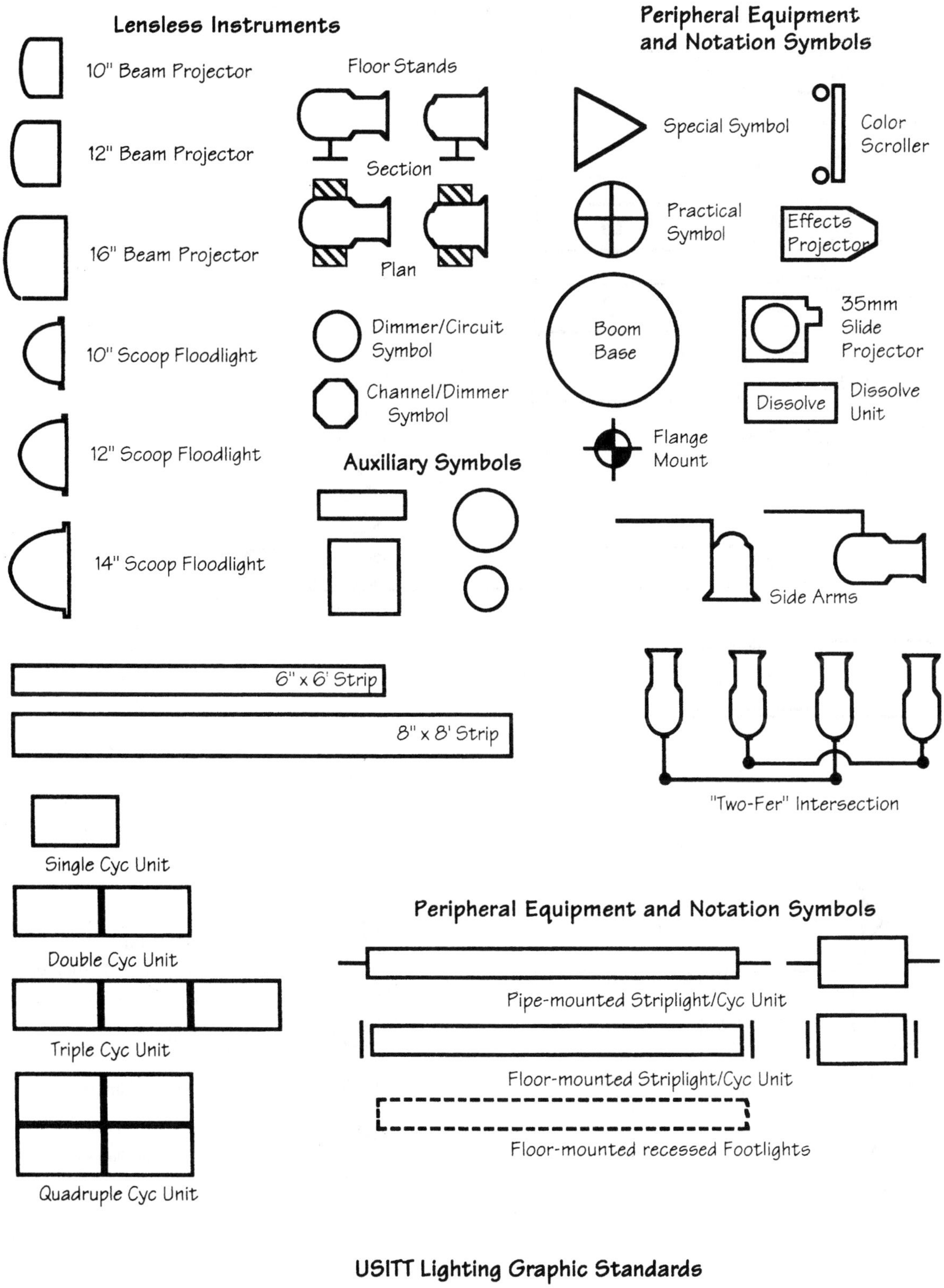

Lensless Instruments

10" Beam Projector

12" Beam Projector

16" Beam Projector

10" Scoop Floodlight

12" Scoop Floodlight

14" Scoop Floodlight

Floor Stands

Section

Plan

Dimmer/Circuit Symbol

Channel/Dimmer Symbol

Auxiliary Symbols

6" x 6' Strip

8" x 8' Strip

Single Cyc Unit

Double Cyc Unit

Triple Cyc Unit

Quadruple Cyc Unit

Peripheral Equipment and Notation Symbols

Special Symbol

Practical Symbol

Boom Base

Flange Mount

Color Scroller

Effects Projector

35mm Slide Projector

Dissolve

Dissolve Unit

Side Arms

"Two-Fer" Intersection

Peripheral Equipment and Notation Symbols

Pipe-mounted Striplight/Cyc Unit

Floor-mounted Striplight/Cyc Unit

Floor-mounted recessed Footlights

USITT Lighting Graphic Standards

FIGURE B–2
USITT lighting graphic standards.

221

Instrument Notation

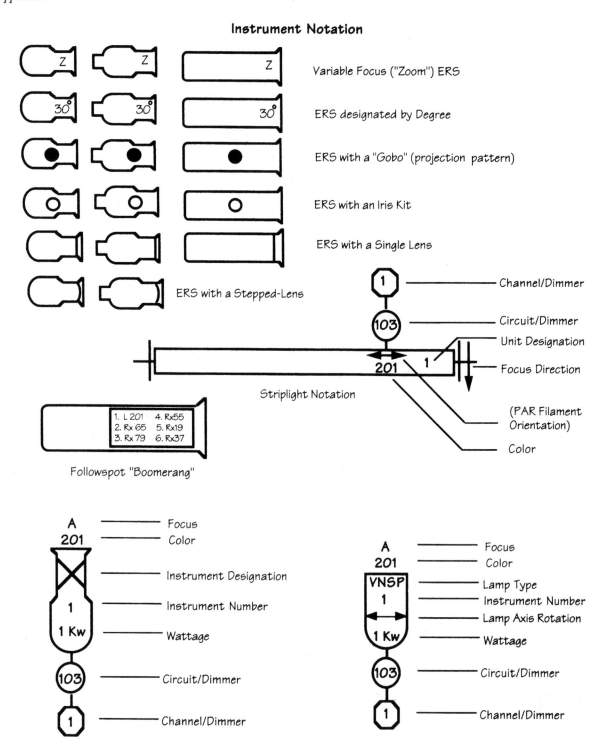

Variable Focus ("Zoom") ERS

ERS designated by Degree

ERS with a "Gobo" (projection pattern)

ERS with an Iris Kit

ERS with a Single Lens

ERS with a Stepped-Lens

Channel/Dimmer

Circuit/Dimmer

Unit Designation

Focus Direction

(PAR Filament Orientation)

Color

Striplight Notation

Followspot "Boomerang"

1. L 201   4. Rx55
2. Rx 65   5. Rx19
3. Rx 79   6. Rx37

Focus
Color
Instrument Designation
Instrument Number
Wattage
Circuit/Dimmer
Channel/Dimmer

Focus
Color
Lamp Type
Instrument Number
Lamp Axis Rotation
Wattage
Circuit/Dimmer
Channel/Dimmer

USITT Lighting Graphic Standards

FIGURE B–3
USITT lighting graphic standards.

Bibliography

Bay, Howard. *Stage Design.* New York: Drama Book Specialists, 1974.

Clay, James H., and Daniel Kremple. *The Theatrical Image.* New York: McGraw-Hill, 1967.

Glerum, Jay 0. *Stage Rigging Handbook.* Carbondale: Southern Illinois University Press, 1987.

Lee Filters. *Color Conversion Guide.* Burbank, CA: Lee Filters, nd.

McCandless, Stanley. *A Method of Lighting the Stage, 4th ed, revised.* New York: Theatre Arts, 1958.

Moody, James L. *Concert Lighting: Techniques, Art and Business.* Boston: Focal Press, 1989.

Pilbrow, Richard. *Stage Lighting, rev. ed.* New York: Drama Book Publishers, 1979.

Richter, H. P. *Wiring Simplified, rev. ed.* Minneapolis: Park Publishing, nd.

Rosco Laboratories, Inc. *The Color of Light.* Port Chester, NY: Rosco Laboratories, 1985.

Rosenthal, Jean, and Lael Wertebaker. *The Magic of Light.* Boston: Little, Brown & Co., 1972.

Rossol, Monona. *Stage Fright: Health & Safety in the Theatre.* New York: Allworth Press, 1991.

Smith, Fran Kellog, and Fred J. Bertolone. *Bringing Interiors to Light: The Principles and Practices of Lighting Design.* New York: Whitney Library of Design, 1986.

Stern, Lawrence. *Stage Management: A Guide of Practical Techniques, 2nd ed.* Boston: Allyn and Bacon, 1982.

Sweet, Harvey. *The Complete Book of Drawing for the Theatre.* Boston: Allyn and Bacon, 1994.

Sweet, Harvey. *Handbook of Scenery, Properties, and Lighting, Vol. 1, 2nd ed.* Boston: Allyn and Bacon, 1994.

Thompson, George (Ed.). *The Focal Guide to Safety in Live Performance.* London: Oxford, 1993.

Uva, Michael G., and Sabrina Uva. *The Grip Book.* Los Angeles: M.G. Uva, 1988.

Watson, Lee. *Lighting Design Handbook.* New York: McGraw-Hill, 1990.

Wilfred, Thomas. *Projected Scenery: A Technical Manual.* New York: Drama Book Specialists, 1965.

Index